MARY AND JOHN GRAY LIBRARY
LAMAR UNIVERSITY

Purchased
with the
Student Library Use Fee

DISCARDED

# The Marketization of Social Security

HD
7091
M235
2001

# The Marketization of Social Security

EDITED BY
John Dixon AND Mark Hyde

A Policy Studies Organization Book

**QUORUM BOOKS**
Westport, Connecticut • London

**Library of Congress Cataloging-in-Publication Data**

The marketization of social security / edited by John Dixon, Mark Hyde.
    p. cm.
  "A policy studies organization book."
  Includes bibliographical references and index.
  ISBN 1-56720-325-6 (alk. paper)
    1. Social security.  2. Social security—Government policy.  3. Pension trusts.  4. Privatization.  I. Dixon, John E.  II. Hyde, Mark, 1958–
HD7091.M235   2001
368.4'3—dc21        00–042565

British Library Cataloguing in Publication Data is available.

Copyright © 2001 by John Dixon and Mark Hyde

All rights reserved. No portion of this book may be
reproduced, by any process or technique, without
the express written consent of the publisher.

Library of Congress Catalog Card Number: 00–042565
ISBN: 1-56720-325-6

First published in 2001

Quorum Books, 88 Post Road West, Westport, CT 06881
An imprint of Greenwood Publishing Group, Inc.
www.quorumbooks.com

Printed in the United States of America

The paper used in this book complies with the
Permanent Paper Standard issued by the National
Information Standards Organization (Z39.48–1984).

10 9 8 7 6 5 4 3 2 1

# Contents

| | | |
|---|---|---|
| Illustrations | | vii |
| Preface | | ix |
| 1. | Welfare Ideology, the Market and Social Security: Toward a Typology of Market-Oriented Reform<br>*Mark Hyde and John Dixon* | 1 |
| 2. | The Market Appropriation of Statutory Social Security: Global Experiences and Governance Issues<br>*John Dixon and Alexander Kouzmin* | 27 |
| 3. | Chile's Pioneering Privatization<br>*Silvia Borzutzky* | 43 |
| 4. | The Market Orientation of Social Security: The Brazilian Case<br>*Sônia Miriam Draibe and Milko Matijascic* | 65 |
| 5. | Marketization of Sickness and Disability Insurance in the Netherlands: A Review of the Polder Route<br>*Ruud Muffels and Henk-Jan Dirven* | 87 |
| 6. | The Forms of Privatization of Social Security in Britain<br>*Carol Walker* | 123 |
| 7. | A Hydra-Like Creature? The Marketization of Social Security in New Zealand<br>*Michael O'Brien* | 143 |

8. "Almost 12 People an Hour Leaving Welfare": The Marketization of Welfare in Ontario and the Decline of the Public Good  167
*Hugh Shewell*

9. Why Privatization Is Not on the United States' Social Security Policy Agenda  187
*Max J. Skidmore*

10. An Assessment of the Marketization of Social Security in Zimbabwe  205
*Edwin Kaseke*

Index  215

About the Contributors  219

# Illustrations

**TABLES**

| | | |
|---|---|---|
| 1.1 | Ideology and Approaches to Social Security Provision | 5 |
| 1.2 | Ideology, De-commodification and Social Security | 18 |
| 4.1 | Brazil: Dimensions of the Social Security System—Public Sector | 68 |
| 4.2 | Brazil: Contributions to the General Social Security Regime | 69 |
| 4.3 | Brazil: Private Closed Pension Funds—General Indicators | 73 |
| 4.4 | Social Security Financial Balances: General and Special Regimes for Civil Servants, by Level of Government (U.S.$ Millions) | 74 |
| 4.5 | The Brazilian Social Security System: Financial Needs in 2005 and 2030 under Different Ceilings and Scenarios (as a Percentage of GDP) | 80 |
| 4.6 | Estimated Impacts of 1998 Social Security Reform and Fiscal Adjustments on Budgetary Savings | 82 |
| 5.1 | The Expansion of the Dutch Social Security System, 1970–1998 | 90 |
| 5.2 | Sickness and Disability Beneficiaries as a Percentage of the Total Population, 1990 and 1995 | 91 |
| 5.3 | Social Security Expenditure in the Netherlands and the European Union, 1996 | 92 |
| 5.4 | Administration Costs and Flow Percentages for Sickness and Long-Term Disability Insurance for the Netherlands, 1993–1998 | 113 |
| 5.5 | Incidence of Sickness Leave by Insurance Type, 1998 | 114 |

7.1 Framework of Social Security in New Zealand     146
7.2 Base Payment Rates for Each Form of Income Support     149

**FIGURE**

4.1 The Brazilian Social Security System Structure     68

# Preface

The pressures to introduce market reforms to public social security systems are shifting the prevailing collectivist social security paradigm toward individual responsibility, with a view to divesting government of some of its public social security responsibilities. Social security needs relating to old age, disability, death, sickness, maternity, employment injury, unemployment and children and families may be determined and met by the individual (individual provision)—whether by purchase of relevant insurance and savings products (voluntary provision) or by accessing support from family and the community (informal provision)—and/or by the state (statutory provision)—whether directly (public provision), jointly with the private sector (joint provision) or by mandating the private sector (mandatory private provision)—whether as defined-benefit provision or as defined-contribution (money purchase) provision. In the jurisdictions we are reviewing, the state has built a public–private partnership to deliver mandatory social security provision, primarily by means of statutory compulsion (the mandatory purchasing of private–occupational or individual) plans to complement public provision, or statutory deregulation (permitting mandated private plans to compete with public programs for market share). Market reform of public social security provision thus seeks to redefine the public–private boundary.

This volume contains commissioned papers from authors from a variety of countries who explore the ideological, policy, administration, governance and consequences of the marketized provision of statutory social security. The papers gathered here are diverse in their scope, content and intellectual foundations; their commonality is their reflective focus on national experiences with the marketization of social security.

It is commonly believed that marketization is the exclusive preserve of neoliberalism and the radical right, but Mark Hyde and John Dixon take issue with this view. In Chapter 1, they examine the ideological foundations of social security, developing a typology of market-orientated reform measures. While some reform approaches unreservedly express support for state withdrawal from social security provision, others are more pragmatic, seeing the respective roles of state and market in the context of two public policy dilemmas: "market failure" and "state failure." Reflecting this, many of the recent statutory social security restructuring initiatives have been framed within "reluctant individualist" and "reluctant collectivist" welfare ideologies, and their aim is not a simple state withdrawal, as suggested by many contemporary observers, but a judicious balance of collective and individual responsibility. Hyde and Dixon argue that this typology can be used to contextualize the recent market-orientated statutory social security reforms.

John Dixon and Alexander Kouzmin, in Chapter 2, review the economic underpinnings of the market appropriation of social security. In doing this, they raise public governance concerns about the ways in which the public interest needs to be protected in perpetuity when private provision is mandated to supplement, or replace, public social security programs. They also anticipate the circumstances under which privatization could well give rise to the specter of government subsidies, and finally they argue that the "hollowed-out" state must become a "smart" state if the public interest is to be protected in perpetuity.

Silvia Borzutzky, in Chapter 3, discusses Chile's privatization of the pension system that took place in 1980. Reflecting this, the chapter examines the political and economic context in which the process of privatization of the pension system took place and the main characteristics of this reform. Since the reform has been in place for almost 20 years, the chapter concludes with an assessment of its socio-economic impact. Special attention is given to its impact on the insured, the state and the national economy. Central to this analysis is the notion that Chile's privatization of its pension system resulted from, and was a by-product of, an authoritarian regime. The only base of legitimacy for policy makers was their access to and close relationship with an authoritarian dictator.

Sônia Miriam Draibe and Milko Matijascic, in Chapter 4, examine the market-oriented proposals for retirement income protection reform that have been present in the Brazilian social agenda for the last decade. Since the 1980s, market reformers have advocated the de-monopolization of benefit provision; that is, the creation of a market for the provision of mandatory complimentary benefits in which both private and public institutions (such as private and public banks) would compete. The main issues at the center of the proposals for and opposition to such a project are the definition of the ceiling for pension values, the constitution of one or two levels of mandatory complementary benefits, the privileges under existing special regimes for civil servants and the constitution of a more reliable and efficient regulatory framework than the present one. It is from this perspective of reforms and transformations that the Brazilian social security system is examined.

Ruud Muffels and Henk-Jan Dirven, in Chapter 5, discuss the role of the private sector in the Netherlands. Dutch social security provision has evolved into a three-pillar system: flat-rate social assistance operating as a safety net for the non-insured, earnings-related programs for employees, and private provision for those who can afford it. This distribution of responsibilities between the state and its citizens is clearly reflected in the pension system, but is less evident in social insurance and health care. Moreover, although this sectoral division of welfare may be the best option for pensions provision, Muffels and Dirven remain skeptical about its appropriateness for the social security system as a whole. They demonstrate that a privatized system cannot work efficiently and equitably without public intervention. This debate on the most appropriate public–private sector mix is ongoing.

Considerable steps have been taken to increase the role of the private sector in both the provision and administration of social security in Britain in the last 20 years. In Chapter 6, Carol Walker examines the underlying imperatives that have been driving this move toward privatization, which includes a growing concern about the cost of the social security system; an ideological commitment toward reducing state intervention to support people in times of adversity by instead making individuals more responsible for their own financial security and and that of their families; and by a presumption that the private sector is, de facto, more efficient than the private sector in delivering services. The main architects of privatization were the successive Conservative governments between 1979 and 1997 under the leadership of Margaret Thatcher and then John Major. However, the social security policy of the new Labour government elected in 1997 reflects many of the same values that underpinned its predecessors' strategy.

Michael O'Brien, in Chapter 7, examines the main areas of New Zealand's statutory social security provision in which marketization reforms have been pursued during the course of the last 15 years: categorical assistance for lone parents, the unemployed, widows, the sick and disabled; superannuation provision for older people; housing assistance and wage subsidy; and accident compensation coverage. Quite different processes of change have occurred in each of these areas, and current provision reflects both these different processes and the impact of political and ideological struggles. The chapter concludes with a discussion of the lessons and implications of the New Zealand experience of marketization.

Since the mid to late 1970s, Canada, as elsewhere, has witnessed a steady decline in the idea of collective responsibility for welfare. In Chapter 8, Hugh Shewell examines this shift by focusing on the recent introduction of "workfare," an approach that requires the unemployed to participate in employment programs as a condition of eligibility for social security benefits. In a critical departure from the emerging global orthodoxy on the desirability of work-welfare programs, Shewell argues that workfare is merely the late twentieth century's re-invention of the parish workhouse and entails the secularization of a so-called moral issue by turning it into a profoundly ideological project: the marketization of government. Workfare is not simply a solution for welfare dependency; it is a transformation of the idea of the public good and of public responsibility.

Max J. Skidmore, in Chapter 9, looks at the recent campaign in the United States, orchestrated by neoliberal policy think tanks and journalists, to privatize America's contributory social insurance income maintenance programs. A number of organizations have sought to replace Social Security with private accounts—sometimes supplemented with a minimal government program for the needy. Others advocate private programs that at first would supplement, and then gradually replace, social insurance. There is also a related movement to secure changes that in themselves would not make the system private but would so revise the nature of the system that privatization would be the likely ultimate result. Considering the speed with which developments can occur in American politics, these factors could result in a shift of policy. Nevertheless, the counterforces that exist are strong. They and the enormous popularity that Social Security has sustained through its nearly three-quarters of a century's existence continue to suggest that privatization is unlikely.

Finally, Edwin Kaseke, in Chapter 10, makes an assessment of the market-driven approach to the provision of social security in Zimbabwe. The discussion provides a socio-economic and political profile of Zimbabwe before examining the forces that have molded the market-driven approach to social security. It then describes and assesses the market-driven approach, identifying some of the lessons to be drawn from Zimbabwe's experience.

It is evident from the chapters included in this collection that it is far too simplistic to presume that the desire by government to marketize social security is always, and inevitably, driven by the achievement of neoliberal, anti-statist policy goals, as advocated by the radical right, and implemented by means of privatization. Certainly, national social security policy discourses are dominated by economic efficiency concerns generated by the anticipated threats that might flow from increasingly globalized commodity, labor and capital markets and by the real threats that accompany demographic aging. As a policy response to the perceived limitations of public provision in these circumstances, marketization of mandatory (statutory) social security provision offers the promise of reduced dependency on the state, reduced public expenditure and thus lower taxes, enhanced international competitiveness, more efficient delivery of social security and more economically sustainable and effective social security provision. Whether these promises are deliverable would seem to depend on a variety of factors, particularly the level of development and sophistication of the capital market, the degree of market competition achieved and sustained and the capacity of the state to develop and implement governance mechanisms to ensure that private providers act in the public interest. The national experiences with the marketization of mandatory social security documented in this volume suggest that a degree of skepticism is justified about whether marketized provision can deliver its promised efficiency gains. They also suggest that any efficiency gains are at a significant opportunity cost in terms of diminished social justice outcomes. So far, no country reviewed has found the right public–private sector balance in the provision of mandatory social security. The search continues. Lessons can be drawn, and must be learned, from cross-national experiences. This volume is intended to contribute to this global policy discourse.

We would like to thank all the contributors for their enthusiastic support for this volume and for dealing with our nit-picking queries with the good humor that we perhaps did not deserve.

# The Marketization of Social Security

*Chapter 1*

# Welfare Ideology, the Market and Social Security: Toward a Typology of Market-Oriented Reform

## Mark Hyde and John Dixon

**INTRODUCTION**

A specter is haunting statutory social security around the world! Since the early 1980s, there has been a discernible policy shift from the state to the market in responsibility for meeting social security needs. This has been accompanied by a profound shift in the ideology underpinning social security from collective to individual responsibility. The importance of these shifts is suggested by the attention that they have received from social policy analysts. Two explanations have emerged.

To some analysts, the increased role of the market as a way of meeting statutory social security needs in developed countries is the product of unsustainable fiscal pressures that have been engendered by the state's prior permissive commitment to public provision. Public expenditure growth over the last 30 or so years reflects the juxtaposition of three factors (Cantillon, 1990; Carter and Shipman, 1996; Dornbusch, 1997; Glennerster and Hills, 1998; Gustafsson and Klevmarken, 1988; Hagemann and Nicoletti, 1989; ILO, 1989; Jordan, 1996; MacKeller and Bird, 1997; Rosa, 1982a and 1982b; Simanis, 1989; Tanzi and Schuknecht, 1996; Taverne, 1995). The first is population aging—associated with the post-war baby boom, increasing life expectancy, declining fertility rates and declining workforce participation rates among the older age groups—long seen as remote prospects. The second is a slowing down of economic growth—long the victim of unrealistic expectations. The third is the emergence of intractable unemployment—long dismissed as the fault of the unemployed. Addressing this escalating public social security cost burden, in the face of a diminishing workforce, constitutes the supreme challenge. The prophets of doom, with their rhetoric of crisis and their "doom-laden tracts" (Littlewood,

1998: 1) assert, with a certainty that belies the complexities of the constellation of political, economic, demographic and social dimensions that impact on public social security policy, that without radical market-oriented reform, social security's future is bleak.

Kotlikoff maintains that unless public social security reforms are made, "it will mean our kids paying almost 20 percent of their earnings for pensions" which would "further transfer from young savers to old spenders in our society and reduce our perilously low rate of savings" (1996: 22) (see also Genovese, 1990; Gramlich, 1996; Marrota, 1997; Schobel, 1992). In the Austrian setting, Prinz puts this potential inter-generational conflict argument another way: "Inequities between the baby-boom and after baby-boom cohorts could indeed threaten the implicit [social security] generational contract" (1995: 17). In this view, the central aim of public social security restructuring in favor of the market is to reduce the burden of existing expenditures, thereby averting a fiscal crisis of the state.

An equally influential explanation proffered is that market-oriented statutory social security reform, whether in developed, developing or post-socialist countries, needs to be understood in the context of a global political movement that aims to redistribute power and resources away from workers and their organizations to capitalists and their organizations (Byrne, 1999; Deacon et al., 1997; Mishra, 1990). This goal has been pursued through a variety of labor strategies, including the promotion of work incentives through reductions in public social security protection. Essentially, it is argued, these measures have aimed to bring about productive relations which are unfettered by the demands of organized labor and which are conducive to highly profitable investments. This perspective gains credibility from the views expressed by the international financial institutions that the privatized provision of social security is an integral part of any national economic restructuring strategy aimed at stimulating economic development in a globalized competitive environment (World Bank, 1994).

Both the unsustainable fiscal pressures explanation and the global political movement explanation share in common a belief that global public social security restructuring reforms have been informed and justified by a distinctive set of political ideas and social values. For Mishra,

Neo-conservatism, which broadly represents the response of capital, suggested the return to a pure form of capitalism—the rigor and discipline of the marketplace—including unemployment as natural and inevitable in a market society, privatization, a lean even if not mean social welfare system, and reliance on non-government sectors for meeting social needs. (1990: 14)

In a similar vein, Martin (1993: 6) argues that the market-oriented public social security reforms have been guided by a global neoliberal alliance of

economists, accountants or lawyers . . . the big banks and management consultancies; the World Bank and the IMF; regional financial institutions, such as the Inter-American

Development Bank (IADB) and the European Bank for Reconstruction and Development; and bilateral agencies, notably the United States Agency for International Development (USAID). Others again are attached to universities or policy pressure groups sometimes referred to as think tanks. Their broadly shared outlook is that the free market knows best and the private sector does best, that the state's main task in economic and social development is to minimize impediments and maximize inducements to private capital accumulation.

Essentially, the many market-oriented public social security reforms that have been introduced in different countries over the last 20 years are seen to be part of a cohesive welfare restructuring initiative that draws its ideological inspiration from the New Right.

We take issue with this view. An examination of the main welfare ideologies that have influenced contemporary statutory social security provision suggests that the market is not the exclusive preserve of the New Right. Reflecting different value configurations, the market is central to a range of distinctive approaches to social security provision. While some approaches unreservedly express support for state withdrawal from social security provision (Murray, 1990; Nozick, 1974), others are more pragmatic, seeing the respective roles of state and market in the context of two public policy dilemmas: "market-failure" and "state-failure." Reflecting this, many of the recent statutory social security restructuring initiatives have been framed within reluctant individualist and reluctant collectivist welfare ideologies, and their aim is not a simple state withdrawal, as suggested by many contemporary observers, but a judicious balance of collective and individual responsibility. This suggests, as Midgley and Tang note, that

an analysis based on a simple juxtaposing of individualism and collectivism does not adequately explain the way that ideological beliefs create policy options for social security. These ideologies should be more carefully examined for the way they sustain and facilitate state intervention in social security and provide new policy options more suited to current economic, demographic and social realities. (2001 forthcoming)

This chapter looks at the five main welfare ideologies that have influenced the development of statutory social security systems. Along a collectivist-individualist spectrum they are Communist Collectivism, Social Reformism, Reluctant Individualism, Reluctant Collectivism and the New Right. All of these ideologies endorse a role for market principles, and at least three insist that they should have a significant role. In consequence, it is important to look at the degree to which market principles are endorsed when assessing the significance of particular social security reforms. Drawing on Esping-Andersen's recent (1990) deliberations on de-commodification, we develop a five-fold typology of approaches to the role of the market in the provision of social security. We argue that this typology can be used to contextualize the recent market-oriented statutory social security reforms.

## IDEOLOGY, THE MARKET AND SOCIAL SECURITY

Although the market is often linked with the ideas of the New Right, the sheer diversity of market-oriented social security reform initiatives—incentive-driven public provision, contracting-out of public administration, joint public–private provision, mandatory private provision, and encouraged voluntary provision—defies such a simple association. The market has had a substantial—if variable—role in most social security systems, suggesting the need to look at a number of ideological influences. In this section, we look at the main welfare ideologies that have had the greatest influence on the development of modern social security systems. These are summarized in Table 1.1.

### Communist Collectivism

Social security in the context of Communist Collectivism may be likened to putting a patch on the status quo in the pious hope that an ideal society would ultimately emerge, as a matter of dialectical inevitability. Thus, public social security becomes a means to a set of ideological ends rather than an end in itself. The inevitable socialist revolution that Marx envisioned would, of course, have obliterated any vestige of capitalism. His robust cosmology predicted an egalitarian future society in which every member would have an equal share in future abundance and an equal opportunity to contribute to that prosperity (Dixon, 1981; Dixon and Kim, 1992; Elliot, 1987; George and Manning, 1980; Machan, 1988). In this scenario, labor becomes a prime necessity of all members of society, and the socialist principle of distribution according to work, a principle that would find support among the New Right, gives way to the communist principle of distribution according to need, a principle that would find support among the Social Reformists. This leads to the eradication of all remnants of inequality based on property.

Marx, however, said very little about the precise nature of the society that would emerge from the ruins of capitalism, but he did, rather simplistically, suggest that there would be "a fund for people unable to work, etc. In short for what today [1875] comes under so-called poor relief" (Marx, [1875] 1970: 31). This public consumption fund, Marx argued, should be financed by deductions from the total value of production before the payment of earnings, but its administration was left to the imagination. Indeed, it was left to Lenin to articulate the guiding principles of public social security under socialism.

Lenin's conceptualization of public social security was somewhat more sophisticated and strongly and positively influenced by the early European experience with social insurance. He envisioned the new socialist society providing cradle-to-grave protection by means of a broad-based labor insurance system with both universal employment coverage and complete income replacement, administered by insured workers themselves on a territorial basis but financed by the state and state enterprises (George and Manning, 1980: 33). Of course

Table 1.1
Ideology and Approaches to Social Security Provision

| Criteria | Communist Collectivism | Social Reformism | Reluctant Individualism | Reluctant Collectivism | New Right |
|---|---|---|---|---|---|
| Core values | Social solidarity | Freedom, equality and fellowship | Freedom, equality, fellowship, individual responsibility | Freedom, efficiency, individual responsibility | Freedom, efficiency, individual responsibility |
| Source of welfare problems | Affordability | Market failure, inequality and alienation | Market failure, state failure | Market failure, inefficiency, social costs | State failure, inefficiency, coercion, moral hazard |
| Role of the state | Provide social benefits; consolidate society and promote economic development | Provide universal social benefits | Provide social benefits, enforce citizenship obligations, regulate market provision | Provide social benefits to a minimum standard, encourage voluntary provision | Provide a residual safety net based on market principles |
| Role of the market | None | Minimal, confined to primary income distribution | Substantial but bounded by public/private governance structures | Substantial; all social security benefits beyond a minimum standard | Provides all forms of income maintenance |

these state enterprises operated in an economic environment where production costs were more illusory than real and where economic efficiency was always subservient to communist ideology.

Stalin's major contributions to the development of public social security under the Communist Collectivist ideology was to insist on incentive-driven public provision, thereby ensuring that public social security contributed not only to economic development—a New Right value taken to the extreme—but also to the consolidation of socialism. He fused public social security to work discipline and work incentives, by rewarding work effort and punishing perceived malingerers. The underlying psychological premise is that it is only through work that human nature can be transformed so as to be compatible with that required for the coming egalitarian communist society.

Communist Collectivist values suggest a number of social security principles. The first is that public social security provision should be an integral part of a socialist society and should be a practical manifestation of class solidarity. Second, employer-financed public provision should be a fundamental right of all loyal and hard-working socialists and their families. Third, public provision should not have the intention of equalizing the earnings of those who make different work contributions, for that would be contrary to the socialist distribution principle of income allocation in accordance with labor contribution (Marx, [1875] 1970). Fourth, public provision should not be made available to anyone capable of self-support through work. Fifth, socialist trade unions should have a prominent role in the public social security administration in order to promote labor discipline and productivity by directly relating the receipt of benefits to work history, work performance and work attitude. Sixth, eligibility for benefit entitlements should be dependent, in part, on the political attitudes and activities of the applicant. Finally, both individual eligibility and the generosity of the benefits provided depended upon past work histories.

The legacy of Communist Collectivist ideology is the challenge of reducing the public social security cost burden born by the state and state enterprises in post-socialist countries, albeit in a way that does not generate social and political instability. The policy response engendered is to reconfigure the public social security by imposing employee contributions and by introducing incentives (especially tighter eligibility criteria and reduced benefit generosity) that encourage work engagement wherever possible.

**Social Reformism**

Social Reformism refers to a number of strands of socio-political thought, the intellectual antecedents of which can be found in romanticism (evoking a sentimental melancholy for the dignity and rights of the individual), humanism (evoking the ultimate ethical premise of the greatest happiness for the greatest number), and functionalism (evoking the need to ensure a society's survival, stability and well-being) (Jones, 1974; Lamont, 1965; Pinker, 1983). Historically, the ideology of Social Reformism has been used in liberal democracies to justify the removal of that which Freud described as "the social sources of our distress" (1951: 44) by the use of state intervention. This, it is argued, also promotes social cohesion, integration and inclusion, and so permits progress to be made toward a free, equal and more secure society. In such a milieu, exemplified by the Welfare State, citizenship guarantees every individual a secure lifestyle (Marshall, 1964 and 1965) with a minimum degree of insecurity and the wherewithal to develop to the greatest possible extent as an individual and as a member of society (Alber, 1988; Allardt, 1987; Baldwin, 1990a and 1990b; Barry, 1998; Briggs, 1965). The outcome was a significant role for the state in the provision of social security (Bernstein, [1896] 1961; Korpi, 1983; Lister, 1989; Marshall, 1950; Titmuss, 1973; Townsend, 1993; Walker, 1984; Walker and Walker, 1997). What these strands of socio-political thought share in common, therefore, is a faith in the virtues of equality and social cohesion and a belief that both may be achieved by the state. The social reformist case for universalism rests on a trenchant critique of the market as a basis for facilitating human welfare, and it subscribes to three core values: freedom, equality and fellowship (Williams, 1989).

The value of freedom is often associated with the New Right, but Social Reformists have long had their own distinct definition—positive liberty or "freedom to"—which rests on three key assumptions: that all individuals have capacities, or latent but desirable qualities; that positive freedom consists of the realization of these capacities, which may therefore be conceptualized, in the broader sense, as individual autonomy; and that social conditions are the decisive influence on the realization of these capacities. It is argued that the social conditions engendered by the market undermine these capacities in a number of significant ways: they deprive low income households of the material prerequisites for a satisfactory quality of life; they require individuals to engage in relentless competition, thus depriving them of their capacity for moral impartiality; they deprive some individuals of the capacity to make appropriate life course decisions; and, in leaving the amelioration of social problems to the vicissitudes of competition, they deprive people of their capacity to act on seriously held moral principles (Goodin, 1982: 156–69; see also Heald, 1984: 77–82). It follows that social conditions should be arranged so as to facilitate the realization of these capacities. Positive freedom may best be promoted through public provision of social security that embraces collectivist values. The attainment of freedom then is, inherently, a collective rather than an individual pursuit.

Although equality is clearly sometimes a prerequisite for enhanced positive freedom, it is possible to imagine circumstances where the patterned resource distribution required by equalitarian social policies may conflict with individual autonomy. For Social Reformists, then, equality is a value in its own right and not merely a means to the attainment of other ends. A number of arguments have been advanced in favor of equality. First, although there are vast disparities of income and wealth in contemporary societies, all individuals have a set of common characteristics (shared language, the capacity to experience pain and affection, the capacity to reflect, the need for self-respect and the capacity to pursue moral purposes) (see Heald, 1984 for a fuller discussion). Social security should, therefore, reinforce rather than detract from these aspects of a common humanity. Second, although existing unequal resource endowments may sometimes be justified through appeals to merit, they often reflect arbitrary circumstances—for example, unequal starting points and the different valuations that society assigns to individual aptitudes. The state should seek to address these arbitrary inequalities, not through the equal distribution of resources, but by extending the range of socialized consumption. Social Reformists have argued that public social security provision should thus focus on the major life contingencies and aim to ensure equality of treatment for all. Because the market is a powerful mechanism for the transmission of inequalities, its role in the provision of social security should be a restricted one.

Fellowship—or social cohesion—rests on the psychological premise that individuals are inherently social, a condition that engenders distinct needs: the need to co-operate, the need to express altruism, and the need to be integrated into broader social collectivities. The hierarchical and competitive nature of the market undermines these needs: the requirement to compete undermines co-operation, the requirement to attend exclusively to self-interest negates altruism and the exclusion of the poor from mainstream standards of living precludes the possibility of social integration. In contrast, it is argued, social cohesion may be effectively promoted through the provision of universal public social security provision. Universalism fosters social integration directly because it requires individuals to access public provision on equal terms, regardless of their socioeconomic background and status. Similarly, universalism facilitates the expression of altruism. In removing the cash nexus from welfare relations, universalism encourages individuals to make unilateral transfers—voluntary and unconditional gifts to others including strangers (see Titmuss, 1973 for a fuller discussion). In short, Social Reformists endorse universalism on the grounds that it meets the fundamental human needs: social integration and altruism.

The values underpinning Social Reformism suggest a number of social security principles. First, and perhaps of greatest importance, social security should be regarded as a right of citizenship. Second, public social security should be allocated exclusively according to the principle of need, with no other restrictions on eligibility (such as prior earnings, prior contributions and work motivation). Third, benefits should be universal, with benefit levels and the administrative processing of claims being the same for all that meet the relevant need eligibility criteria. Finally, a regulated market should play only a minimal role in the provision of social security, although the market does have an important role in generating the primary income distribution. Overall, then, Social Reformists reject the supremacy of the market and its socially divisive values.

The legacy of Social Reformist ideology is to address the challenge of reducing public social security provision's burgeoning cost burden on society without raising social tensions, especially those associated with anomie and despair, and without losing electoral support. The policy response engendered is to redesign the tax-financed public social security system by tightening eligibility criteria and reducing benefit generosity, thereby enforcing market engagement or the accessing of informal provision.

**Reluctant Individualism**

Reluctant Individualism is an ideology that questions public social security provision in the face of state-failure, but only reluctantly looks to the individual and the marketplace as the panacea. It has two modalities. The first, Authoritarian Reluctant Individualism, emerged in the 1980s as a response to the inevitable demise of communism (and with it the concomitant demise of Communist Collectivism). The second, Liberal-democratic Reluctant Individualism, emerged in the early 1990s as a response to the growing and conspicuous cost burden of the Welfare State (and with it the concomitant threat to Social Reformism).

*Authoritarian Reluctant Individualism*

The contemporary threat to the values of Communist Collectivism from within the communist movement emerged in the late 1970s in China, when Deng Xiaoping opened China's doors to the outside worlds and sought to introduce market socialism with Chinese characteristics (Dixon, 1981; Dixon and Newman, 1998). Deng, undoubtedly a very Authoritarian Reluctant Individualist, acknowledged state economic failure, but his desire to have the Chinese Communist Party retain political power, and his concern for social stability, meant that market reform needed to be phased in gradually without any concomitant shift toward democratization, although the dismantling of the "iron rice bowl" of state provision of basic human needs was more forthcoming in order to encourage market engagement (Leung, 1994). As a result, the social fabric in China was rent by economic and social dislocations, as also happened, subsequently, in those post-socialist countries that followed more robust roads to capitalism. Common to all is a recognition that the once ideologically sacrosanct state-owned enterprises should be shielded from the immediate and full shock of market adjustments, which constrain, even reduce, the degree to which post-socialist societies can afford to protect those who have been made most vulnerable by this transition process, especially the aged, disabled people and the unemployed (see for example Chan and Chow, 1992; Chow, 1988a, 1988b, and 1995; George and Rimachevskaya, 1993; Maydell,1994; Sredkova, 1996). The democratization of some post-socialist countries has produced political parties with Authoritarian Reluctant Individualist values. They have their roots in the old discredited communist regimes, who look back to the old Communist Collectivism ideology, in an effort to position themselves as the sole protector of working class interests. Thus the key elements of this ideology are market pragmatism, political authoritarianism and the recognition that the lost socialist lifeworld has yet to be replaced by another (Gregova, 1996).

The values of Authoritarian Reluctant Individualism suggest a number of social security principles. First, social security should be the fundamental right of all citizens and an integral part of a post-socialist society. Second, public social security provision should at least protect those who have been made most vulnerable by the socio-economic transition process embarked upon. Finally, individuals should be encouraged, if not required, to take responsibility for meeting at least some of their own social security needs in a regulated marketplace.

The legacy of Authoritarian Reluctant Individualist ideology is the challenge of dismantling an inherited social security system, once the envy of many, but which can now no longer be afforded, while still preserving a safety net for the vulnerable that does not have gaping holes, and without loosing political power, which means also addressing Sztompka's (1996: 38) prevalent syndrome of distrust, particularly of public institutions (Barr, 1994; Deacon and Szalai, 1990; George, 1991; Maret and Schwartz, 1994; Myles and Brym, 1992; Myles, 1996; Paul, 1991; Rajnes and Turner, 1996; Rossler,1996; Rys, 1994; Voirin, 1993; Zukowski, 1994). The policy response engendered is to reconfigure public social security provision by imposing employee contributions and means tests, and by introducing incentives (especially tighter eligibility criteria and reduced benefit generosity) that promote work engagement wherever possible; and to compliment, or even replace, distrusted public provision with private provision.

### *Liberal-Democratic Reluctant Individualism*

A growing number of erstwhile Social Reformists began in the 1980s to question and revise their commitment to the role of the liberal democratic state in providing welfare (U.K. Commission on Social Justice, 1994; Etzioni, 1995a and 1995b; Field, 1996 and 1998; Giddens, 1998; Layard, 1997; Mead, 1986 and 1998). While they continue to accept the main value premises of Social Reformism—particularly the commitment to social cohesion—Liberal-democratic Reluctant Individualists are sensitive to the problem of state-failure and they are therefore amenable to a limited role for a regulated market in meeting social security needs. Their principal argument—that social rights should be matched by individual responsibilities—has been particularly influential in the 1990s and has informed recent social security policy developments in the United Kingdom (see Jordan, 1998).

On the whole, Liberal-democratic Reluctant Individualists continue to accept a dominant role for the state in the provision of welfare, but they argue that an exclusive emphasis on collective social rights is problematic. First, it undermines legitimate individual obligations, such as the obligation to maintain economic independence through participation in paid employment. Mead (1998) believes that the existence of perverse incentives in social security systems has been the leading cause of growing poverty in the urban ghettos of Western societies since the 1970s. Second, it is out of step with social change. For Giddens (1998), the development of collective social rights was a practical expression of the collectivist sentiment that was forged under conditions of economic scarcity and austerity during the Second World War. Since then, rising household incomes have fuelled the demand for greater personal responsibility in the consumption of welfare. Third, it contradicts human nature, which is essentially founded upon self-interest. For Field, "Welfare is pitted against self-interest in a way in which the public good can only be the loser. Hard work is penalized by the loss of entitlement. Incentives reinforce welfare dependency. Honesty is punished by a loss of income" (1996: 20). Fourth, an exclusive emphasis on social rights is politically unsustainable. Etzioni in this context argues that "We need to remind one another that each newly minted right generates a claim on someone. . . . Unless we want to generate a universal backlash against rights, we need to curb rights inflation and protect the currency of rights from being further devalued" (1995a: 6). For these reasons, Reluctant Individualists insist that existing social rights should be qualified by personal obligations, particularly the obligation to maintain economic independence where this is feasible.

It may be suggested that the Reluctant Individualist's endorsement of individualism negates equality, but they disagree. In a challenge to both traditional Social Reformism and the New Right, Mead (1998) argues that true equality has less to do with distributive outcomes and more to do with equal citizenship—a clearly defined set of rights and responsibilities that apply to all.

Liberal-democratic Reluctant Individualism attempts to steer a path that combines elements of individualism and collectivism and suggests a number of specific social security principles. First, social security should be provided by a private-public partnership, where some benefits may be provided by the market but where private provision is regulated by socio-political governance mechanisms (Kooiman, 1999) (for a discussion of recent British initiatives see Hewitt, 1999). Second, public provision should be targeted to ensure that it is restricted to those who are genuinely unable to achieve a measure of economic independence (for a discussion of recent British initiatives see Hyde et al., 1999). Similarly, it is argued, social security should be targeted on those who are actively discharging their citizenship obligations—essentially by working. Third, public provision should be incentive-driven, so as to remove those perverse incentives that reward dependency and punish initiative and self-help (for a discussion of recent British and United States initiatives see Jordan, 1998; Mead, 1998). The threat of penalization, it is argued, "begins to affect the culture in which people consider how they respond and, indeed, what their responsibilities are" (Field, 1998: 62). Finally, public provision must be tied into mechanisms that provide practical advice and assistance to help people meet their citizenship obligations, especially those on short-term out-of-work benefits.

It is clear, then, that Liberal-democratic Reluctant Individualists endorse a significant role for market values in the provision of social security. However, unlike the New Right, they do not propose to roll back the frontiers of the state. Instead, they aim to use the regulated market as a mechanism to address state failure—principally, to qualify existing social rights with citizenship obligations. Their individualism is, indeed, reluctant.

The legacy of Liberal-democratic Reluctant Individualist ideology is the challenge of ensuring that the state's involvement in social security provision ensures that social rights are matched by individual responsibilities. The policy responses engendered are to build a private-public partnership that will jointly deliver statutory social security provision in a tightly regulated environment and to ensure that dominant public social security provision contains no perverse incentives that produce the moral hazards that undermined work and self-help ethics.

**Reluctant Collectivism**

Reluctant Collectivism, be it derived from Western (colonial) values (Galbraith, 1969; Heald, 1984; Hutton, 1995, 1997a and 1997b; Keynes, 1927; Pinker, 1991 and 1999) or Asian (Confucian) values (Chow, 1985), has exerted a powerful influence on the expansion of social security systems since the Second World War. Unlike Social Reformists, Reluctant Collectivists are generally well disposed toward the competitive market as an efficient producer of wealth and as the basis for allocating economic rewards. They also generally accept as core values the principles of individual and family (clan) responsibility. They recognize, however, that the competitive market engenders avoidable social costs which ultimately undermine economic and social stability. These failures of the marketplace take a variety of forms.

The first is the market's failure to ensure full employment. Writing during the boom and bust of the inter-war years, Keynes (1927 and 1936) took issue with the classical economists who explained mass unemployment in terms of supply-side factors such as wage rigidities. In contrast, Keynes argued that unemployment is sustained by deficient aggregate demand for goods and services, a phenomenon, which, in his view, is integral to the capitalist business cycle, and indeed, which is compounded by laissez-faire approaches to economic policy. On a contemporary note, Keynesian economists believe that this problem has been exacerbated by technological developments which have given rise to a longer gestation period for the production and consumption of commodities (Galbraith, 1969; Hutton, 1995). Demand, whether domestic or foreign, is the principal factor influencing business confidence and cannot be ensured by the market alone, so government intervention is needed to ensure full employment. Alone, the market generates business cycles and thus regular peaks of inflation and troughs of unemployment, the most important cause of mass poverty and social exclusion in contemporary society.

The second is the market's failure to allocate resources in the public interest. Although this theme runs throughout Reluctant Collectivist thought, it is particularly characteristic of John Kenneth Galbraith. He argues that modern consumer capitalism promotes "private affluence and public squalor"—an imbalance between private consumption and public services—resulting in a range of avoidable social costs including road traffic congestion, environmental pollution and heightened levels of social conflict (Galbraith, 1970). These problems arise from the privileged position that industrialists occupy in relation to public servants and the policy process. The disproportionate influence of economic elites in the public arena distorts public policy priorities, preventing the state from adequately serving the broader collective interest.

The third is the market's failure to achieve an acceptable distribution of income. This gives rise to high levels of material deprivation—for example, Beveridge's five giants of want, idleness, ignorance, disease and squalor. Under circumstances where notions of equity and collective responsibility have been marginalized, the affluent are inevitably resistant to redistributive tax-transfer measures. As Galbraith notes:

Self-regard is . . . the dominant, indeed the controlling, mood of the contented majority. This becomes wholly evident when public action on behalf of those outside this electoral majority is the issue. If it is to be effective, such action is invariably at a public cost. Accordingly, it is regularly resisted as a matter of high, if rather visibly contrived, principle. (1992: 17)

In this way, mass poverty and social exclusion are integral to capitalist economic development; they are self-perpetuating. In addressing these problems, Reluctant Collectivists acknowledge that individuals may well have the potential for free and independent action, for self-reliance, for enterprising initiative and for moral autonomy; but their attitudes and behavior are more often than not constrained by socio-economic forces beyond their control. Thus they advocate an interventionist social security role for the state, albeit one that aims to supplement rather than substitute for competitive private enterprise and family responsibility.

Reflecting these Reluctant Collectivist values, a number of social security principles are clearly discernible. First, the state should seek to provide a macroeconomic framework that achieves economic development with full employment, thereby reducing the need for long-term social security dependency. Second, the state should permit, if not encourage, individuals to make their own voluntary social security provision through competitive but regulated private and occupational savings and insurance plans, where this is practicable. Indeed, Reluctant Collectivists believe that voluntary initiative should provide the foundation for social security provision, a notion that has been reflected in the rapid growth of occupational and private pension plans since the Second World War, but they acknowledge the realities of under-consumption due to shortsightedness, adverse selection and imperfect information. Third, the state should aim to promote minimum standards in public social security provision, providing a safety net below which no one should fall but at the same time, being sufficiently parsimonious as to encourage individuals to make their own additional private arrangements. Fourth, the state should require work participation as a condition of eligibility for public social security provision. Finally, private enterprise should become more involved in the administration of public social security provision because of its presumed efficiency vis-à-vis the public sector.

The legacy of Reluctant Collectivist ideology is the challenge of ensuring that the state's involvement in social security provision supports individual and family responsibility and encourages market provision. The policy responses engendered are to ensure that baseline public social security provision contains no perverse incentives that produce the moral hazards that undermined work and self-help ethics, and that private enterprise is engaged in its administration to the greatest degree possible, and to facilitate the market delivery of mandatory social security provision in a way that is in the public interest.

## The New Right

The New Right is a useful rubric because it is couched at a level of generality that is sufficient to incorporate the diverse ideas of a range of contributors (Barry, 1999; Bell et al., 1994; Friedman, 1962 and 1999; Glennerster and Midgley, 1991; Himmelfarb, 1995; Hayek, 1944; Marsland, 1996; Murray, 1990). In spite of their differences, New Right perspectives share in common an antipathy toward the public social security provision and a strong belief in the virtues of competitive private enterprise and individual responsibility. The case for the withdrawal of the state from social security rests on a powerful critique of collectivist approaches to social security provision, particularly, but not exclusively, those which predominated in Western industrial societies during the first two decades following the Second World War. This critique involves three discourses.

The first discourse is on freedom and argues forcefully that state welfare—negative liberty or "freedom from"—is defined simply as the absence of external constraints on individual action. Heald explains:

The wider the area of non-interference possessed by the individual, the wider is his freedom. Liberty, in this sense, means freedom from: the absence of interference beyond a shifting and recognizable, though disputed, frontier drawn between the area of private life and that of public authority. (1984: 59–60)

Freedom, as defined, is perhaps the most important value for the New Right, which it justifies on three grounds: that individuals require the space to identify appropriate personal goals and ambitions; that goals and ambitions have value only if they are freely chosen; and that voluntary action—choice and personal responsibility—enables individuals to meet important spiritual needs. Although negative liberty may take a number of forms, it is market freedom—freedom to engage in voluntary market exchange—that takes primacy. Similarly, while there are many possible sources of constraint on negative liberty, it is the activities of the state in the field of social security provision that are seen as being the most onerous. Public social security provision undermines freedom by imposing uniformity, which prevents people from exercising freedom of choice, and so denies them the right to exercise personal responsibility by expressing a preference for alternative modes of income support. It also subjects people to mandatory contribution requirements and to excessive bureaucratic regulation (see Goodin, 1982; also Heald, 1984). It follows, then, that negative liberty may best be promoted through a radical withdrawal of the state from social security provision and a much greater reliance on the voluntary effort of individuals.

The second discourse is couched in terms of economic efficiency. The fundamental ideological underpinning of this neoliberalism is a set of beliefs that claims legitimacy by drawing heavily upon Adam Smith's *Wealth of Nations* (1776) infused with the interpretations of the Austrian school of economic thought (Gretschmann, 1991: 47–67). At its heart is the idealized and stylized competitive marketplace. It is posited as an efficient and impersonal distributor of society's resources, a belief held, despite the reality of market-failure, because of the inherent imperfections of democracy (Arrow, 1963 and 1976); and the inherent limitations of government supply and policy implementation (Weimer and Vining, 1992: 131–38; Wolf, 1979). The resultant pursuit of the most efficient means of achieving exogenous socio-economic goals is often ruthless, sometimes stultifying, and occasionally heartless, but it is always pragmatic and, to the neoclassical economist, a disinterested and value-free exercise (O'Brien, 1981).

The third discourse is on human nature, which asserts the proposition that state involvement in the social security provision undermines individual capacities for self-reliance and personal responsibility. Marsland believes:

The most damaging impact of the Welfare State is on the character, motivations and behavior of individual men and women subjected to its comprehensive expropriation of their capacity for free and independent action, for self-reliance, for enterprising initiative and for moral autonomy. The Welfare State creates and reproduces dependency. (1996: 109)

In this view, welfare dependency—and thus poverty—is a product of the moral hazards that are built into the "hand-out culture" of public social security provision. The indiscriminate provision of benefits to those of working age who are not in employment has undermined the work ethic, giving rise to significant and sustained levels of voluntary unemployment. For Murray (1990, 1994), these perverse incentives have been the principal cause of growing unemployment in Western societies since the late 1970s. Most significantly, it is claimed, the availability of long-term out-of-work benefits has encouraged large numbers of young working class women to have children out of wedlock, fostering the growth of a ghetto underclass of lone-parent households. Although this is a burden on taxpayers, who are required to finance public expenditures on social security, its most onerous impact is on the well-being and future life-chances of underclass children. Young men in particular are deprived of the role-model of an employed father and are socialized into a culture of unemployment and long-term benefit dependence, thus giving rise to inter-generational poverty. Although well intentioned, the Welfare State undermines the core values of the market and thus gives rise to profound dis-welfares.

These New Right values point to a number of clear principles for social security provision. First, social security should be provided mainly—if not exclusively—by means of an unfettered competitive market. For libertarians (see Nozick, 1974) and conservatives (see Murray, 1994), the state should withdraw entirely from social insurance, leaving income replacement to the voluntary effort of individuals. Second, public social assistance provision should be strictly means tested to ensure that scarce public resources are targeted on those most in need of them. While accepting the primacy of individual responsibility, Friedman (1962) also advocates a residual public safety net for those who are genuinely unable to rely on their personal (and perhaps even family) resources. Third, the state should deploy administrative criteria to distinguish between those who are genuinely unable to work—and who are therefore deserving of public charity—and the able-bodied poor—who should be vigorously encouraged to seek paid employment. Fourth, public social security provision should be based on the Poor Law principle of "less eligibility," which requires that benefit levels are less than the wages of the lowest paid in employment so as to avoid the problem of moral hazard.

The New Right legacy is the challenge of ensuring that voluntary social security provision is sufficient to indemnify individuals overcome by social security maladies, despite the well-rehearsed market-failure arguments of shortsightedness, adverse selection and imperfect information. The policy response engendered is to encourage voluntary market provision, leaving the state with, at best, only a minimalist residual safety-net role.

## DEGREES OF MARKET ENGAGEMENT WITH SOCIAL SECURITY?

All key ideological perspectives on social security endorse a role for market principles—not just the New Right—and at least three of them endorse a significant role. When assessing global social security shifts in favor of the market, it makes sense to look at the degree to which market principles have been reflected in particular reforms. This question of degree is neatly expressed in Esping-Andersen's concept of de-commodification, which he defines as "the degree to which individuals, or families, can uphold a socially acceptable standard of living independently of [labor, capital and commodity] market participation" (1990: 37). Esping-Andersen suggests that de-commodification has three core dimensions: contingency coverage, access and income replacement, to which we would add population coverage. Contingency coverage refers to the range of social security contingencies covered by a public social security system;

the fewer they are, the greater the extent of market dependency. Population coverage refers to the scope of the protection provided; the larger the proportion of the population excluded from coverage, the greater degree of market dependence. Access refers to the eligibility criteria that govern people's access to social security benefits; the more restrictive those criteria, the greater the degree of market dependence. Income replacement refers to the extent to which social security benefits replace prior earnings; the lesser the extent of income replacement, the greater the degree of market dependence.

These criteria can be used to assess the de-commodification potential of each of the key ideological perspectives on social security. This is outlined in Table 1.2.

Communist Collectivism acknowledges no role of the market in the provision of social security, and thus it has a very considerable de-commodification potential. But, until the ultimate transformation from socialism into communism is achieved, social rights are constrained, and thus some people are placed beyond state protection. Contingency coverage is expected to preclude only unemployment on the ground that this risk is only a trait of capitalism, which, of course, fails to acknowledge the reality of unemployment due to state (labor assignment) failure. Population coverage is expected to preclude only those who had never been in the workforce. Eligibility criteria are expected to exclude those with poor work histories, work performances, work attitudes, or political attitudes. Income replacement is expected to be generous. Although the market plays no role in the primary distribution of resources or the generation of primary income, those few who are precluded from state protection are expected to fend for themselves as best they can with informal family and community provision.

Social Reformism acknowledges only a voluntary and supplementary role for the market in the provision of social security, and thus it has a considerable de-commodification potential. Contingency coverage is expected to be all embracing. Population coverage tends toward the inclusiveness of the universal. Eligibility criteria are expected to preclude those without citizenship rights—resident recent migrants are punished. Income support is expected to be sufficient to ensure a satisfactory standard. Although the market plays a considerable role in the primary distribution of resources or the generation of primary income, income distribution is expected to be modified substantially by universalist taxation and transfer policies. Those few who fail to benefit from the full largesse of public provision are expected to fend for themselves as best they can by means of voluntary market provision or informal family and community provision.

Reluctant Individualism, whether Authoritarian or Liberal-democratic, endorses forms of public social security provision that encourage market engagement, and sees the market as having a supplementary-support or a joint-delivery role in the provision of social security. Its de-commodification potential is therefore ambivalent: high for those who meet their citizenship obligations, less

Table 1.2
Ideology, De-commodification and Social Security

| Design Feature | Communist Collectivism | Social Reformism | Reluctant Individualism | Reluctant Collectivism | New Right |
|---|---|---|---|---|---|
| Contingency coverage | High except unemployment | High | High | High | High |
| Population coverage | Employees and dependants | Universal | Universal | Excludes those with a poor work record | Excludes dependants |
| Access | Eligibility restrictions based on work motivation and performance | Few eligibility restrictions | Eligibility restrictions based on work capacity | Eligibility restrictions based on work performance | Eligibility restrictions based on income and work motivation |
| Income replacement | High | High | High for some, low for others | Low | Very low |
| De-commodification potential | High | High | Ambivalent | Low | Very low |
| Marketization strategies | IDPP | IDPP | CP, CM, CBP, IDPP, EVP, ACO | CBP, IDPP, EVP, CM, CP | IDPP, ACO |

so for those that do not. Contingency coverage is expected to be all embracing. Population coverage is expected to tend toward the universal. Eligibility, however, is expected to be restricted to those who meet their citizenship obligations by working wherever possible. Income replacement is expected to be sufficient only to maintain a minimally acceptable standard of living, reflecting the tension between a commitment to social cohesion and a desire to maintain market engagement. Those who are precluded from statutory or voluntary social security provision are expected to fend for themselves as best they can by means of informal family and community provision.

Reluctant Collectivism also endorses forms of public social security provision that are clearly based on market principles, a condition that considerably reduces its de-commodification potential, which, however, remains significant because of the state's perceived role in correcting failures generated by the market. Contingency coverage is expected to be all embracing. Population coverage is expected to tend toward those in employment, with a residualist safety net provided for the rest. Eligibility, however, is expected to be restricted to those who can satisfy employment or contribution requirements. Income replacement is expected to be parsimonious, reflecting a desire to ensure that individuals make their own voluntary provisions. Those who are precluded from statutory or voluntary social security provision are expected to fend for themselves as best they can by means of informal family and community provision.

The New Right endorses, at best, only limited public social security provision in the form of a minimalist residual safety net and thus has extremely limited de-commodification potential. Contingency and population coverage are expected to be minimalist, as appropriate for public provision that only provides a residualist safety net. Eligibility is expected to be based on means, needs, worthiness and work motivation. Income support is expected to be parsimonious, conforming to the Poor Law "less eligibility" principle, with, no doubt, time-limited benefits for recipients of working age. Those who fail to provide for their own social security needs on a voluntary basis, and who fall through or entirely miss the residual safety net, are expected to fend for themselves as best they can by means of informal family and community provision.

## A TYPOLOGY OF MARKET-ORIENTED SOCIAL SECURITY REFORMS

The market-driven social security reforms can be classified by their degree of market orientation and by the degree of competition they introduce. Competitive marketization occurs when private provision is developed in the context of a competitive or at least a contestable market environment. Partially competitive marketization occurs where private provision to a particular industry or occupational group is only in competition with a public social security agency. These contrast with non-competitive marketization, where private provision to a particular industry or occupational group is by a regulated monopolist.

### Incentive-Driven Public Provision

This is the weakest of the market-oriented social security reforms for it does not challenge the concept of collective responsibility. The policy response is to reform public provision by removing perverse incentives that discourage work and savings and to ensure that benefits are not so generous as to discourage voluntary provision.

### Encouraged Voluntary Provision

As a form of social security reform, encouraged voluntary provision can have a weak market orientation (if it is intended only to complement public provision) or a strong one (if it is intended to replace or stand in lieu of public provision). The policy response is typically to make individual and/or employer contributions tax deductible and/or to impose regulatory regimes intended to build public confidence in voluntary provision.

### Administrative Contracting-Out

This form of market-oriented reform involves private sector engagement in public social security provision. The policy response is for specific administrative and other services undertaken by a public social security agency to be contracted out to service providers operating in a market environment (such services typically relate to health care, investment portfolio management, the administration of benefit payments, benefit advice provision and work testing).

### Complementary Benefit Privatization

This occurs when governments mandate the private provision (including provision by other non-governmental organizations) of complementary social security benefits (whether mandated as defined-benefit or defined-contribution in form) to supplement those that are publicly provided. The policy responses are two-fold. The first is to permit mandated private provision to compete with the public provision. The second is to obligate employers and/or individuals (perhaps as employees) to purchase mandated complementary benefits in a market environment, as a replacement for, or in lieu of, public provision.

### Coverage Privatization

This occurs when government mandates private provision (including provision by other non-governmental organizations) of existing publicly provided primary social security benefits (whether mandated as defined-benefit or defined-contribution in form). The policy responses are two-fold. The first is to permit mandated private provision to compete with public provision. The second is to obligate employers and/or individuals (perhaps as employees) to purchase mandated primary provision in a market environment, as a replacement for public provision.

### Coverage Marketization

This occurs when government creates a market for the private provision (including provision by other non-governmental organizations) of primary social security benefits (whether mandated as defined-benefit or defined-contribution in form) that have never been publicly provided. The policy response is to obligate employers and/or individuals (perhaps as employees) to purchase mandated primary provision in a market environment, in lieu of public provision.

## CONCLUSION

The global shift toward the market in the provision of social security is typically associated with the New Right, but we take issue with this view. An examination of the main welfare ideologies that have influenced the development of contemporary social security systems—Communist Collectivism, Social Reformism, Reluctant Individualism, Reluctant Collectivism and the New Right—suggests that the market has a role to play in a range of approaches to public social security reform. While some approaches unreservedly endorse the market—in a way which moves toward the ideas of the New Right—other approaches adopt a pragmatic market orientation based on a recognition of two public policy dilemmas, namely, market-failure and state-failure. Drawing upon Esping-Andersen's recent work on de-commodification, we have constructed a typology of normative approaches to the public provision of social security, which we have used to contextualize examples of market-oriented reform of public social security. This we argue is necessary to avoid the over-simplified dichotomy between individualism and collectivism, which is typical of so much recent literature on social security reform.

## NOTE

This chapter is a considerably expanded version of a paper to be published in the *Policy Studies Review* symposium on "The Marketization of Social Security: A Cross-National Perspective" (forthcoming).

## REFERENCES

Alber, J. 1988. Continuities and Change in the Idea of the Welfare State. *Politics & Society* 16 (4): 451–68.

Allardt, E. 1987. The Civic Conception of the Welfare State. In Rose, R. and Shiratorie, R. (eds.), *The Welfare State—East and West*. Oxford: Oxford University Press.

Baldwin, P. 1990a. Class Interests and the Post-War Welfare State in Europe: A Historical Perspective. *International Social Security Review* 43 (3): 255–69.

Baldwin, P. 1990b. *The Politics of Social Solidarity*. Cambridge: Cambridge University Press.

Barr, N. 1994. Income Transfers: Social Insurance. In Barr, N. (ed.), *Labor Markets and Social Policy in Central and Eastern Europe*. New York: Oxford University Press.

Barry, N. 1998. *Welfare*. Milton Keynes: Open University Press.

Barry, N. 1999. Neoclassicism, the New Right and British Social Welfare. In Page, M. and Silburn, R. (eds.), *British Social Welfare in the Twentieth Century*. London: Macmillan.

Bell, M., Butler, E., Marsland, D. and Pirie, M. 1994. *The End of the Welfare State*. London: Adam Smith Institute.

Bernstein, E. [1898] 1961. *Evolutionary Socialism*. New York: Schocken.

Briggs, A. 1965. The Welfare State in Historical Perspective. In Zald, M. N. (ed.), *Social Welfare Institutions: A Sociological Reader*. New York: Wiley.

Byrne, D. 1999. *Social Exclusion*. Buckingham: Open University Press.

Cantillon, B. 1990. Socio-demographic Changes and Social Security. *International Social Security Review* 43 (4): 399–425.

Carter, M. N. and Shipman, W. G. 1996. The Coming Global Pension Crisis. *Foreign Affairs* 75 (6): S1–S16.

Chan, C. and Chow, N.W.S. 1992. *More Welfare after Economic Reform: Welfare Development in the People's Republic of China*. Hong Kong: University of Hong Kong, Department of Social Work and Social Administration.

Chow, N.W.S. 1985. Social Security Provisions in Singapore, Hong Kong, Taiwan and South Korea. *Journal of International and Comparative Social Welfare* 2 (1 and 2): 1–10.

Chow, N.W.S. 1988a. *The Administration and Financing of Social Security in China*. Hong Kong: Centre of Asian Studies, University of Hong Kong.

Chow, N.W.S. 1988b. Scope for Reform in the Social Security System of the People's Republic of China. *Asia News Sheet* (International Social Security Association) 18 (3): 22–28.

Chow, N.W.S. 1995. Social Security Reforms in China. In Dixon, J. and Scheurell, R. P. (eds.), *International Perspectives on Social Security*. Westport, CT: Greenwood.

Deacon, B., with Hulse, M. and Stubbs, P. 1997. *International Organizations and the Future of Welfare*. London: Sage.

Deacon, B. and Szalai, J. 1990. *What Future for Socialist Welfare?* Aldershot: Avebury.

Dixon, J. 1981. *The Chinese Welfare System: 1949–1979*. New York: Praeger.

Dixon, J. and Kim, H. S. 1992. Social Welfare under Socialism. In Dixon, J. and Macarov, D. (eds.), *Social Welfare in Socialist Countries*. London: Routledge.

Dixon, J. and Newman, D. 1998. *Entering the Chinese Market: The Risks and Discounted Rewards*. Westport, CT: Quorum.

Dornbusch, R. 1997. Japan's Pension Crisis: Growth the Only Way Out. *Business Week* 35 (11) (January 27): 18.

Elliott, J. E. 1987. Moral and Ethical Considerations in Karl Marx's Robust Vision of the Future Society. *International Journal of Social Economics* 14 (10): 3–26.

Esping-Andersen, G. 1990. *The Three Worlds of Welfare Capitalism*. Cambridge: Polity.

Etzioni, A. 1995a. *The Spirit of Community: Rights, Responsibilities and the Communitarian Agenda*. London: Fontana.
Etzioni, A. (ed.). 1995b. *New Communitarian Thinking: Persons, Virtues, Institutions, and Communities*. Charlottesville: University of Virginia Press.
Field, F. 1996. Stakeholder Welfare. In Deacon, A. (ed.), *Stakeholder Welfare*. London: Institute of Economic Affairs.
Field, F. 1998. Re-inventing Welfare: A Response to Lawrence Mead. In Deacon, A. (ed.), *From Welfare to Work: Lessons from America*. London: Institute of Economic Affairs.
Freud, S. 1951. *Civilization and Its Discontents*. London: Hogarth Press.
Friedman, M. 1962. *Capitalism and Freedom*. Chicago: University of Chicago Press.
Friedman, M. 1999. Speaking the Truth about Social Security Reform. *Cato Institute Briefing Papers* 46: 1–3.
Galbraith, J. K. 1969. *The New Industrial State*. London: Hamish Hamilton.
Galbraith, J. K. 1970. *The Affluent Society*. Harmondsworth: Penguin.
Galbraith, J. K. 1992. *The Culture of Contentment*. London: Sinclair-Stevenson.
Genovese, F. C. 1990. The Deficit and Social Security. *American Journal of Economics and Sociology* 49: 151–52.
George, V. 1991. Social Security in the USSR. *International Social Security Review* 44 (4): 47–64.
George, V. and Manning, N. 1980. *Socialism, Social Welfare and the Soviet Union*. London: Routledge and Kegan Paul.
George, V. and Rimachevskaya, N. 1993. "Poverty in Russia." *International Social Security Review* 46 (1): 67–78.
Giddens, A. 1998. *The Third Way*. Cambridge: Polity.
Glennerster, H. and Hills, J. (eds.). 1998. *The State of Welfare: The Economics of Social Spending*. Oxford: Oxford University Press.
Glennerster, H. and Midgley, J. (eds.). 1991. *The Radical Right and the Welfare State*. London: Harvester Wheatsheaf.
Goodin, R. E. 1982. Freedom and the Welfare State: Theoretical Foundations. *Journal of Social Policy* 11: 149–76.
Gramlich, E. M. 1996. Different Approaches to Dealing with Social Security. *American Economic Review* 86 (2): 358–62.
Gregova, M. 1996. Restructuring of the "Life-world of Socialism." *International Sociology* 11 (1): 63–78.
Gretschmann, K. 1991. Analyzing the Public Sector: The Received View of Economics and Its Shortcomings. In Kaufmann, F. X. (ed.), *The Public Sector: Challenge for Coordination and Learning*. Berlin: Walter de Gruyter.
Gustafsson, B. A. and Klevmarken, N. A. 1988. *The Political Economy of Social Security*. Amsterdam: Elsevier.
Hagemann, R. P. and Nicoletti, G. 1989. Population Ageing: Economic Effects and Some Implications for Financing Public Pensions. *OECD Economic Studies* 12: 59–110.
Hayek, F. 1944. *The Road to Serfdom*. London: Routledge and Kegan Paul.
Heald, D. 1984. *Public Expenditure*. Oxford: Martin Robertson.
Hewitt, M. 1999. New Labour and Social Security. In Powell, M. (ed.), *New Labour, New Welfare State?* Bristol: The Policy Press.

Himmelfarb, G. 1995. *The De-moralisation of Society: From Victorian Virtues to Moral Values*. London: Institute of Economic Affairs.
Hutton, W. 1995. *The State We're In*. London: Jonathan Cape.
Hutton, W. 1997a. *Stakeholding and Its Critics*. London: Institute of Economic Affairs.
Hutton, W. 1997b. *The State to Come*. London: Vintage.
Hyde, M., Dixon, J. and Joyner, M. 1999. "Work for Those That Can, Security for Those That Cannot": The United Kingdom's New Social Security Reform Agenda. *International Social Security Review* 52 (4) (October): 69–86.
ILO (International Labor Office). 1989. *Social Security Protection in Old-Age*. Geneva: ILO.
Jones, H. M. 1974. *Revolution and Romanticism*. Cambridge, MA: Harvard University Press.
Jordan, B. 1996. *A Theory of Poverty and Social Exclusion*. Cambridge: Polity.
Jordan, B. 1998. *The New Politics of Welfare*. London: Sage.
Keynes, J. M. 1927. *The End of Laissez-Faire*. London: Hogarth.
Keynes, J. M. 1936. *The General Theory of Employment, Interest and Money*. London: Macmillan.
Kooiman, J. 1999. Socio-political Governance: Overview. Reflection and Design. *Public Management* 1 (1): 67–92.
Korpi, W. 1983. *The Democratic Class Struggle*. London: Routledge and Kegan Paul.
Kotlikoff, L. 1996. Rescuing Social Security. *Challenge* 39 (6): 21–22.
Lamont, C. 1965. *The Philosophy of Humanism*. New York: Friedrich Ungar.
Layard, R. 1997. *What Labour Can Do*. London: Warner.
Leung, J.C.B. 1994. Dismantling the "Iron Rice Bowl": Welfare Reform in the People's Republic of China. *Journal of Social Policy* 23 (3): 341–61.
Lister, R. 1989. Social Benefits-Priorities for Redistribution. In Alcock, P., Gamble, A., Gough, I., Lee, P. and Walker, A. (eds.), *The Social Economy and the Democratic State: A New Policy Agenda for the 1990s*. London: Lawrence and Wishart.
Littlewood, M. 1998. *How to Create a Competitive Market in Pensions*. London: Institute of Economic Affairs.
Macham, T. R. 1988. Marxism: A Bourgeois Critique. *International Journal of Social Economics* 15 (11/12): 1–131.
MacKeller, L. and Bird, R. 1997. Global Population Ageing, Social Security and Economic Growth: Some Results from a 2-Region Model. Paper presented at a *Project LINK* meeting, New York, March.
Maret, X. and Schwartz, G. 1994. Poland: Social Protection and the Pension System During the Transition. *International Social Security Review* 47 (2): 51–70.
Marotta, G. 1997. Social Security: Generational Equity. *Vital Speeches of the Day* 63 (12) (April): 364–65.
Marshall, T. H. 1950. *Social Class and Citizenship*. Cambridge: Cambridge University Press.
Marshall, T. H. 1964. Citizenship and Social Class. In Marshall, T. H., *Class, Citizenship and Social Development*. Garden City, NY: Doubleday.
Marshall, T. H. 1965. The Right to Welfare. *Sociological Review* 13 (3): 261–72.
Marsland, D. 1996. *Welfare or Welfare State? Contradictions and Dilemmas in Social Policy*. London: Macmillan.
Martin, B. 1993. *In the Public Interest? Privatisation and Public Sector Reform*. London: Zed.

Marx, K. [1875] 1970. Critique of the Gotha Programme. In Marx, Karl and Engels, Frederick, *Selected Works*. Moscow: Progress Publishers.
Maydell, B. von. 1994. Perspectives on the Future of Social Security. *International Labor Review* 133 (4): 501–10.
Mead, L. 1986. *Beyond Entitlement: The Social Obligations of Citizenship*. New York: The Free Press.
Mead, L. 1998. From Welfare to Work: Lessons from America. In Deacon, A. (ed.), *From Welfare to Work: Lessons from America*. London: Institute of Economic Affairs.
Midgley, J. and Tang, K. 2001. Individualism, Collectivism and the Marketisation of Social Security: Chile and China Compared. *Policy Studies Review*, forthcoming.
Mishra, R. 1990. *The Welfare State in Capitalist Society: Policies of Retrenchment and Maintenance in Europe, North America and Australia*. London: Harvester Wheatsheaf.
Murray, C. 1990. *The Emerging British Underclass*. London: Institute of Economic Affairs.
Murray, C. 1994. *Underclass: The Crisis Deepens*. London: Institute of Economic Affairs.
Myles, J. 1996. When Markets Fail: Social Welfare in Canada and the United States. In Esping-Andersen, G. (ed.), *Welfare States in Transition: National Adaptions in Global Economies*. London: Sage.
Myles, J. and Brym, R. J. 1992. Markets and Welfare: What East and West Can Learn from Each Other. In Ferge, Z. and Kolberg, J. E. (eds.), *Social Policy in a Changing Europe*. Frankfurt am Main, Germany: Campus Verlag; Boulder, CO: Westview.
Nozick, R. 1974. *Anarchy, State and Utopia*. Oxford: Blackwell.
O'Brien, J. C. 1981. The Economist's Quandary: Ethical Values. *International Journal of Social Economics* 8 (3): 26–46.
Paul, G. 1991. *Poverty Alleviation and Social Safety Net Schemes for Economies in Transition* (Working Paper, WP/91/14). Washington, DC: International Monetary Fund.
Pinker, R. 1983. "Traditions of Social Welfare." In Dixon, J. and Jayasuriya, D. L. (eds.), *Social Policy in the 1980's*. Canberra: Canberra College of Advanced Education, in conjunction with the Australasian Social Policy and Administration Association.
Pinker, R. 1991. On Discovering the Middle Way in Social Welfare. In Wilson, T. and Wilson, D. (eds.), *The State and Social Welfare: Objectives of Policy*. Harlow: Longman.
Pinker, R. 1999. New Liberalism and the Middle Way. In Page, M. and Silburn, R. (eds.), *British Social Welfare in the Twentieth Century*. London: Macmillan.
Prinz, C. 1995. Population Ageing and Intergenerational Equity in the Austrian Pension System: A Long-term Analysis of Cohorts Born in the Twentieth Century. Paper presented at *The European Population Conference*, 1995, Session IV (3), Vienna.
Rajnes, D. M. and Turner, J. A. 1996. Retirement Income System Reform in Central and Eastern Europe. *Benefits Quarterly* 12 (1): 49–58.
Rosa, J. J. (ed.). 1982a. *The World Crisis in Social Security*. San Fransisco: Institute for Contemporary Studies.

Rosa, J. J. 1982b. France. In Rosa, J. J. (ed.), *The World Crisis in Social Security*. San Fransisco: Institute for Contemporary Studies.
Rossler, N. 1996. Eastern Europe: How Supplementary Retirement Provision Fits into the New Philosophy. *Benefits and Compensation International* 25 (8): 15–19.
Rys, V. 1994. Social Security Reform in Central Europe: Issues and Strategies. *Journal of European Social Policy* 3 (3): 163–75.
Schobel, B. D. 1992. Sooner Than You Think: The Coming Bankruptcy of Social Security. *Policy Review* 62: 41–42.
Shapiro, D. 1998. The Moral Case for Social Security Privatisation. *Social Security Privatisation* 14: http://www.socialsecurity.org/pubs/ssps/ssp-14es.html.
Simanis, J. G. 1989. National Expenditures on Social Security and Health in Selected Countries. *Social Security Bulletin* 52 (12): 18–26.
Sredkova, K. 1996. Unemployment Insurance in Bulgaria and Other East European Countries: The Transition to a Market Economy. *International Social Security Review* 49 (4): 38–52.
Stoesz, D. and Lusk, M. W. 1995. From Welfare State to Social Compact: Welfare Transformation in Poland. *Journal of Sociology and Social Welfare* 22 (4): 85–98.
Sztompka, P. 1996. Trust and Emerging Democracy: Lessons from Poland. *International Sociology* 11 (1): 37–62.
Tanzi, V. and Schuknecht, L. 1996. Reforming Government in Industrial Countries. *Finance and Development* 33 (September): 2–5.
Taverne, D. 1995. *The Pension Time Bomb in Europe*. London: Federal Trust.
Titmuss, R. 1973. *The Gift Relationship*. Harmondsworth: Penguin.
Townsend, P. 1993. *The International Analysis of Poverty*. London: Harvester Wheatsheaf.
United Kingdom. Commission on Social Justice. 1994. *Social Justice: Strategies for National Renewal*. London: Vintage.
Voirin, M. 1993. Social Security in Central and Eastern European Countries: Continuity and Change. *International Social Security Review* 46 (1): 27–66.
Walker, A. 1984. *Social Planning*. Oxford: Basil Blackwell.
Walker, A. and Walker, C. 1997. *Britain Divided: The Growth of Social Exclusion in the 1980s and 1990s*. London: Child Poverty Action Group.
Williams, F. 1989. *Social Policy: A Critical Introduction*. Cambridge: Polity.
Weimer, D. and Vining, A. R. 1992. *Policy Analysis: Concepts and Practice* (2nd ed.). Englewood Cliffs, NJ: Prentice Hall.
Wolf, C. 1979. A Theory of Nonmarket Failure. *Journal of Law and Economics* 22 (1): 107–39.
World Bank. 1994. *Averting the Old Age Crisis*. New York: Oxford University Press.
Zukowski, M. 1994. Transformation of Economic Systems and Social Security in Central and Eastern Europe. In Maydell, B. von and Hohnerlein, E. M. (eds.), *The Transformation of Social Security Systems in Central and Eastern Europe*. Louvain: Peeters.

*Chapter 2*

# The Market Appropriation of Statutory Social Security: Global Experiences and Governance Issues

John Dixon and Alexander Kouzmin

### INTRODUCTION: THE GLOBAL MARKET APPROPRIATION OF SOCIAL SECURITY

The idea of the provision of mandatory social security by the private sector has acquired a cult status over the last 15 or so years, feeding on the reaction to what is seen as the uneconomic excesses of the state welfare paternalism (Dixon, 1999; Voirin, 1995). This chapter reviews the economic underpinning of the market appropriation of social security. It raises public governance concerns about the ways in which the public interest needs to be protected in perpetuity when private provision is mandated to supplement, or replace, public social security programs. It also anticipates the circumstances under which privatization could well give rise to the specter of government subsidies. Finally, it argues that the "hollowed-out" state must become a "smart" state if the public interest is to be protected in perpetuity. Social security's appropriation by the private sector makes imperative the designing of corporate capacities capable of surviving through "inter-generational infinity." Designing organizational capacity of a "high reliability" (La Porte, 1996) necessitates long-term horizons (Goodman, 1973) and learning capacities that provide corporate sanction and steering that effectively permits the abdication of contractual responsibilities.

The market provision of statutory social security benefits, either as a compliment to, a substitute for, a replacement for (or in lieu of) public (and employer) provision, had happened in 33 countries by the late 1990s (Dixon, 1999; U.S., SSA, 1999; see also Horlick, 1987; Voirin, 1995).

### Complementary Benefit Privatization

The use of approved occupational plans to provide mandatory complementary (supplementary) benefits in relation to long-term contingencies first occurred in

Finland (1961) and France (1960s) and, somewhat later, in Bolivia (1972), Côte d'Ivoire (1976), Switzerland (1985), Liechtenstein (late 1980s), Australia (1988), Venezuela (1990), Mexico (1992), Argentina (1994), Denmark (1998) and Hong Kong (1998). Such mandated market provision typically covers all the long-term contingencies (the exceptions being Argentina [old-age only] and Denmark [old-age and survivors only]) on a defined-contribution basis (the exceptions being Finland where entitlements are based on average pensionable earnings and contribution periods and Denmark where maximum flat-rate old-age entitlement is payable, proportionally reduced, if the contribution period is less than the specified maximum), financed by employer and employee contributions (except in Australia and Venezuela, where only employer contributions are mandated).

**Coverage Contracting-Out**

Contracting-out public old-age, disability and survivor program coverage by contributors to approved occupational plans that provided equivalent (typically defined-contribution) benefits was first permitted in Greece and Malaysia (1951), then India (1952), Singapore (1953), Japan (1954), Sri Lanka (1958), followed by Fiji (1966), Zambia (1973), the Solomon Islands (1976), Papua New Guinea (1980) and Vanuatu (1987) and, finally, the United Kingdom (1988).

The contracting-out of public social security program coverage by contributors to approved personal plans began in Chile (1981) with respect to its sickness and maternity insurance programs. This approach was subsequently adopted in the United Kingdom (1988), with respect to its public old-age, disability and survivor insurance programs; in Peru (1991), with respect to both its public old-age, disability and survivor insurance programs and its public sickness and maternity programs; and then in Argentina (1994) and Colombia (1994), both with respect to their public old-age, disability and survivor programs. Colombia (1995) also permits contracting-out of its public healthcare insurance program into individual healthcare plans.

**Mandatory Market Provision**

Replacing the public provision of long-term contingency social insurance programs with mandatory personal (defined-contribution) programs first began in the early 1980s in Chile (1981) and, a decade later, in Peru (1991), then subsequently Uruguay (1996), Bolivia and Mexico (1997), El Salvador and Hungary (1998), and Poland (1999). Mandatory personal (defined-contribution) programs have also been used to replace mandatory employer-liability measures in Afghanistan (1987) for its employment-injury programs and in Colombia (1991) for its unemployment program.

**Coverage Marketization**

Guatemala (1991) established a mandatory personal (defined-contribution) program to provide its only form of unemployment provision.

## THE MARKETIZATION AGENDA

Advocates of marketization seek to shift the mode of delivery of mandatory social security provision from public provision (which reflects a collective responsibility that enhances social cohesion, integration and inclusion) to market provision (which reflects an individual responsibility that enhances choice and produces enforceable contractual rights). This paradigmatic shift is intended to move the social security debate away from issues of social justice, social inclusion and equality of opportunity toward issues related to the technical realignment of boundaries that demarcate public–private responsibilities for social security, especially regarding funding. Reflecting on market-driven social security systems, Maydell (1994: 506) ponders:

one question that should be asked is whether [such] a system will guarantee the safety of the long-term capital investment for old age and whether it can achieve a measure of equality between the weak and the strong.

At risk are the weak and vulnerable—the poor, the sick and the unemployed—because they are inherently bad insurance risks, which, of commercial necessity, must be culled from the good and profitable risks wherever possible. Only the latter are a good business opportunity. If good risks can be distinguished from bad, why should the former cross-subsidize the latter at the expense of paying higher premiums? This, of course, may become the basis for a clarion call for government subsidies. Thus, those who are most vulnerable, and most in need, confront the prospect of paying contributions they can ill afford or even becoming the new underclass of the uninsurables—if they are excluded from the social security protection available to others—because the insurance risks are being spread across a narrower risk spectrum to minimize contributions and/or to maximize profits (see, for example, Burchardt and Hills, 1997). After all, vertical income redistribution is not a function of the laissez-faire marketplace; it is a task for the state.

The advocates of market provision propagate the view that the marketplace can deliver social security outcomes more cost-efficiently or, even, more cost-effectively than the public sector. Cynics, however, might be tempted to conclude, as Silburn (1998: 244) does, that "the mantra of the unregulated free market forces may act as little more than ideological cover for sectional advantage and, at the extreme, of unbridled corporate greed." Confidence in traditional public provision of long-term pensions (in the event of old-age, disability and death) and short-term benefits (in the event of sickness, maternity, unemployment and dependent support), based on public administration and public financing, has been eroded by the apparent failure of public provision (Caiden, 1991; Hult and Walcott, 1990; Kooiman, 1993) and by assertions of unaffordability (see, for example, Gramlich, 1996; Schieber and Shoven, 1996). The neoliberal advocates of market reform have sought to shift the prevailing social security paradigm away from community solidarity through risk pooling toward individual (not to mention family) responsibility through work and savings, with a view to divesting government of its statutory social security responsibilities. The market reform pressures that have blossomed over the last two decades drew strength from the spirit of liberalism and the apparent virtues of the marketplace, particularly individual responsibility, contractual rights, efficiency and depoliticization. The policy dream is that the marketization of mandatory social security will allow governments to limit tax and contribution burdens and, thus, prevent these burdens from penalizing future generations (Holzmann, 1996; Montas, 1983; Tanner, 1996). The premises upon which this dream rests are that a market infrastructure either exists or can be created in order to implement privatization, that the market can be disciplined by state-sanctioned incentives and disincentives to achieve public social security policy goals, and that the market can deliver public policy goals more efficiently than the public sector.

In developed countries, market reform has its advocates because national social security systems are perceived to be heading rapidly toward financial crisis—the pre-commitment of future generations to unsustainable forced transfers, especially those needed to support an aging population. This is a view, propagated by prophets of doom, with their rhetoric of crisis and their "doom-laden tracts" (Littlewood, 1998: 1), that gives credence to the neoliberal new orthodoxy of anti-statism (Freeden, 1978) and justifies the call, with almost missionary zeal, for radical systemic surgery, however politically unpalatable that may be.

In less developed countries, market reform has its advocates because it offers the hope, if not the promise, of enhanced economic performance—increased domestic savings; enhanced domestic capital market efficiency, depth and liquidity; and reduced labor-market distortions (World Bank, 1994).

## THE MARKETIZATION RHETORIC

Advocates of market reform advance the proposition that individuals should, in their self-interest, fend for themselves in the face of social security risks. They should not depend on governments for "cradle-to-grave" protection that bloats the public social security budget. This brings into focus a rebalancing of the equity and efficiency dimensions of social security. The market reform thrust draws support from neoclassical economic theory: the myth of the marketplace (Engler, 1995), which is, of course, at its neoliberal heart, and which is posited by its neoliberal adherents as being "morally right and economically efficient" as an impersonal distributor of a society's resources (Muller, 1994: 46).

The inevitable neoclassical economic presumption—ideological prejudice—is, in the classical Benthamite tradition (Bentham, [1789] 1970), that the public sector is bloated, inefficient and wasteful, and thus not giving value for money because the absence of any automatic disciplining mechanism permits rent-seeking behavior (Tullock and Eller, 1994) by bureaucrats, their clients and the politicians who govern them, perhaps even with a Machiavellian flair (Gilman et al., 1993; Terrell 1993). Premised on a set of simplistic notions of bureaucratic behavior and theories about democracy, principal–agent relationships, transaction costs, property rights and government failure (see, for example, Arrow, 1963 and 1976; Bryson and Ring, 1990; Coarse, 1937; Weimer and Vining, 1992; Williamson, 1985; but also Self, 1993), there emerges a concern about "opportunism" in public administration. Self-serving, even deceitful and dishonest behavior by bureaucrats contrives with the equally self-serving behavior by politicians and voters to develop public social security programs that distribute benefits to maximize voter support, financed by tax mechanisms that spread the cost across the entire population. The outcome of these neoclassical presumptions is a predisposition toward opposing state provision. They invariably favor market reform, particularly privatization (Donahue, 1989; Gormley, 1994)—"the shifting of a [government] function, either in whole or in part, from the public sector to the private sector" (Butler, 1991: 17)—or, at the very least, the adoption of policy instruments that cause the least "market distortion" (Howlett and Ramesh, 1993). This redrawing of the boundaries around the public sphere does not, however, mean the retreat of the state (see, for example, Dixon, 1988; Dixon and Kouzmin, 1994; Dixon et al., 1995; Kouzmin and Dixon, 1993), for even neoclassical economists accept that public regulation or even public subsidization of private economic activity may be justified if there is market failure or if it produces a merit good. Others would, of course, go further (see, for example, Majone, 1994).

Neoliberals, of course, also accept, quite uncritically, the public choice explanation of the development of the public sector in terms of vote-maximization behavior by politicians and benefit-maximization behavior by voters (Bridges, 1978; Browning, 1975; Velthoven and Winden, 1985; Verbon, 1988). They have a deep suspicion of populist democracy and the proposition that the will of the people should be sovereign. Riker (1982: 238) has pronounced that government does not, and, more importantly, cannot know what the people want. Neoliberals present a broad presumption that individual decision-making is preferred to collective decision-making. Thus, they advocate that the boundaries around state intervention must be redrawn more tightly; the state must thus retreat to create market opportunities for commercial exploitation. As Cerney (1990: 230) notes, the state itself is having to "act increasingly like a market player, shaping its policies to promote, control and maximize returns from market forces in an international setting." It is as if private managerial authority is, without doubt, legitimate, while government authority is a malevolent burden (Rowlands, 1990: 267). Harris and Seldon (1979: 23) captured the spirit of this malevolence when they remarked: "The Welfare State has gradually changed from the expression of compassion to an instrument of political repression unequaled in British history and in other Western industrial societies." Of the neoliberal reform agenda, Cerney (cited in Kouzmin et al., 1997: 19) has observed: "The central policy objective has been to shift public policy from the 'social goal' to the 'economic goal'; from the 'welfare state' to the 'competitive state' " (see also Rieger and Leibfried, 1998).

Neoliberalism, with its penchant for economic models and actuarial predictions, and its specious epistemological dualism of objectivism–subjectivism, is disdainful of irrational values discourse because it involves abhorrent "subjective" judgments. Instead, it prefers to conceptualize social security as a set of purely technical issues. This allows efficiency considerations, essentially supply-side preoccupations, to be stressed and kept well separated from the down-played equity considerations (see, for example, Reichlin and Siconolfi, 1996; but see also Taylor-Gooby, 1999; LeGrand, 1990). Kingson and Williamson (1996: 30) make the pertinent observation:

There is a disturbing tendency in public discourse to reduce social security discussions to mere accounting exercises on the financial costs of the [social security] program, overlooking its value as a source of national social cohesion and as an expression of the obligations of all to each member of the national community, especially those at greatest risk.

Yet neoliberalism does embody a set of politically conservative values (O'Brien and Penna, 1998), the principal tenets of which in the social security context are individual and family responsibility, personal choice, dignity based on contractual relationships, fair returns and economic efficiency. These are, of course, fundamental to neoliberalism's analytical premises and presumptions, which are taken to be axiomatic, requiring no justification. It is as if the economic efficiency of social security systems is all that matters (Ippolito, 1986; Kotlikoff, 1989).

## MARKET APPROPRIATION OF THE PUBLIC INTEREST

The shift from direct public provision of mandatory social security to regulated private provision in a decentralized public policy environment, which, of course, redefines the public–private boundary, moves the state into the realms of "governing without government" (Rhodes, 1997: 46; see also Bolderson, 1985; Peters and Pierre, 1998). The state's seal-of-approval on market provision creates a need for state regulatory intervention, so as to ensure that market providers conduct their affairs in the public interest (Drover, 1999; Mitnick, 1980), but does it have the will, and the wherewithal, to meet that need?

What the public interest is, and how it differs from private interest, may be problematic, as public choice theorists have argued (Arrow, 1963; Olson, 1965).

On the other hand, as communitarians (MacIntyre, 1983; Sandel, 1982; Walzer, 1983) and idealists (Wolff, 1973; Williams, 1985) have insisted, the public interest is grounded in a notion of the collectivity, or the "common good," which is different from, and greater than, the sum of the parts. In this sense, the public interest is constitutive of the individual partly because the common good reflects shared values and creates a social cohesion and identity (Elster, 1991; Plant, 1991).

Liberal democracies are in the midst of a crisis of government legitimacy because there is little belief in the "common good" (Brown, 1994), for as Rouseau (1974) predicted more than two centuries ago, "private interests" regularly prevail over "public interests." Indeed, Rouseau's (1974: 17) long-standing dilemmatic governance challenge remains:

[How] to devise a form of association which will defend and protect the person and possessions of each associate with all the collective strength, and in which each is united with all, yet obeys only himself and remains as free as before.

Faced with this crisis of legitimacy, it is essential that there be a restoration of the fiduciary principle of public interest, which holds that it is the duty of the state to serve and enhance the well-being of all its citizens; thus citizenship rights and obligations must be expounded clearly, assets must be conserved and enhanced, the vulnerable must be protected and diversity must be recognized and acknowledged. Reflecting on the role of independent organizations in a democratic society, Dahl (1982) has argued that the public interest involves a balance between autonomy and control. What, then, is in the public interest is a matter of public policy.

Where the marketplace—with its egotistical assumptions and individualistic presumptions—has become the dominant ideology and the centerpiece of the privatizing state, its obligation is to define an enabling environment for the market provision of mandatory social security that ensures that market providers contribute to the "common good" by achieving public social security policy goals. In so doing the state must address an array of fundamental social security policy issues, including

- appropriate population coverage (such as, whether private provider coverage exemptions should exist for employees in particular industries, occupational groups or employee categories, for the self-employed);
- appropriate forms of benefits (such as, whether defined-contribution or defined-benefit programs should be mandated and whether lump sum benefits should be permitted);
- appropriate contribution rates (such as, whether contribution floors and ceilings should be set, whether contribution rates, including minimum or maximum rates, should be specified);
- appropriate public financial support (such as, whether taxation benefits, minimum benefit guarantees, targeted or general subsidies should be provided); and

- appropriate administrative and financial constraints on private providers (such as institutional management constraints, portfolio management constraints, the public accountability (reporting and disclosure) requirements, the statutory records-keeping requirements, the statutory right-of-access by contributors and beneficiaries to information stored by private providers, the statutory guarantee of confidentiality of such information, the probity (auditing) requirements, the statutory sanctions (at the corporate and responsible-individual level) available to government in the event of institutions acting contrary to the current and future public interests, the statutory winding-up provisions in the event of private providers being unable to meet their financial obligations).

The market provision of mandatory social security also raises concerns that the public interest can only be protected by regulatory compliance within the context of a socio-political governance mechanism (Ward, 1983; Wilks, 1996). Kooiman (1999: 70) defines socio-political governance as "All those interactive arrangements in which public as well as private actors participate aimed at solving societal problems or creating societal opportunities and attending to the institutions within which these governing activities take place." Kooiman (1999: 83–84) distinguishes between three regulatory modes: self-regulation (where the regulated are their own regulators, perhaps by state delegation or default); co-governing (where the regulated voluntarily cede some autonomy to the state in return for agreed common rights and acceptable common obligations); and hierarchical governing (where the regulated are subject to a set of state-imposed rights and obligations). Hierarchical governing involves the design and implementation of regulatory regimes embodying both structural regulations and conduct regulations (Majone, 1994; Wright, 1992). Structural regulations determine the characteristics of acceptable private providers. Conduct regulations determine what are the acceptable forms of institutional behavior and private governance practices in the marketized mandatory social security industry.

The achievement of public social security policy goals in a market environment requires a socio-political governance mechanism that co-ordinates, steers, influences and balances pluralist interactions (Gilbert and Gilbert, 1989; Wright, 1994; Rose, 1996), with the civil service acting as the trustee of the public interest (Ott and Goodman, 1998) although there has long been debate about the governability of modern societies (see Foucault, 1991; Maynetz, 1993; Willke, 1990), about whether any governance mechanism can even be, and remain, focused on the public interest (Edelman, 1964; Lowi, 1969; Peltzman, 1976; Schubert 1960) and about the causes of regulatory failure (Donahue, 1989; Gormley, 1994; Kettle, 1993). The design features of regulatory regimes (their requirements, structures, culture and processes) determine the degree to which there is a threat of asymmetrical information (the regulated actors distorting or withholding the information needed by regulators to regulate effectively) and the degree of risk of agency capture (the regulated actors manipulating the regulators by, perhaps, strategic agenda setting or compromise bargaining at the political or administrative levels to achieve their ends) (Bernstein, 1955; Majone, 1994; Wright, 1992). Thus a governance regime for a marketized mandatory social security industry to oversight should have the following features. First, it should be flexible enough to allow the regulated market providers to respond to the challenges of complexity, diversity and the dynamics of modern society (Lamour, 1997). Second, it should place the private and the public sectors as a co-operative continuum rather than a conflictual dichotomy (LeGrand and Robinson, 1984). Third, it should be transparent, so as to engender public trust (Taylor-Gooby, 1999) in an environment where the assessment of future social security risks and the market products available to meet them is problematic and to foster co-ordination and co-operation between the community-at-large, the regulated market providers and the public regulators. Fourth, it should acknowledge that participation as a precondition for human action and interaction (Doyal and Gough, 1991; Drover and Kerans, 1993). Fifth, and finally, it should foster equitable outcomes (Rees et al., 1993).

The private sector's interest in achieving profit goals and the public sector's interest in achieving public policy goals are not good bedfellows: this is the privatization dilemma. Whether the public interest is appropriated by the market depends crucially on whether the state is willing and able to design and implement a regulatory mechanism that ensures mandatory market provision that meets promised needs when contracted to do so, that fosters equitable outcomes, that requires losses as well as profits to be privatized without detriment to current and future beneficiaries, and that produces the expected budgetary savings on public social security expenditure. These policy and governance imperatives are central to the maintenance of public trust and confidence in privatized mandatory provision. There is little reason to be confident that the state can resist the appropriation of the public interest by the market, and, perhaps, the appropriation of public revenue to market providers.

## MARKET APPROPRIATION OF TAX REVENUE

The market provision of mandatory social security could well give rise to the specter of government subsidies. It should be noted that Argentina, Chile (Borzutzky, 1990 and 1993; Castaneda, 1992) and Colombia already subsidize their personal retirement pension plan systems to guarantee a minimum pension rate (see also Queisser, 1995). Subsidization could emerge under two sets of circumstances.

First, pressures for government subsidies to be paid to mandated defined-contribution (money purchase) plans would build up if their achieved levels of accumulated savings (or equivalent annuities) are so inadequate, or so much below community expectations, as to be fiscally and politically unacceptable. Because defined-contribution plans place the burden of the risk of asset value variations on their members (covered employees), then members' interests may not be congruent with those of the plan administrators and investment fund managers. The cost of any financial mismanagement or malfeasance is carried by members unless the government acts as a guarantor, which might, of course, only encourage greater risk taking by commission-driven investment fund managers. Members also carry the cost of not minimizing administrative charges, unless government provides some form of administrative subsidy, which might encourage inefficiency. Members, furthermore, carry the cost of unpaid contributions from insolvent employers unless government subsidizes this group, which might encourage voluntary insolvency by employers as an acceptable way of avoiding their statutory social security obligations. Making mandatory the membership of what were previously voluntary defined-contribution plans thus places a responsibility on government to design and administer an appropriate regulatory regime in order to reconcile the inherent tensions generated by using profit-making organizations to deliver statutory social security outcomes, so as to ensure both their long-term solvency and the adequacy of their benefits (Daykin, 1995; Dixon, 1995). As Wright (1992: 1031) observes "welfare and profit-maximization are not good bedfellows." Any socio-political governance failure may well encourage the specter of government subsidization.

Second, pressures for government subsidies to mandated defined-benefit plans would emerge with any diminution of the profitability (or financial viability) of such plans. Such subsidies, of course, may be, initially, politically more acceptable to enacting, endorsing or, even, merely permitting either increases in the employee and/or employer contribution rates or decreases in benefit generosity. Such subsidized plans may even, eventually, become cheaper than reintegrating their covered employees back into the public social security system. With any such subsidization, however, comes the prospect of efficiency distortions, which may well overshadow any efficiency benefits gained. In these circumstances, the government subsidization ghost will come to haunt countries as they confront the prospect of a fragmented, inefficient and costly social security system.

## WHAT A SMART STATE MIGHT DO

Any re-positioning of the state along the public–private spectrum in market economies requires a recognition of the importance of the social dimension to economic growth and development, for it is one of the resources relied upon by governments to minimize social dislocation when markets expand beyond the moral and political boundaries within which they operate (Dertouzos et al., 1989; Boyer and Drache, 1996).

Public domains define the institutional capacities to bring about consensus, to achieve equity, and to protect the public interest. The key challenge thus confronting the "hollowed out," post-Keynesian, privatized Welfare State is how it can efficiently and effectively manage the failures of the marketplace and the social distortions that flow from state-mandated private social security provision. New policy and administrative capabilities are required if desirable public policy outcomes are to be achieved and if the public interest is to be protected.

The challenge confronting a diminishing public social security domain is to re-invent itself in such a way as to ensure the state's continued legitimacy and its effectiveness in protecting the public interest in perpetuity—by ensuring that mandatory market provision meets promised needs when contracted to do so, by fostering equitable outcomes, by requiring losses as well as profits to be privatized without detriment to current and future beneficiaries and by producing the expected budgetary savings on public social security expenditure. These policy and governance imperatives are central to the maintenance of public trust and confidence in privatized mandatory provision. There is, thus, a need for clarification and empirical verification of the relationship between residual public provision, governance practices and the market in order to appropriately frame critical public policy debates and discourses (Cable, 1995). This requires a close scrutiny of the strengths and weaknesses of, and the threats and challenges posed by, private sector encroachment into an established public social security domain. The resultant re-positioning of the state—from being a direct public provider to being a regulator of mandatory private provision—requires governments to have a comprehensive sense of

- how the public domain has changed—functions foregone, whether privatized or outsourced—and the impact that that has had on the state's capacity to deliver its residual functions because of the resultant organizational de-skilling; and
- whether any structural and administrative reforms initiated to enhance the public domain's cost-effectiveness have gone far enough, too far or are about right.

Moreover, the public social security domain must be administered by agencies with characteristics that have not always been in evidence in the public sector. They must be capable of learning—from their own experiences and the experiences of other institutions in other jurisdictions. They must focus on long-term and strategic policy perspectives—the privatized delivery of desirable policy outcomes in perpetuity. They must facilitate modes of policy reasoning—essentially, when private interest in achieving profit goals comes into conflict with the public interest in achieving public policy goals.

## CONCLUSION

The shift from public provision of mandatory social security (which reflects a collective responsibility that enhances social cohesion, integration and inclusion) to market provision (which reflects an individual responsibility that enhances choice and produces enforceable contractual rights) has moved the social security policy debate away from issues of social justice, social inclusion and equality of opportunity toward issues related to the demarcation of public–private responsibilities. These market appropriation pressures have blossomed over the last two decades. The policy dream is that the privatization of mandatory social security will allow governments to limit tax and contributions burdens and thus prevent them from penalizing future generations or current privileged sectors of society.

The daunting twin challenges facing governments grappling with the market appropriation of their public social security systems are, first, to design a set of regulatory arrangements that can protect the public interest in perpetuity, and, second, to resist calls for government subsidies to support the economic rent expectations of privatized providers. To meet these challenges the "hollowed-out" state must become a "smart" state.

## NOTE

This chapter is a considerably expanded version of a paper to be published in the *Policy Studies Review* symposium on "The Marketization of Social Security: A Cross-national Perspective" (forthcoming).

## REFERENCES

Arrow, K. J. 1963. *Social Choice and Individual Values* (2nd ed.). New York: Wiley.
Arrow, K. J. 1976. Values and Collective Decision-making. In Laslett, P. and Runciman, W. G. (eds.), *Philosophy, Politics and Society*. Oxford: Basil Blackwell.
Bentham, J. [1789] 1970. *An Introduction to the Principles of Morals and Legislation*. London: Athlone.
Bernstein, M. H. 1955. *Regulating Business by Independent Commission*. Princeton, NJ: Princeton University Press.
Bolderson, H. 1985. The State at One Remove: Examples of Agency Arrangements and Regulatory Powers in Social Policy. *Policy and Politics* 13 (1): 17–36.
Borzutzky, S. 1990. Chile. In Dixon, J. and Scheurell, R. P. (eds.), *Social Welfare in Latin America*. London: Routledge.
Borzutzky, S. 1993. Social Security and Health Policies in Latin America: The Changing Roles of the State and the Private Sector. *Latin American Research Review* 28 (2): 246–56.
Boyer, R. and Drache, D. (eds.). 1996. *States against Markets: The Limits of Globalization*. London: Routledge.
Bridges, S. 1978. Why the Social Insurance Budget Is Too Large in a Democracy: A Comment. *Economic Inquiry* 16 (January): 133–42.
Brown, P. 1994. *Restoring the Public Trust*. Boston: Beacon Press.
Browning, E. K. 1975. Why the Social Insurance Budget Is Too Large in a Democracy. *Economic Inquiry* 13 (September): 373–87.
Bryson, J. and Ring, P. S. 1990. A Transaction-Based Approach to Policy Intervention. *Policy Sciences* 23 (3): 205–29.
Burchardt, T. and Hills, J. 1997. *Private Welfare Insurance and Social Security*. York: York Publishing Services in association with the Roundtree Trust.
Butler, S. 1991. Privatization and Public Purposes. In Gormley, W. T. (ed.), *Privatization and Its Alternatives*. Madison: University of Wisconsin Press.

Cable, V. 1995. The Diminished Nation-State: A Study in the Loss of Economic Power. *Daedalus* 124 (2) (Spring): 23–53.
Caiden, G. E. 1991. *Administrative Reform Comes of Age*. Berlin and New York: de Gruyter.
Castaneda, T. 1992. *Combating Poverty: Innovative Social Reform in Chile during the 1980s*. San Francisco: ICS Press.
Cerney, P. 1990. *The Changing Architecture of Politics: Structure, Agency and the Future of the State*. London: Sage.
Coarse, R. 1937. The Nature of Firms. *Economica* (new series) 4 (3): 386–405.
Dahl, R. 1982. *Dilemmas of Plural Democracy*. New Haven, CT: Yale University Press.
Daykin, C. D. 1995. Financial Management and Control of Supplementary Pension Schemes. *International Social Security Review* 48 (3–4): 75–89.
Dertouzos, M. L., Lester, R. K. and Solow, R. M. 1989. *Made in America*. Cambridge, MA: MIT Press.
Dixon, J. 1988. The Changing Nature of Public Administration in Australia. *Public Personnel Management* 17 (2): 231–36.
Dixon, J. 1995. *Mandatory Occupational Retirement Savings: Towards a Program Design Agenda for Hong Kong*. Working Paper 17 (2/95). Hong Kong: Center for Public Policy Studies, Lingnan College.
Dixon. J. 1999. *Social Security in Global Perspective*. Westport, CT: Praeger.
Dixon, J. and Kouzmin, A. 1994. Management Innovations for Improving Governance: Changes and Trends in Australian Public Administration and Finance. *Asian Review of Public Administration* 6 (1 and 2): 33–91.
Dixon, J., Kouzmin, A., and Wilson, J. 1995. Commercialising "Washminster" in Australia: What Lessons? *Public Money and Management* 15 (1): 1–8.
Donahue, R. 1989. *The Privatization Decision: Public Ends, Private Means*. New York: Basic Books.
Doyal, L. and Gough, I. 1991. *A Theory of Human Need*. London: Macmillan.
Drover, G. and Kerans, P. (eds.). 1993. *New Approaches to Welfare Theory*. London: Edward Elgar.
Drover, G. 1999. Personal correspondence.
Edelman, M. 1964. *The Symbolic Uses of Politics*. Urbana: Univeristy of Illinios Press.
Elster, J. 1991. *The Cement of Society: A Study of Social Order*. Cambridge: Cambridge University Press.
Engler, A. 1995. *Apostles of Greed: Capitalism and the Myth of the Market*. London: Pluto Press.
Foucault, M. 1991. Governmentality. In Burchaell, G., Gordon, C. and Miller, P. (eds.), *The Foucault Effect: Studies in Governability*. London: Harvester Wheatsheaf.
Freeden, M. 1978. *The New Liberalism: An Ideology of Social Reform*. Oxford: Clarendon Press.
Gilbert, N. and Gilbert, B. 1989. *The Enabling State*. Oxford: Oxford University Press.
Gilman, S. C., Stupak, R., Jr., and Collier, T. J., Jr. 1993. Machiavelli Reinvented: Integrity, Power, and Democratic Responsibility. *Public Manager* 22 (3): 24–26.
Goodman, R. A. 1973. Environmental Knowledge and Organizationnal Time Horizons: Some Functions and Dysfunctions. *Human Relations* 26 (2): 54–65.
Gormley, W. T., Jr. 1994. Privatization Revisited. *Policy Studies Review* 13 (3/4): 215–34.

Gramlich, E. M. 1996. Different Approaches to Dealing with Social Security. *American Economic Review* 86 (2): 358–62.
Harris, R. and Selden, A. 1979. *Over-ruled on Welfare: The Increasing Desire for Choice in Education and Medicine and Its Frustration by Representative Government* (Hobart Papers 13). London: Institute of Economic Affairs.
Holzmann, R. 1996. *Pension Reform, Financial Market Development, and Economic Growth: Preliminary Evidence from Chile.* IMF Working Paper WP/96/94 (August). Washington, DC: International Monetary Fund.
Horlick, M. 1987. The Relationship between Public and Private Pension Schemes: An Introductory Overview. *Social Security Bulletin* 50 (7): 3–6.
Howlett, M. and Ramesh, M. 1993. Patterns of Policy Choice: Policy Styles, Policy Learning and the Privatization Experience. *Policy Studies Review* 12 (1/2): 3–24.
Hult, K. and Walcott, C. 1990. *Governing Public Organizations.* Belmont, CA: Brooks/Cole Publishing Company.
International Social Security Association (ISSA). 1993. Complementary Retirement Pensions in Europe. *International Social Security Review* 46 (4): 67–71.
Ippolito, R. A. 1986. *Pensions, Economics and Public Policy.* Homewood, IL: Dow Jones.
Kettle, D. F. 1993. *Sharing Power: Public Governance and Private Markets.* Washington, DC: Brookings Institution.
Kingson, E. R. and Williamson, J. 1996. Undermining Social Security's Basic Objective. *Challenge* 39 (6): 28–30.
Kooiman, J. 1993. *Modern Governance: New Government-Society Interactions.* Beverly Hills, CA: Sage.
Kooiman, J. 1999. Socio-political Governance: Overview. Reflection and Design. *Public Management* 1 (1): 67–92.
Kotlikoff, L. J. 1989. On the Contribution of Economics to the Evaluation and Formation of Social Security Policy. *American Economic Review* 79 (2): 184–90.
Kouzmin, A. and Dixon, J. 1993. The Dimensions of Quality in Public Management: Australian Perspectives and Experiences. In Hill, H. and Klages, H. (eds.), *Qualitats und Erfolgsorientierte Vervaltung: Aktualle Tendenzen und Entwurfe* [Quality and Success-Oriented Administrative Management: Current Trends and Models]. Berlin: Dunker and Humbolt.
Kouzmin, A., Leivesley, R. and Korac-Kakabadse, N. 1997. From Managerialism and Economic Rationalism: Towards "Reinventing" Economic Ideology and Administrative Diversity. *Administrative Theory and Praxis* 19 (1): 19–46.
Lamour, P. 1997. Models of Governance and Public Administration. *International Review of Administrative Science* 63 (3): 383–94.
La Porte, T. D. 1996. High Reliability Organizations: Unlikely, Demanding and at Risk. *Journal of Contingency and Crisis Management* 4 (2): 60–71.
LeGrand, J. 1990. Equity versus Efficiency: The Elusive Trade-off. *Ethics* 100 (4): 554–68.
LeGrand, J. and Robinson, R. 1984. *Privatisation and the Welfare State.* London: Macmillan.
Littlewood, M. 1998. *How to Create a Competitive Market in Pensions* (Choice in Welfare, 45). London: Institute of Economic Affairs, Health and Welfare Unit.
Lowi, T. 1969. *The End of Liberalism.* New York: Norton.
MacIntyre, A. 1983. *After Virtue.* Notre Dame, IN: University of Notre Dame.

Majone, G. 1994. The Rise of the Regulatory State in Europe. *West European Politics* 17 (3): 77–101.
Maydell, B. von. 1994. Perspectives on the Future of Social Security. *International Labor Review* 133 (4): 501–10.
Maynetz, R. 1993. Governing Failure and the Problem of Governability: Some Comments on a Theoretical Paradigm. In Kooiman, J. (ed.), *Modern Governance: New Government-Society Interactions*. London: Sage.
Mitnick, B. M. 1980. *The Political Economy of Regulation*. New York: Columbia University Press.
Montas, H. P. 1983. Problems and Perspectives in the Financing of Social Security in Latin America. *International Social Security Review* 36 (1): 70–87.
Muller, W. C. 1994. Political Traditions and the Role of the State. *West European Politics* 17 (3): 32–51.
O'Brien, M. and Penna, S. 1998. *Theorising Welfare: Enlightenment and Modern Society*. London: Sage.
Olson, M. 1965. *The Logic of Collective Action*. Cambridge, MA: Harvard University Press.
Ott, J. S. and Goodman, D. 1998. Government Reform or Alternative Bureaucracy? Thickening Tides and the Future of Governing. *Public Administration Review* 58 (6): 540–45.
Peltzman, S. 1976. Towards a General Theory of Regulation. *Journal of Law and Economics* 19 (August): 2–40.
Peters, B. G. and Pierre, J. 1998. Governance without Government? Rethinking Public Administration. *Journal of Public Administration Research and Theory* 8 (3): 223–43.
Plant, R. 1991. *Modern Political Thought*. Oxford: Basil Blackwell.
Queisser, M. 1995. Chile and Beyond: The Second Generation Pension Reforms in Latin America. *International Social Security Review* 48 (3 and 4): 23–40.
Rees, S., Rodley, G. and Stilwell, F.J.B. (eds.). 1993. *Beyond the Market: Alternatives to Economic Rationalism*. Sydney: Pluto Press.
Reichlin, P. and Siconolfi, P. 1996. The Role of Social Security in an Economy with Asymmetrical Information and Financial Intermediaries. *Journal of Public Economics* 60 (2): 153–75.
Rhodes, R.A.W. 1997. *Understanding Governance: Policy Networks, Governance, Reflexivity and Accountability*. Buckingham: Open University Press.
Rieger, E. and Liebfried, S. 1998. Welfare State Limits to Globalization. *Politics and Society* 26 (3): 361–85.
Riker, W. H. 1982. *Liberalism against Populism: A Confrontation between the Theory of Democracy and the Theory of Social Choice*. San Francisco: W. H. Freeman.
Rose, N. 1996. The Death of the Social? Re-figuring the Territory of Government. *Economy and Society* 25 (3): 327–56.
Rousseau, J. (1974). The Social Contract. In Blair, L. (trans.), *The Essential Rousseau*. New York: New American Library.
Rowlands, D. 1990. Privatization and Managerial Ideology. In Kouzmin, A. and Scott, N. (eds.), *Dynamics in Australian Public Management: Selected Essays*. Melbourne: Macmillan.
Sandel, M. 1982. *Liberalism and the Limits of Justice*. Cambridge: Cambridge University Press.

Schieber, S. J. and Shoven, J. B. 1996. Social Security Reform: Around the World in 80 Ways. *American Economic Review* 86 (2): 373–77.

Schubert, G. 1960. *The Public Interest*. New York: Free Press.

Self, P. 1993. *Government by the Market? The Politics of Public Choice*. London: Macmillan.

Silburn, R. 1998. United Kingdom. In Dixon, J. and Macarov, D. (eds.), *Poverty: A Persistent Global Reality*. London: Routledge.

Tanner, M. 1996. It's Time to Privatize Social Security. *Challenge* 39 (6): 19–20.

Taylor-Gooby, P. 1999. Markets and Motives: Implications for Welfare. *Journal of Social Policy* 28 (1): 97–114.

Terrell, K. 1993. Public–Private Wage Differentials in Haiti: Do Public Servants Earn a Rent? *Journal of Development Economics* 12 (2): 293–314.

Tullock, G. and Eller, K. 1994. *Rent Seeking*. London: Edward Elgar.

United States. Social Security Administration (U.S. SSA). 1999. *Social Security Programs throughout the World*. Washington, DC: Social Security Administration, Office of Policy, Office of Research, Evaluation and Statistics.

Velthoven, B. van and Winden, F.A.A.M. van. 1985. Towards a Political-Economic Theory of Social Security. *European Economic Review* 27: 263–89.

Verbon, H. 1988. *The Evolution of Public Pension Schemes*. Berlin: Springer-Verlag.

Voirin, M. 1995. Private and Public Pension Schemes: Elements of a Comparative Approach. *International Social Security Review* 48 (3–4): 91–141.

Walzer, M. 1983. *Spheres of Justice: A Defense of Pluralism and Justice*. New York: Basic Books.

Ward, E. J. 1983. *An Exploration of the Public Interest Concept: Towards an Enhanced Theoretical and Practical Understanding*. Ann Arbor, MI: UMI Dissertation Information Service.

Weimer, D. L. and Vining, A. R. 1992. *Policy Analysis: Concepts and Practice* (2nd ed.). Englewood Cliffs, NJ: Prentice Hall.

Wilks, S. 1996. Regulatory Compliance and Capitalist Diversity in Europe. *Journal of European Public Policy* 3 (4): 536–59.

Williams, B. 1985. *Ethics and the Limits of Philosophy*. London: Collins.

Williamson, O. E. 1985. *The Economic Institutions of Capitalism: Firms, Markets, Rational Contracting*. New York: Free Press.

Willke, H. 1990. Disenchantment of the State: Outline of a Systems Theoretical Argumentation. In Ellwein, T., Mayntz, R. and Scharpf, F. (eds.), *Yearbook in Government and Public Administration*. Baden-Baden: Nomos.

Wolff, R. P. 1973. *The Autonomy of Reason*. New York: Harper Torchbooks.

World Bank. 1994. *Averting the Old Age Crisis*. New York: Oxford University Press.

Wright, V. 1992. The Administrative System and Market Regulation in Western Europe: Continuities, Exceptionalism and Convergence. *Rivista Trimestrale di Diritto Pubblico* (4): 1026–41.

Wright, V. 1994. Reshaping the State: The Implications for Public Administration. *Western European Politics* 17 (3): 102–37.

*Chapter 3*

# Chile's Pioneering Privatization

## Silvia Borzutzky

### INTRODUCTION

Chile's privatization of its public pension system took place in 1980. The first section of this chapter contains a summary of the system that existed before 1980, highlighting its main characteristics and problems. The next section deals with the political and economic context in which the process of privatization of the pension system took place and the main characteristics of the reform. Since the reform has been in place for almost 20 years, the chapter concludes with an assessment of its socio-economic impact. Special attention is given to its impact on the insured, on the state and on the national economy. The chapter concludes with a socio-political analysis of the reform and the lessons that can be drawn from the Chilean case. Central to the analysis presented here is the notion that Chile's privatization of its pension system resulted from, and was a by-product of, an authoritarian regime. The only base of legitimacy of the policy makers was their access to and close relationship with the authoritarian ruler.

### POPULIST POLITICS AND POLICIES: CHARACTERISTICS AND PROBLEMS OF THE OLD SYSTEM, 1924–1973

Between 1924 and 1925 Chile experienced major political and economic transformations. During those two years, a flurry of legislation prompted by Chile's social and economic crisis created a new constitution and enacted a set of social and political laws that would become the backbone of Chile's political organization for the next 48 years. While the constitution of 1925 established a presidential-type democracy, what emerged was a form of populism structured around a multiparty system. The labor and social laws of 1924 set the bases for the new social security system, which included old-age and retirement pensions as well as maternity and health benefits. The various political parties represented different sectors of the urban society. While the right wing parties represented the interest of the urban bourgeoisie, the center and leftist parties developed strong ties with the most vocal sections of the working class. The labor and social laws of 1924 set the bases for the new social insurance system. Its subsequent evolution was simply a result of the nature of the political system created in 1924–1925 and the persistent problems of the Chilean economy.

The social insurance system created in 1924 was inspired by the need to provide a minimum pension, family allowances, and maternity and health benefits to selected groups of the population. The pension system was organized around four funds, each of which covered a specific occupational group. The original funds provided benefits to blue-collar workers, white-collar workers, civil servants and the armed forces. The self-employed and the peasants were excluded from the system (Borzutzky, 1983: 89–97).

Central to the expansion of the system over the next 50 years were two dichotomies: the divisions between dependent and independent workers and between urban and rural workers. The system evolved toward the protection of the dependent, urban worker. By 1973, 92.4 percent of the workers in this group had pension benefits while only about 50 percent of the rural population was covered. Only 10 percent of the independent workers were entitled to pensions. The system provided old-age, disability and survivors' pension benefits to over 70 percent of the population making the Chilean system one of the most comprehensive systems in Latin America.

Between 1925 and 1973 the original four funds became fragmented into hundreds of small funds providing special benefits to selected groups. A dynamic evolved in which small sub-groups separated themselves from the basic funds and secured the legislative creation of their own pension system. Alternatively, a group would stay in the main fund but would acquire special privileges that in fact amounted to having a separate fund. The size and power of the group depended entirely on the political circumstances and on the relations of the group with key members of congress. This resulted in the creation of 160 different funds and a legal labyrinth of about "1600 laws, decrees, and regulations [which] remained uncompiled and uncoordinated" (Mesa-Lago, 1978: 33).

Originally the pension system was financed through contributions from employers, workers and the state. Between 1925 and 1973 the four funds evolved into about 50 financial subsystems. This resulted in skyrocketing costs and constant deficits that demanded direct government financing. Different governments dealt with this deficit either through direct transfers from the fiscal budget or by establishing new taxes directly earmarked for social security. The end result was an anarchic and unfair financial system. For instance, in the public sector employers' contributions fluctuated between zero and 52 percent of the salary, while in the private sector they fluctuated between 49 and 285 percent (Borzutzky, 1983: 98). In the final analysis the most salient characteristics of the financial structure were inequality and regressiveness. Carmelo Mesa-Lago, for instance, concluded that of the four main occupational groups, the armed forces received the most generous benefits while contributing the least to the system. The top administrative agency, the Superintendencia of Social Security reached similar conclusions (Mesa-Lago, 1978: 49; Briones, 1968: 71–79).

The same kind of unfairness and anarchy was found in the benefits system. The original systems provided old-age and disability pensions as well as health care and maternity benefits to the four groups. Over the years special benefits were created for particular groups. Among the most expensive were the so-called *perseguidoras* and pension schedules based on the number of years of service. *Perseguidoras* were a special type of pension that were tied to the value of the salary received by the person currently performing the job. The pensions, based on the length of service, were granted after the beneficiary had completed a certain number of years of service regardless his or her age. They were extremely costly, and they were paid directly out of public revenues. Both benefits were granted to special groups among the civil servants and the white-collar workers.

The dismemberment of the funds and the chaotic structure of benefits and finance resulted from the clientele ties developed between a divided but organized working class and the political system. Especially important were the ties developed by the different groups with different members of congress. Also important was the unequal distribution of income and wages and the inflationary process that characterized the Chilean economy. High inflation and income inequalities were responsible for both poverty and inadequate pensions (Hirschman,1963; Mamalakis, 1976; Pinto, 1962; Stallings, 1978).

The system also provided family allowances and health and maternity benefits. Both systems were organized around the main occupational groups. While family allowances were financed by employer contributions, the health system was financed through a combination of state, employer and employee contributions. The system also provided benefits in cases of occupational accidents.

President Alessandri (1958–1964) and President Frei (1964–1970) tried to reform the system, but they failed. Reforming social security entailed a direct attack on the benefits and privileges of powerful interest groups and the nature of the electoral and political processes simply impeded the reform. As a consequence, the system continued to grow in a dismembered form, costs skyrocketed, the financial crisis deepened and the regressive nature of the social security system continued to affect the poorest sectors of the society.

In contrast to these earlier attempts to reform the social security system, President Allende (1970–1973) sought only its expansion. Thus, between 1970 and 1973, coverage continued to expand in the same piecemeal fashion, and existing problems only became worse. The most important problem, the fiscal crisis, was reinforced by the growing phenomenon of the "massification" of benefits and exemptions (Mesa Lago, 1978). Massification of benefits produced the constant expansion of the benefits received by the different groups while the massification of exemptions reflected the power of the entrepreneurial groups and their ability to create a system of legalized evasion.

The 1973 coup marked the end of a long period of democracy in Chile. The new regime was able to reform the system without having to deal with the views and interests of the society. The new rulers also destroyed Chile's democratic institutions and political leadership.

## AUTHORITARIAN POLITICS AND POLICIES

The bloody coup of September 11, 1973, put an end to Chile's long democratic tradition. The actions and policies pursued by General Pinochet and his associates in the following weeks led to the death of President Allende and destroyed Chile's democratic institutions. Congress was closed, political parties and other political organizations were banned, and Chilean society experienced the full force of General Pinochet's repressive policies. Political leaders were killed, imprisoned or forced into exile.

The military regime faced two fundamental tasks: the disarticulation of the remnants of the previous system and the reorganization of the society. The reorganization involved the total transformation of the economic functions of the Chilean state in accordance with neoliberal principles. The central proposition here is that there was a great deal of complementarity between the authoritarian nature of the political system and the adoption of the neoliberal economic principles on the part of General Pinochet's policy makers. The adoption of the neoliberal economic model, in turn, resulted from the influence of a group of Chilean economists trained at the University of Chicago who had developed very close ties with the Pinochet regime.

It is important to note that since the beginning, the Pinochet regime demonstrated a strong interest in the problems of the social security system. This resulted in partial reforms to the family allowances system that led to the unification of the funds in 1973 and the enactment of Decree 2448 in 1978 that eliminated the *perseguidoras* and the pensions based on years of service. An early attempt to carry out a total reform of the system failed due to the opposition of members of the ruling Junta, particularly Commander in Chief of the Air Force, General Gustavo Leigh (Borzutzky, 1983: 286–95).

The enactment of the 1980 reform resulted from changes to the internal structure of the Pinochet regime. On the one hand, General Pinochet was able to consolidate his personal power through a series of political moves that included the 1978 plebiscite and the subsequent elimination of General Leigh from the Junta. From an economic standpoint, 1978 was the year in which the neoliberal economists trained in Chicago were able to obtain full control of the centers of economic decision making. Between 1978 and 1980, the "Chicago boys" were able to carry out substantial economic reforms, known as the "modernizations." The pension reform was the product of the ideas of a group of economists led by the former Minister of Labor, Jose Piñera, and the Director of the National

Planning Office, Miguel Kast, and it was a key component of the process of economic modernization (Borzutzky, 1991; Piñera, 1991; Valdes, 1989). Minister Piñera was in charge of transforming labor law and the social security and health systems.

The privatization of the pension system in Chile has two major dimensions: the elimination of the social security tax paid by the employer and the transfer of the administration of the funds to private-for-profit enterprises. The new system is characterized by the establishment of private corporations charged exclusively with the administration of pension funds; by the creation of a compulsory, individual, pension fund; and by a system of minimum pensions financed either totally or partially by the state. According to Minister Piñera, the reform was intended to strengthen the private sector, disperse economic power, diminish the size and functions of the state and reduce the financial burden of the state (Piñera, 1991).

## FINANCIAL STRUCTURE

The 1980 legislation introduced a number of substantial reforms which changed the very basis of the financial system underpinning Chilean pensions, undermined the principle of solidarity and reinforced individualism. It involved the elimination of the employer's contributions to the pension system and the transformation of the common fund system, *sistema de reparto*, formed by the contributions of employers, employees and in some cases the state, into individual funds.

The reduction of the employer's contribution to the pension system had begun in 1975 when contributions were reduced from 43.3 percent of the taxable wages to 20.3 percent in 1980 (Arellano, 1981). The 1980 legislation maintained only a 1 percent contribution to the workmen's compensation fund, and a temporary, 2.85 percent tax to finance the family allowance and the unemployment insurance programs. By 1988, all employer contributions had been eliminated. The purpose of the elimination of the social security tax was to lower the cost of labor and, in turn, reduce unemployment rates. Employee contributions to the system were also reduced, but only for those workers who transferred their social security funds to the new system.

In the late 1990s, the insured were paying a 10 percent contribution to the old-age pension system. Additional contributions of 2.5 percent to 3.7 percent were required to finance the invalidity and survivors' pensions. The insured could also make additional contributions of up to 10 percent to augment the old-age pension fund, and they had to deposit another 7 percent of wages to obtain health and maternity benefits. Consequently, the total compulsory contribution in the private sector amounted to between 19.5 percent and 20.7 percent, while the contribution in the public sector was about 27 percent (Mesa-Lago, 1994: 18).

This large reduction in contributions to the pension system resulted from the reduction in social security expenditures that was mandated by Decree (D. L.) 2448. Specifically, the elimination of the pensions based on years of service, the increase in the retirement age to 60 years for women and 65 for men, and the elimination of the *desahucio* or cash benefit paid in relation to the years of service, all produced a sizable reduction in expenditures. Better compliance with the laws produced an increase in revenues (Arellano, 1981: 15; Cóstabal, 1981: 10).

Officials in the administration argued that the elimination of the social security tax would reduce the cost of labor, which in turn would reduce unemployment. Martin Cóstabal, a close associate of Minister Piñera, Chairman of the Reform Commission and Director of the National Budget Office, argued that the reform would produce in the medium and long range between 100,000 and 200,000 jobs (Cóstabal, 1981: 10).

The common fund system, which had been under attack from the neoliberals since 1974, was replaced by the individual capitalization fund. For Píñera (1980: 2) the common fund had not only failed to achieve its fundamental purpose, social solidarity, but it had generated and encouraged social inequalities, economic inefficiencies and insufficiencies that characterized the whole social security system.

Logically, then, the problem had to be attacked at its roots: replacing a system based on the collectivist ideology with one based on a reluctant collectivist ideology, which "establishes a clear relationship between the personal effort and reward" and which "gives the individual the freedom of choosing and deciding" (Piñera, 1980: 6). The elimination of the common fund system complemented the elimination of the social security tax and established a system that might be defined as a mandatory individual capitalization system.

There is little doubt that the main factor underlying the replacement of the common fund by the individual fund was the individualistic ideology sustained by the regime. Piñera's argument was that the old system failed to achieve its goal, and instead of creating a better society for all, it created a better system for those with enough power to get the benefits from the politicians. For the others it created simply a hope and also a deception, a mirage formed by unattainable benefits. However, in the new system the nature and extent of the social security fund and benefits are mediated by the market and by the individual's position in the market. There is no question that every Chilean has the right to have a substantial pension; the requirement for this is simply having a well-paid, permanent job that allows savings to be made for the future. Unfortunately, not all Chileans can meet this requirement.

It is important to mention that the Armed Forces were not incorporated to the new system, but maintained their own older system. Why did the military seek exclusion from the new system? Although there is very little information on this question, it is quite obvious that the military would rather have the safety and security of a system financed by the state than the uncertainty of a system based on personal effort. That the military acted as an interest group within the regime is also quite obvious.

## THE ADMINISTRATIVE REFORM

The principles of subsidiarity of the state, the need to enhance the role of the private sector, and the need to improve administration, all led Piñera to argue that the social security funds should be put in the hands of the private sector. The administrative reform was expected to reduce administrative costs and to integrate the social security system into the national economy.

It is important to note that for the government economists one of the major obstacles to Chile's economic development was the low national savings rate, which the market approach has been unable to resolve. This resulted from the underdevelopment of local capital markets. The pension reform was thus crucial both for the development of capital markets and consequently to achieve economic growth. As Martin Cóstabal argued:

The growth of the capital markets produced by the new pension system will be oriented, by and large, to produce long-term effects. The long term characteristics of the social security savings will be geared to develop long-term credit instruments, which would contribute to structure a more integral capital market, something we have not had until now.... The development of these long-term capital markets would bring stability and longer terms to the credit system, improving credit conditions for activities such as housing, and for medium and small entrepreneurs, who are intensive credit users. (Cóstabal, 1981: 64)

The transference of the administration of the pension funds to the private sector involved the creation of a new type of enterprise. The *Administadoras de Fondos de Pensiones* (AFP) or Pension Funds Managing Corporations. They are exclusively charged with the administration of the individual funds and the provision of the mandatory social security benefits established by statute.

In order to understand the nature and functions of these new private entities, one has to keep in mind that the new legislation contained both free market and regulatory principles. The free market principles encouraged the formation of a plurality of AFPs that would compete among themselves, offering the highest interests in the capital accounts and charging the lowest commissions. AFPs are lucrative corporations which accrue profit from the commissions they charge for the administration of the funds. Originally, those commissions could be structured either as a flat rate, as a percentage of the insured deposit or as a combination of both. In order to insure efficiency and the lowest commissions, the insured were free to move from one AFP to another.

Given the underdevelopment of the Chilean economy, and especially the underdevelopment of the capital markets, the state chose to regulate the investments of the newly created corporations. The law prescribed that each AFP had to maintain two separate funds: a minimum capital fund was required to establish an AFP, and a second capital fund contained the individual account deposits. The law also prescribed investment policy constraints and the profitability of the latter fund (Illanes, 1981: 48).

As for benefits, the 1980 legislation, as amended in August 1987, established that once the basic pension eligibility requirements have been met, the applicant has three different benefit options: first, to buy an immediate life annuity from an insurance company with the funds accumulated in the account; second, to obtain the pension directly from the AFP, provided that the individual capitalization fund is large enough to provide for a pension that is at least equal to 120 percent of the value of the minimum state pension; and third, to combine a temporary annuity paid by the AFP with a deferred life annuity bought from an insurance company. In the case of disability and death prior to retirement, the disability and survivors' pensions are not paid by the AFP but by the insurance company contracted for that purpose. The disability pensions fluctuate between 50 and 70 percent of the average earnings of the last 10 years depending on the extent of the disability. Survivors' pensions are paid to widows or disabled widowers, to children below age 18 (24 if they are students or regardless of age if they are disabled) and to parents if there are no other beneficiaries (Mesa-Lago and Arenas de Mesa, 1999: 63–64).

Finally, there is a system of minimum pensions for those affiliated to the individual capitalization system to be applied in case of depletion of the individual capital account, or if the rent produced by the fund is smaller than the minimum pension. In order to qualify for this pension, the insured must have at least 20 years of contributions. The original minimum pension was about U.S.$45 monthly and in 1999 it was U.S.$103.

## THE MANDATORY INDIVIDUAL CAPITALIZATION SYSTEM IN OPERATION

Launching the system involved the actions of both the private and the public sector: the former had to create the AFPs while the latter had not only to make the affiliation to the new system compulsory for all first-time employees after December of 1982 but also to ensure that all transference to the new system was permanent. The state also created two new agencies, the *Superintendencia* of AFPs and the *Instituto de Normalización Previsiónal*, or Institute for the Normalization of the Social Security System, charged with coordinating the transition from the old to the new system.

### The AFPs and the Mandatory Coverage of the New System

The launching of the reform in May 1981 was followed by the massive adoption of the new system. In the first month, half a million people changed to the new system. By December of 1981, 1.6 million people, out of an economically active population of 2.9 million (some 55 percent) had moved to the new social security system. Neither the government nor the leadership of the AFPs had predicted such a large move. Four factors seem to have prompted people to abandon the old social security system. First, a very expensive and well-orchestrated propaganda campaign was conducted by the government. Second, there was a net increase in the salary to those that moved to the new system. Third, the contributors to the old system faced poor pension prospects. Finally, the pressure was applied to employees by some employers who were connected either financially or personally to the AFPs.

Both the AFPs and the government launched what was the most expensive publicity campaign in Chile's history. This campaign stressed the "modernity" and "self-reliance" involved in the new system, as opposed to the "politicization," "chaos" and "crisis" involved in the old one. During the months of May and June in 1981, all of the AFPs spent over U.S.$8 million in advertising (Borzutzky, 1983: 314–18). The acceptance of the new system can be explained in terms of the skillful propaganda campaign, the changes in societal values stressed in the publicity and the importance of propaganda in the context of an authoritarian regime in which the society is deprived of alternative views or ideas.

The net salary increase obtained by those workers who transferred to the new system also contributed to their decision to move. The salary increase ranged from 7.6 percent for those that belonged to the Blue-Collar Workers Fund to 17.1 percent for the Bank Employees. The salary increase was well publicized by both the government and the AFPs. It is reasonable to believe that the desperate situation of retirees associated with the old system might have also acted as an incentive for contributors to the old system to move to the new system. The combined effect of several years of high inflation, declining real wages and the system used to compute entitlements had withered away their pensions.

The beginning of the new system was preceded by the creation of several AFPs. However, the large degree of ownership concentration of the Chilean economy thwarted the free market principles that inspired the reform. Of the 12 corporations that were originally created, nine were owned by Chile's largest economic cartels (known in Chile as the economic groups), and they covered 92 percent of the affiliates that changed to the new system (the other three belonged to the Teachers Association, the Copper Workers Association and the Builders Association). Furthermore, the two largest AFPs—*Provida* and *Santa María*—owned by the two largest economic groups, captured 63 percent of the insured. By the end of 1987, *Provida* had 30 percent of the affiliates while *Santa María* had 20 percent. By the end of 1998 one-third of the insured population were contracted to *Provida* while about of one-half were affiliated with *Habitat*. *Santa María* was ranked third, with about one-sixth of the insured population (Mesa-Lago 1985: 114; SAFP, 1987: 17; SAFP, 1998: 57).

## THE ROLE OF THE STATE

The 1980 reform did not eliminate the role of the state, as might have been expected given the neoliberal rhetoric, but rather transformed it. The new role of the state exhibits three important characteristics: enforcement, bureau creation and deficit budgeting.

Because of the new system's compulsory nature, the state had to enforce it. The law obliged all new workers to join the new system while the old workers were forced to remain in it once they had decided to change. The establishment of a state-regulated, mandatory individual capitalization system was certainly unique in the early 1980s. Its creation reflects some of the contradictions that the application of neoliberal principles with extensive state involvement can exhibit, especially in the context of authoritarian politics. In order to understand the extent of this contradiction, it must be remembered that the government has consistently claimed that the new system was designed to enhance the freedom of the Chilean workers. The compulsory aspects of the system reflect both the authoritarian nature of the regime as well as a paternalistic approach to policy making. Both created a perception among policy makers that the state needs to be able to make critical decisions for society because the individual is unable to do it.

From an institutional perspective, two new bureaucracies were created: the *Superintendencia de Administradoras de Fondos de Pensiones*, and the *Instituto de Normalización Previsiónal*. The *Superintendencia de Seguridad Social* was maintained to control the old system. The *Superintendencia* of AFPs was created to control the newly established AFPs, authorize their constitution, supervise the structure of commissions, control the pension funds, regulate the agreements with the insurance companies and dissolve the AFP in case of violation of the law. Why did the government create this new supervisory agency? The question is particularly relevant since the regime had done the utmost to reduce the size of the bureaucracy and to reduce government involvement in the economy. Behind the stated technical reasons seems to be a political motive: to create an institution responsive to the needs and ideas of the neoliberal economists and to put an end to the life of the old *Superintendencia* (Piñera, 1980: 12).

The *Instituto de Normalización Previsiónal* has financial functions. It was created to facilitate the transition from one system to another. Its fundamental function is to administer a social security fund formed with all the funds received by the old pension funds, or *Cajas*, which had ceased to be autonomous. The creation of the institute was the culmination of a process of fiscal centralization that began in 1978 and that drastically reduced the power and functions of the *Cajas*. The *Instituto* also administers the *Bono de Reconocimiento*, or recognition bond. The bond represents the number of years that the insured contributed to the old system, and it is given to the AFP at the time of retirement, invalidity or death (*La Segunda*, 1981: 23).

## THE IMPACT OF THE REFORM

As Píñera correctly argued:

The social security reform has been one of the most important steps taken by the present regime. It constitutes a new and original scheme which will contribute decisively to change the economic, social and political culture of all Chileans. (Piñera, 1980: 12)

Of the seven modernizations carried out by the government, this one stands out as having both a profound societal and individual impact, as being significant to Chile's economy and to its politics and as one that touches not only the present but also the future of the entire population. The impact of this reform has to be analyzed in at least two ways: first, from an economic perspective, regarding both the public and the private sector of the economy; and second, from a socio-political perspective. In order to assess the economic impact we will compare and analyze data from the late 1980s and the late 1990s.

### The Economic Impact

It is useful to distinguish two levels of the reform's economic impact: the impact on pensions and on the general economy. Regarding the first we will look at the reform's effects on coverage and the value of pensions, as well as its impact on women. Regarding the second one, the analysis will focus on those areas identified as critical by the proponents of the reform, such as the impact on the state and on both the capital and labor markets.

The question of coverage appears to be quite complex. While in the old system Chile had about 80 percent of the labor force covered, in the new one the measurement of the coverage has been problematic. In 1996, the *Superintendencia* reported that 107 percent of the labor force was covered by the new system, which did not take into account that 89 percent of the self-employed were not covered, that a small percentage remain in the old system, and that the armed forces have their own separate system. After a preliminary revision of the data, the *Superintendencia* argued that the figures were marred by statistical deficiencies produced by the constant changes from one AFP to another one. The agency now estimates that about 80 percent of the labor force is covered, 90 percent of which is in the private system. However, this data is still being revised (Mesa-Lago, 1998a). The data for 1998 indicates that the total number of people registered in the AFP system amounts to 5.97 million while the active contributors to the system are 3.15 million. This means that only 62 percent of the insured were actually paying monthly contributions, which entails a substantial reduction in the number of people actually covered by the private pension system (SAFP, 1998: 373–74). Since the basic coverage statistics remain problematic, it is impossible to analyze the impact of the reform in terms of coverage. Tentatively, we can conclude that the actual percentage of population covered has decreased because only 62 percent of the insured are actually paying the monthly contributions. The decline in the number of those who pay their contributions can be the result of evasion and payment delays, temporary workers that enter and leave the workforce and flaws in the data on affiliation. The self-employed that, by and large, did not have coverage in the past still remain outside the system.

### Pension Values

The value of the pension received by the insured depends on the contributions paid plus the interest accrued, less the commissions charged by the AFP. The pensions awarded under the new system are, therefore, the direct result of the level of wages and the real rate of capital return. Between 1981 and 1987 at least two contradictory phenomena can be observed: the decrease in the real value of wages, which by 1985 were estimated to be 13 percent below their 1970 level, and the high real yield of the pension fund investments, which on average amounted to 13.8 percent per year. The situation changed dramatically in the 1990s. Between 1990 and 1998, the real value of wages increased by 35 percent (CEPAL, 1998). On the other hand, the real yield of the investments decreased. The performance of the pension funds has been quite unstable, oscillating from a real yield of 28.6 percent in 1991 to $-2.5$ percent in 1995. There were moderate gains in 1996 and 1997, but the real yield was again negative in 1998 ($-1.6$ percent). The average yield from the inception of the system to December of 1998 has been 10.9 percent (SAFP, 1988: 13; SAFP, 1998: 340).

The *Superintendencia de Administradoras de Fondos de Pensiones*, in 1987, estimated that the average value of a pension paid by the new system was 1.24 times higher than those paid by the old system, while the invalidity pensions are 2.23 times higher. However, it is important to note that by the time this estimate was done, the AFP had granted only 10,099 old-age pensions and 12,383 invalidity pensions out of an insured population of almost 3 million people. By the end of 1998, the system was paying 290,000 pensions, and the average value of a retirement pension was about U.S.$200, while the average value of an invalidity pension was about U.S.$280 (SAFP, 1988: 42–53; SAFP, 1998: 142–402).

### Gender Inequalities

The reform also raises the question of gender inequities. The central issue here is that the reform reinforces existing gender inequalities. To the extent that the value of the pension depends on the value of the wages, the years of contributions and the life expectancy after retirement, the situation of retired women is certainly worse than that of retired men. As Arenas de Mesa and Montecinos argue:

women should clearly understand that... every year in the labor market is considered in the calculation of their pensions. This means that women who take time off the labor market... will receive lower pensions than those who have worked without interruptions. ... Women should also know that the actuarial factors used to calculate their pensions are different from the ones used for men's pensions. The pensions that women receive in the new system are lower than the pensions of men because the average life expectancy of women is longer than men's life expectancy. Women should consider that although the system allows them to retire five years earlier than men, early retirement reduces even further the amount of their pensions. (Arenas de Mesa and Montecinos, 1996: 24)

The government, as well as women and those interested in women's rights, have entirely ignored this critical issue. The value of the pensions has a direct effect on the life of women and also on state finances. One can expect that a very large number of women will not qualify for a retirement pension due to the fact that they earned less, left covered employment for child bearing and caring or simply because they live longer than men. Those women thus qualify for a state-funded minimum pension. Consequently, women are being penalized and discriminated against and nothing has been done to remedy the situation.

### Administration Commissions

The structure and size of the commissions charged by the AFPs for the administration of the fund impinges directly on pension values. The insured must pay the AFPs two commissions: a fixed sum deducted from the contribution for old age pension and a variable percentage, which covers the premium for disability and survivor benefits. Changes in the law introduced in January of 1988 brought greater transparency in the structure of the commissions that allowed the insured to compare charges. This, in turn, has caused a drop in the commissions. However, the main problem, the regressive nature of the flat rate, remains unchanged. For instance, at the beginning of 1988 *Provida* charged $954 to administer the fund when the taxable wage was $20,000, and $3,728 when the taxable wage was $100,000 (SAFP, 1988: 5–11; SAFP, 1998: 404). This regressive impact affects not only the poorest sectors of the population but also the fiscal deficit since the government subsidizes those pensions that are smaller than the minimum pension.

Data for 1998 indicate that the regressive effects of the commission structure and the high administrative costs continue. For instance, for an insured person with an income of about U.S.$160, the administrative costs fluctuate between 25.6 percent and 37.9 percent, while the cost for an insured with an income of U.S.$1,300 fluctuates between 24.1 percent and 30.2 percent (SAFP, 1998: 28–32). The data also indicates that in spite of the reforms and the freedom of the insured to move from one AFP to another, administrative costs have not declined.

What has decreased is the premium for disability and survivor insurance that is managed by commercial insurance companies. The premium decreased from 1.22 percent to 0.62 percent from 1990 to 1998, but the commission rose from 1.73 percent to 2.34 percent from 1990 to 1995 and then declined to 2 percent, which is still a higher rate than in 1990. Conversely, the commission for old-age insurance has oscillated but tended to increase in the long run. The net result has been rising or at best stagnant administrative costs, a strong indication that competition does not work properly (Mesa-Lago, 1996: 786).

Strongly related to the question of commissions is the overall nature of the administrative system designed by those who framed the program. Essential to the reform was the notion that the private sector would create pension fund managing companies and that the public would be free to choose among them and to change from one to another. Ideally, this would create a system characterized by low administrative costs and high coverage and efficiency. In practice, the number of AFPs has not changed much. There are today thirteen AFPs; initially there were twelve, with 69 percent of the insured concentrated in the three largest. The insured are permitted to change AFPs as often as they wish, and the data indicates that people have massively changed their AFPs.

According to Mesa-Lago (1998b: 120), between 1984 and 1996 the percentage of insured changing their AFPs increased from 10 percent to 52 percent, some 1.3 million transfers. Since most of these changes are the result of the promotional activities of the AFP, the key element in the change is the activity and number of sales personnel involved in the process. The number of salespeople reached almost 19,000 by 1996, or one per 160 insured. The costs of the salespeople amounted to 37 percent of the total operating costs of the AFPs and 60 percent of the commissions charged by the AFPs to the insured (Mesa-Lago, 1998b: 120).

Perceptions about the efficiency of the AFPs have changed since the inception of the system. A survey conducted in 1987 indicated that the public image of these institutions was declining (*Centro de Estudios Públicos*, 1987). For instance, over 50 percent of the interviewees indicated that they believed the state was more likely to pay a higher pension and an indexed pension than the AFPs, while only 9 percent preferred to leave the administration of the pension programs to national private enterprises (*Centro de Estudios Públicos*, 1987).

It is interesting to note that during the 1980s the three largest AFPs charged the highest commissions. That, however, has changed, and currently they charge the lowest commissions. During that same period the largest institutions had the lowest rate of return. Consequently, it appears that the selection was not made on the basis of performance or cost, but as a result of marketing, the actions of the sellers and the publicity. It could also be the result of a generalized dissatisfaction with the performance of the AFPs. The economic effects of the reform have not been limited to the pensioners.

The reform has had a substantial impact on the private sector at large because it facilitated a huge transfer of resources from the public to the private sector. By the end of 1985, the capital accumulated by the AFPs amounted to 9.73

percent of gross domestic product (GDP). Three years later the capital accumulated in the AFPs was about U.S.$30 billion which amounts to about 40 percent of the GDP (Iglesias et al., 1986: 115).

In order to protect the solvency of the AFPs, the law closely regulates the investment policies and practices of the pension funds. The AFPs are required to distribute their investment among government instruments, fixed term deposits, mortgage bonds and stocks. By the end of 1985, 42.6 percent of the funds were invested in government instruments, 35.3 percent in mortgage bonds and 20.5 percent in fixed term deposits (Iglesias et al., 1986: 118). In 1987, 1990 and in 1993, some of these regulations were modified in order to liberalize the investment opportunities thereby reducing the investment in government instruments while increasing the investment in stocks and allowing investment in foreign stocks and bonds. By December of 1998, 40.9 percent of the funds were invested in government bonds, 16.6 percent in mortgage bonds, 14.5 percent in stocks and 13.6 percent in fixed term deposits (SAFP, 1998: 405).

The Chicago-trained economists argued that the private pension system would be a critical element in the establishment of a local capital market. Although there is no question about the growth of the capital markets in Chile, there is a strong debate about the role of the AFPs in that process. Some analysts (Cheyre, 1991; Iglesias and Acuña, 1991; Piñera, 1991) argue that the pension funds have had a critical role in that process, promoting foreign investment in the local market and reducing the foreign debt by transforming debt into a capital investment. Others argue that the growth of the Chilean capital market is not different from that of other Latin American markets during the same period and that the pension system did not make a strong contribution to that growth (Gillion and Bonilla, 1992; Mesa-Lago, 1988). Finally, the expected positive impact on national savings is also a matter of intense debate, and there is no conclusive evidence that the new system has had a positive impact on the rate of savings. In fact, a recent study shows that the net effect on national savings has been negative since the fiscal cost was higher than the capital accumulation (Mesa-Lago, 1998a).

In 1980, those who framed the reform argued that the elimination of the employer contribution would reduce the price of labor. In turn, the reduction in the price of labor would produce a drastic reduction in unemployment. The behavior of the unemployment rates between 1981 and 1985 shows that the social security reform did not produce this effect. Again, the neoliberals seemed to have ignored the fact that the high unemployment rates were linked to the very nature of the economic model and its consequences. Unemployment was the result of the reduction in the size of the industrial sector due to the combined effect of the policy of trade liberalization, the reduction or elimination of subsidies to the industrial sector and the reduction in the internal demand produced by the shock therapy. In fact, between 1975 and 1983, unemployment rates were at least three times higher than in the previous decade while the price of labor had dramatically decreased. Unemployment was not the result of the high price of labor, as the reduction or elimination of the social security cost did not affect the rates of unemployment. By the same token, the growth of employment between 1986 and 1997 cannot be attributed to the social security reform but to the modifications introduced in the model and the success of the export sector.

Unemployment has again increased since 1997, and in May of 1998 reached 10 percent, its highest level in a decade. The main reason is the collapse of Asia's demand for copper, which accounts for about 40 percent of Chile's exports. Chile's exports of manufactures have also suffered due to the recession in Argentina and Brazil. The preeminent theme of the reform was the creation of a subsidiary role for the state in the provision of social security. However, the financial impact of the reform on the public finances was never estimated (Arellano, 1981: 412–13). In fact, the reform is having, and will continue to have, a large budgetary impact, which will seriously affect the finances of the Chilean state.

The reform carries a budget deficit which is the result of the transference of the administration and payment of contributions to the private sector, thus producing a net decrease of the government social security receipts, while at the same time the state maintains a high level of expenditures. This reduction in government receipts was not accompanied by a decrease in social security expenditures essentially because, first, in order to allow the AFPs to capitalize, the law established that they would not pay retirement pensions during the first five years. As a result, during those five years, the state was faced basically with the same social security expenditures, since workers close to retirement chose not to move to the new system. Second, after the first five years, the state continued paying pensions to those who chose to remain in the old system and has to pay also the *bono de reconocimiento* (or recognition bond) of those that begin to retire in the new system. This bond, which represents the number of years that the insured contributed in the old system, becomes effective at the time of retirement, invalidity or death. Third, the pattern of transfer to the new system has added a new financial burden; while those affiliated to the civil servants fund, which requires the largest state contribution, were reluctant to move to the new system, those affiliated to the self-financed funds, such as white collar workers and bank employees moved in very large proportion because of the increase in take-home pay. In brief,

The state contributes to the private pension fund through two mechanisms: the recognition bond, that amounts to half to two-thirds of the capital of those who are going to retire before the year 2000; and the difference needed to pay the minimum pension of those individuals who at time of retirement do not have enough funds in the AFP. Furthermore, the state covers the deficit of the civil servant and armed forces funds, pays all the welfare pensions and the unemployment compensation, and the family allowances and health benefits for indigents. (Mesa-Lago, 1994: 22)

Although a comprehensive analysis of the state involvement in the system and the overall cost of the state subsidy has yet to be done, it is clear that built into the new system there is a large state subsidy and thus a projected large, ongoing budgetary deficit. Estimates done by several social security analysts point to a deficit of about 4 or 5 percent of the GDP. It is not clear either how the state is financing the deficit. According to Mesa-Lago, the state has three options: taxes, public debt and a combination of the above. The government has opted, mainly, for the use of public debt, which in turn has increased the public debt to as much as 67 percent of GDP (Mesa-Lago, 1994: 22–23).

In conclusion, the reform has not resulted in a reduction of government expenditures but a very peculiar application of the principle of subsidiarity of the state, as the state maintains a secondary role only in the administration of the funds but not in the financial responsibility.

## Social and Political Impact of the Reform

From a social point of view, the question is to what extent has this reform altered traditional social security principles. There is little doubt that, at the very least, the reform has substantially transformed the principle of social solidarity since the new system is based on the notion of individual capitalization combined with a social system of minimum pensions. In other words, providing for old age is an individual responsibility, except in the case of the military personnel and the extremely poor. As the former Under Secretary of Labor, Patricio Mardones, argued, "the reform transforms the notion of solidarity both in its role and in its content. From now on, solidarity is not a fundamental notion, but a complementary one, as in a system of minimum and welfare pensions" (Interview, Santiago, August 2, 1982). Consequently, it is reserved for those people to whom the principle of individual responsibility cannot be applied. To a large extent, then, the reform has transformed the social security system into a private insurance system in which the state intervenes at two different stages: at the onset by enforcing enrollment into the new system, and at the final stage by providing pensions to the military and to the lowest income groups.

From a political perspective the reform has to be analyzed in the context of the other reforms enacted by the government between 1981 and 1982. It is clear that the neoliberal economic model and the authoritarian regime converged in their need to silence the entire society. It was especially important to silence those groups perceived as having political power, especially the power to interfere with the free functioning of the market, such as organized labor, professional associations and the organizations representing white-collar workers and civil servants.

Throughout the last 50 years, there has been a close relationship between the organization of the labor movement, its pattern of interaction with the state and the evolution of the social security system. After having reformed the role and functions of the state and the nature of the labor movement, the Pinochet regime found it necessary to create a pension system attuned to those reforms. Of course, in an authoritarian context, the reforms came from the regime itself, without the participation of the society.

The pension reform has been crucial to the destruction of large bureaucratic entities such as the pension funds, as well as to the depolitisization of the groups of workers organized around them, who, in the past, have had a major role both in the formulation and the obstruction of public policies. The social security reform during this period, as well as in the past, reflects the existing political organization and the principles that guide the relations between the regime and the society. At the same time, those policies have been a key political mechanism used to shape future political arrangements. In this case the policy has served to atomize society and depolitisize critical groups, reinforcing the power of the authoritarian regime (Borzutzky, 1999).

## Lessons and Conclusions

Chile's social security reform has been in place for almost 20 years. In those years the Chilean government, as well as international organizations and experts, have collated a very impressive amount of information about the Chilean social security system. This chapter contains a detailed analysis and assessment of the performance of the system during the last two decades. The market-oriented reform transformed the common fund into a compulsory, individual capitalization fund administered by private enterprises created with the exclusive purpose of managing pension funds and obtaining a profit from their activities. The state has maintained a regulatory function and provides minimum pensions to those who were unable to save for their old age. The state also provides welfare pensions to the indigents.

The reform needs to be analyzed in the context of the political and economic logic of the Pinochet regime. The reform was the result of a closed-door process in which society could not participate. It was the result of the economic ideas sustained by the Chicago-trained economists that were controlling the process of economic decision making. Most importantly, there was a great deal of complementarity between the authoritarian nature of the government and the neoliberal reform agenda. Neither the political nor the economic leaders of the country had any legitimacy and both behaved in an authoritarian fashion. There was no room for democratic discussion, compromises or negotiations. Neither the political nor the economic decision makers were interested in the views of the majority, and both of them sustained a paternalistic attitude toward the society. The policy makers, nevertheless, were quite responsive to the needs and interests of those groups operating from inside the regime, such as the military, or the powerful economic groups that ended up controlling 70 percent of the pension fund management business and that had direct ties to the regime.

From an economic standpoint, the Chilean system presents a number of problems. As shown above, the percentage of the population covered has declined, the administrative costs in the private sector are very regressive and high and the profitability of the accounts depends on a number of conditions that the majority of the society cannot control. State involvement continues even after 20 years, and the budget deficit generated by the system is large and will continue to be a burden on the economy.

The market-oriented system seems to work very well for those in the high income brackets with a very stable job. The system does not work very well for the poor, for those without a stable job and for women. These groups pay proportionally higher contributions, cannot secure a stable well-paid job and consequently are not able to save enough to have a pension at the time of retirement. They are thus dependent upon the state's minimum pension which, in fact, is not a lot better than those provided by the state in the past. Their economic freedom is reduced to either accepting a state pension of about U.S.$100 a month or having no pension at all.

The full impact of the privatization process is seen in the transference to the private sector of about 50 percent of the country's GDP. To what extent has the private administration of the funds and the profits generated by the management companies had a positive effect in the entire economy? There has been a clear growth of capital markets and a much better integration between the Chilean and the international economy. The excellent performance of the economy between 1985 and 1997 seemed to indicate that the Chilean economy was somehow overcoming the typical problems of the less developed countries thanks to the market-oriented reforms. However, as of 2000, the economic downturn of 1998–1999 casts many doubts, even in those areas in which the market approach seemed to be doing well. Unemployment is again above 10 percent and the economy is in a downward spiral. The reasons are to be found in the crisis in Asia, but the decision to depend on those markets was made in Chile. What is even more troublesome is that the recent recuperation of the Asian markets is not having an impact on the Chilean economy.

The notion of a compulsory private insurance system is a typical result of market-oriented policies implemented by a very authoritarian regime. To the extent that this is the most central characteristic of Chile's social security system, it is not something to be replicated nor used in democratic contexts. In a democratic/capitalist society, individuals need to have choices. The private choice is certainly a very convenient and effective choice for those with the means to save for the future. The others need a system based on the notion of social solidarity and state support.

**REFERENCES**

Arellano, J. P. 1981. Elementos para el analisis de la reforma previsional chilena. *Colección Estudios CIEPLAN* 6: 11–15.

Arenas de Mesa, A. and Montecinos, V. 1996. *The Privatization of Social Security and Women's Welfare: Gender Effects of the Chilean Reform*. Unpublished Manuscript, University of Pittsburgh.

Borzutzky, S. 1983. *Chilean Politics and Social Security Policies.* Ph.D. Dissertation, University of Pittsburgh.
Borzutzky, S. 1991. The Chicago Boys: Social Security and Welfare in Chile. In Glennerster, H. and Midgley, J. (eds.), *The Radical Right and the Welfare State: An International Assessment.* London: Harvester Wheatsheaf.
Borzutzky, S. 1999. Chile: The Politics of Privatization. In Cruz-Saco, M. A. and Mesa-Lago, C. (eds.), *Do Options Exist? The Reform of Pension and Health Care in Latin America.* Pittsburgh: University of Pittsburgh Press.
Briones, C. 1968. Antecedentes básicos y analisis del estado actual de la seguridad social en Chile. *Seguridad Social* 98.
Centro de Estudios Públicos. 1987. Estudio social y de opinión pública en la población de Santiago. *Documento de Trabajo* 83.
Cheyre, H. 1991. *La previsión en Chile ayer y hoy: Impacto de una reforma.* Santiago: Centro de Estudios Públicos.
Comision Económica para America Latina y el Caribe (CEPAL). 1998. *Balance preliminar de las economías de America Latina y el Caribe.* Santiago: Cepal.
Cóstabal, M. 1981. Efectos económicos de la reforma previsional. *Gestión* 64 (6): 1–64.
Gillion, C. and Bonilla, A. 1992. La privatización de un regimen nacional de pensiones: el caso chileno. *Revista Internacional del Trabajo* 3 (2): 120–35.
Hirschman, A. 1963. *Journeys toward Progress: Studies of Economic Policymaking in Latin America.* New York: 20th Century Fund.
Iglesias, A. and Acuña, R. 1991. Chile: Experiencia con un regimen de capitalización 1981–1991. In CEPAL (ed.), *Sistemas de pensiones en America Latina.* Santiago: CEPAL/PNUD.
Iglesias, A., Echeverria, A. and Lopez, P. 1986. Proyección de los fondos de pensiones. In Baeza, S. (ed.), *Analisis de la previsión en Chile.* Santiago: Centro de Estudios Públicos.
Illanes, E. 1981. Inversion de recursos del sistema de pensiones. *Gestión* 63 (6): 48–52.
Mamalakis, M. 1976. *The Growth and Structure of the Chilean Economy.* New Haven, CT: Yale University Press.
Mesa-Lago, C. 1978. *Social Security in Latin América: Pressure Groups, Stratification and Inequality.* Pittsburgh: University of Pittsburgh Press.
Mesa-Lago, C. 1985. *El desarrollo de la seguridad social en America Latina.* Santiago: Estudios e informes de la Cepal.
Mesa-Lago, C. 1988. *Review of Chile, SAL III Conditions: Pension System.* Washington, DC: World Bank.
Mesa-Lago, C. 1994. *Changing Social Security in Latin America: Toward Alleviating the Costs of Reform.* Boulder, CO and London: Lynne Rienner.
Mesa-Lago, C. 1996. *The Reform of Social Security and Pensions in Latin America: Public, Private, Mixed and Parallel Systems.* Unpublished Manuscript, University of Pittsburgh.
Mesa-Lago, C. 1998a. Pension Reform around the World: Comparative Features and Performance of Structural Pension Reforms in Latin America. *Brooklyn Law Review* 64: 289–316.
Mesa-Lago, C. 1998b. La reforma estructural de las pensiones en América Latina: Tipología, comprobacion de presupuestos y enseñanzas. In Bonilla, A. and Conte-Grand, A. (eds.), *Pensiones en America Latina: Dos decadas de reformas.* Ginebra: Oficina Internacional del Trabajo.

Mesa-Lago, C. and Arenas de Mesa, A. 1999. The Chilean Pension System: Evaluations, Lessons, and Challenges. In Cruz-Saco, M. A. and Mesa-Lago, C. (eds.), *Do Options Exist? The Reform of Pension and Health Care Systems in Latin America.* Pittsburgh: University of Pittsburgh Press.

Piñera, J. 1980. *Exposición del Ministro del Trabajo Sr. Jose Piñera en el Seminario sobre reforma previsional y evaluación del plan laboral.* Santiago: Mimeo.

Piñera, J. 1991. *El cascabel al gato: La batalla por la reforma previsional.* Santiago: Zig-Zag.

Pinto, A. 1962. *Chile: Un caso de desarrollo frustrado.* Santiago: Editorial Universitaria.

*Segunda (La).* 1981. March 10: 23.

Stallings, B. 1978. *Class Conflict and Economic Development in Chile, 1958–1973.* Stanford, CA: Stanford University Press.

*Superintendencia de Administradoras de Fondos de Pensiones* (SAFP). 1987. Boletín Estadístico Mensual. Santiago: SAF.

SAFP. 1988. *Boletín Estadistico Mensual.* Santiago: SAFP.

SAFP. 1998. *Boletín Estadistico Mensual.* Santiago: SAFP.

Valdés, J. G. 1989. *La escuela de Chicago: Operación Chile.* Buenos Aires: Grupo Editorial Zeta.

*Chapter 4*

# The Market Orientation of Social Security: The Brazilian Case

## Sônia Miriam Draibe and Milko Matijascic

**INTRODUCTION**

Although market-oriented proposals for retirement income protection reform have been present in the Brazilian social agenda for the last decade, they have become increasingly relevant in recent years. Since the 1980s, market reformers have advocated the de-monopolization of benefit provision; that is, the creation of a market for the provision of mandatory complimentary benefits in which both private and public institutions (such as private and public banks) would compete. The main issues at the center of the proposals for and opposition to such a project are the definition of the ceiling for pension values, the constitution of one or two levels of mandatory complementary benefits, the privileges under existing special regimes for civil servants and the constitution of a more reliable and efficient regulatory framework than the present one. It is from this perspective of reforms and transformations that the Brazilian social security system is examined in this chapter.

**THE BRAZILIAN SOCIAL SECURITY SYSTEM: A BRIEF INSTITUTIONAL HISTORY**

The origins of the Brazilian public social security system may be traced to the 1930s, when the *Institutos de Aposentadorias e Pensões* (IAPs) were created to cover risks related to temporary or permanent loss of ability to work (old age, sickness, disability, and survivors' benefits) and to organize healthcare services. During the previous decade, several organized segments of the labor movement had succeeded in obtaining some state regulation of the relations in the workplace, including legislation regarding work-related disabilities, and the creation of mutual-aid societies organized along traditional anarchist lines.

Structured by occupational category, according to local and regional differences, the IAPs created a heterogeneous system of benefits. After many attempts, and despite strong resistance, this situation was changed in 1961 when the Social Security Reform Law provided uniform benefits for all salaried urban workers registered in the benefit system.

A new centralizing thrust took place in 1967 with the creation of the *Instituto Nacional de Previdência Social* (INPS), the National Social Security Institute, that unified the IAPs. However, the creation of the *Sistema Nacional de Previdência e Assistência* (SINPAS), Social National System of Social Security and Welfare in 1977, introduced extensive restructuring. Under the administration of a new *Ministério da Previdência e Assistência Social* (MPAS), the Ministry of Social Security and Assistance, SINPAS was composed of six units: the *Instituto de Administração Financeira da Previdência Social* (IAPAS), Social Security Financial Administration Institute, which is the accounting agency for the entire system; the *Empresa de Processamento de Dados da Previdência Social* (DATAPREV), the Social Security Data Processing Company; the INPS, which is responsible for the distribution of benefits; the *Legião Brasileira de Assistência* (LBA), the Brazilian Social Aid League and the *Fundação Nacional de Bem-Estar do Menor* (FUNABEM), the National Children's Welfare Foundation's two social aid organizations; and the *Instituto Nacional de Atendimento Médico da Previdência Social* (INAMPS), the administrative unit responsible for public health services. In this manner, a superstructure was constituted with central control at the ministerial level but functionally decentralized through public agencies and institutes that gained increasing autonomy. By the late 1970s, around 250,000 employees worked in this public social security system.

The operational and financial mechanisms of the three traditional areas of the social security system—pension benefits, health services and social assistance—emerged from this process with clearly defined and independent profiles.

## GENERAL CHARACTERISTICS OF THE PUBLIC AND PRIVATE SECTORS OF SOCIAL SECURITY IN BRAZIL

A number of organizational characteristics and entry and eligibility requirements are discernible in the public and private sectors of the Brazilian social security system.

### Structure and Dimensions of the System

Brazilian social security institutions are grouped into two major sectors: the public social security sector—henceforth the mandatory public system—and the voluntary private system—henceforth the private pension funds.

Affiliation to the mandatory public system is compulsory for all salaried employees and optional for self-employed workers. It consists of two types of regimes:

- The General Social Security Regime (henceforth the General Regime), which encompasses all urban and rural employees in the private sector and in state enterprises and is managed by *Instituto Nacional do Seguro Social* (INSS), the National Institute for Social Security;
- The Special Pension Regimes for Civil Servants, designed for federal civil servants serving in the executive, legislative and judicial branches. The other two levels of government—states and municipalities—have their own differentiated social security regimes, not subject to INSS norms and management.

Until very recently, these regimes differed widely, in terms of their own specific financial sources, rules and benefit plans.

The voluntary private system also encompasses two main forms:

- The *Entidades Fechadas de Previdência Privada*, the Closed Private Pension Funds, which are designed for employees in an enterprise, or group of enterprises, with a minimum voluntary affiliation of 50 percent of the employees. Their objective is to complement the public entitlement scheme of the General Social Security Regime by paying beneficiaries, as a rule, the difference between the INSS pension and the final salary.
- The *Entidades Abertas de Previdência Privada*, the Open Private Pension Funds, which are designed for employees who wish to receive supplementary monetary benefits beyond those to which they are entitled upon retirement. The amount of those supplementary benefits varies according to the rules of the chosen benefit plan and is not related to the retirement benefits of the INSS.

The mandatory public system's regimes follow a pay-as-you-go principle while private pension funds operate on an individual capitalization basis. Figure 4.1 summarizes the aforementioned structure.

The vast size of the Brazilian social security system partially reflects the country's demographics and level of economic development, although one of its characteristics is its relatively limited coverage of the economically active population, as shown by the most significant indicators.

In 1997, the mandatory public system (comprising INSS, federal, state and municipal civil service regimes) covered 32 million contributors and has close to 20 million beneficiaries. In 1998, expenditures within this sector reached 10.5 percent of gross domestic product (GDP) and represented approximately 50 percent of total governmental social expenditures. Table 4.1 presents the dimensions of the public sector.

The voluntary private system's dimensions are quite modest, compared to the public system's. There are 1.8 million contributors, with U.S.$65 billion in assets and $3.6 billion in revenues in the Closed Pension Funds for the year 1998. The number of beneficiaries represent 250,000 with U.S.$2.4 billion in expenditures. Closed Pension Funds' beneficiaries in 1997 amounted to 10.7 percent of the total number of beneficiaries of INSS while contributors represented only 6.8 percent of all those insured. In the Open Pension Funds there were 2.5 million

**Figure 4.1**
The Brazilian Social Security System Structure

**Private Sector**

Voluntary affiliation
Capitalization regime

Complementary
Pension Funds

Open Pension Funds

**Public Sector**

General Regime (INSS)

Compulsory affiliation
Pay-as-you-go regime

Mandatory Public System

Closed Pension Funds

**Special Social Security Regimes for Civil Servants**

Federal | States | Municipalities

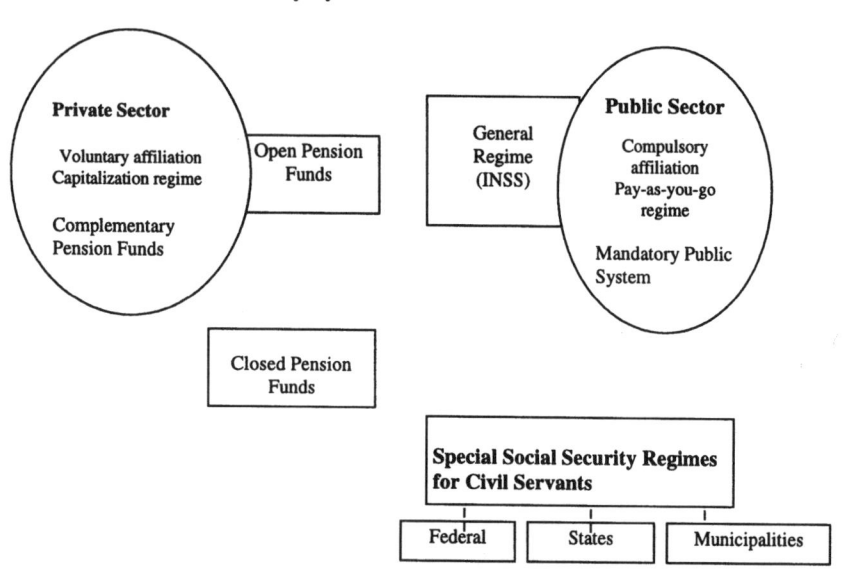

**Table 4.1**
Brazil: Dimensions of the Social Security System—Public Sector

| Dimensions | General Regime (A) | Civil Servants Regime (B) ||| Total A + B |
|---|---|---|---|---|---|
| | | Federal (I) | State/ Municipal (II) | Total (I) + (II) | |
| Contributors—1996 (in 1,000 persons) | 28,278 | 953 | 2,837 | 3,790 | 32,068 |
| Beneficiaries—1996 (in 1,000 persons) | 16,912 | 892 | 2,000 | 2,892 | 19,804 |
| Revenues—1998 (in U.S.$1,000) | 38,347 | 2,197 | 3,351 | 5,548 | 43,894 |
| Expenditures—1998 (in U.S.$1,000) | 44,859 | 17,481 | 16,796 | 34,276 | 79,135 |
| Expenditures (as percent of GDP 1998) | 5.95 | 2.32 | 2.23 | 4.54 | 10.49 |

*Sources*: MPAS, 1997; Brazilian Institute of Geography and Statistics (IBGE).

Table 4.2
Brazil: Contributions to the General Social Security Regime

| Employees | Insured Contribution Rates (%) | Employer Contribution Rates and Base (%) | Government |
|---|---|---|---|
| Urban | 8 to 11% (20% self-employed) | 22% of total payroll | Covers eventual financial deficits |
| Rural | Exempt | 2.5% of sale of results of first harvest | |

*Source*: MPAS, 1997.

contributors with U.S.$4.8 billion in assets and $0.8 billion in revenues for the year 1998. No data is available regarding the expenditures for beneficiaries or their numbers for the Open Pension Funds.

### The Mandatory Public System

#### *Contribution and Eligibility Rules*

Following the logic of the pay-as-you-go model, the General Regime is based on highly differentiated rules that define contributions and the scope and amount of benefits. Contribution rules in the General Regime vary according to the occupational sector in which the insured workers are employed, as shown in Table 4.2.

The ceiling of employee contributions is about 10 times the minimum wage (approximately U.S.$69 in October 1999), as is the ceiling of pension values. In the case of urban employees, there are two other contributions: *Contribuição para o Financiamento da Seguridade Social*, (COFINS), which is 2 percent of an employer's total revenue, and which is earmarked for pensions; and the Net Profit Contribution, which is 10 percent of the employer's net profits, and which is earmarked for healthcare benefits and social assistance.

Finally, it is important to emphasize the important role of the state as a source of financial funds. Although the specific proportion of its participation in the structure of contributions is not predetermined, the state covers the mandatory public system's administrative costs (including staff), pays retirement pensions of federal civil servants and complements the General Regime's resources to cover operational deficits.

The contribution rules of the special regimes for civil servants vary significantly among the three levels of government, especially with respect to contribution rates. The contribution of federal civil servants approaches that of normal contributors in the General Regime (increasing progressively from 8 percent to 12 percent, according to income). As in the case of the federal government, state and municipal governments also cover deficits resulting from differences between collected contributions and expenditures with benefit payments.

Since the 1988 Constitution, the General Regime sets a floor that is equal to the minimum wage and a ceiling of ten times the minimum wage for pension values. These amounts may be adjusted by a legally established index, which accompanies the adjustments of the minimum wage. On the other hand, until the 1998 social security reform, civil servants' benefits under the special regimes were not subject to the ceiling established in the General Regime. According to the Constitution, civil servants' pension values should equal the last full active salary before retirement and should be adjusted at the same time and by the same amount as their active counterparts.

Social security legislation was always permissive with regards to the re-entry of retired employees in the labor market and cumulative pensions. In fact, after retirement, beneficiaries may continue to hold active employment in the labor market without any legal restrictions. Greater restrictions have been placed on civil servants since the 1998 reform.

The General Regime's plan includes more than 60 different types of benefits, mainly covering old age (retirement), disability (disability pensions), death (survivors' pensions) and work injuries. It also includes temporary benefits for sickness, maternity leave, family-related benefits (family salary and family aid), and a large number of less important welfare payments. Unemployment insurance is not included in this plan. It was only introduced in the Constitution of 1988 and is funded by resources from the *Fundo de Amparo ao Trabalhador* (FAT), the Worker's Aid Fund.

Until 1971, rural workers were not included in any social security regime. Since that year and until the promulgation of the 1988 Constitution, they enjoyed very limited coverage consisting of only limited social assistance. They became fully covered by the system in the 1990s and are exempt from contributions.

### *Rules and Types of Pensions*

Until the 1998 reform, the General Regime covered various types of pensions: disability, old-age (65 years), length of employment (35 years), proportional (to length of employment with 30 years) and others of a special nature (from 15 to 30 years). It also includes a special pension—a Lifetime Monthly Income—designed for the destitute elderly and disabled people who were not eligible for normal retirement and pension benefits. The benefit payment is calculated from the average of the last 36 months of contribution, adjusted for inflation. Women may retire five years earlier in all those circumstances. Civil servants enjoy the same types of pensions, except

- they retire with their last full salary;
- adjustment of benefits is indexed by the same proportions and at the same time as active civil servants' salaries.

## The Voluntary Private System

### Structure and Regulation

The legislation regulating the private sector of Brazilian social security covers two types of funds. Open Pension Funds that are managed by private institutions, such as banks, insurance companies or non-profit agencies, and that are available to all interested persons. Benefits provided are practically the same as those of the mandatory public system's General Regime. Their plans may be organized on the basis of defined benefits or defined contributions. A periodic actuarial evaluation must be carried out in the case of defined-benefit plans in order to guarantee adequate financial balances. Closed Pension Funds, on the other hand, are not accessible to all. Managed by closed private social insurance entities, they are constituted by and provide coverage to employees in a specific enterprise or group of enterprises. In contrast to open funds, employers may share the costs of the plan, whether related to administrative expenses or in the contribution base itself. Benefits tend to be identical to those in other sectors of the social security system, but they are based on contracts.

At the regulatory level, different agencies exercise control over different sectors. In the case of Closed Pension Funds, the *Secretaria da Previdência Complementar, Ministério da Previdência e Assistência Social Complementary* (SPC/MPAS), the Social Security Department of the Ministry of Social Security and Social Assistance, approves benefit plans and supervises actuarial operations. Open Pension Funds are supervised by the *Superintendência de Seguros Privados/Ministério da Fazenda* (SUSEP/MF), the Ministry of the Treasury's Department of Private Insurance. Both these supervisory agencies are also kept informed of the composition of investments and the financial situation of each Fund.

The regulation of investments is probably one of the most important aspects of the voluntary private system. According to public policymakers, the lack of maturity and modest dimensions of capital markets require special care to avoid manipulation, which would harm small stockholders, or misappropriation of funds, which would negatively affect the financial interests of the insured. To prevent those problems, legislation regulating Closed Pension Funds and Open Pension Funds determined that Brazil's Central Bank establishes, through resolutions approved by *Conselho Monetário Nacional* (CMN), the National Monetary Council, the minimum and maximum limits in the composition of the funds' portfolios, while the *Comissão de Valores Mobiliários* (CVM), the Securities and Exchange Commission, supervises the operations so as to avoid disloyal practices such as market manipulation.

Since the constitution of the voluntary private system in 1977, Closed Pension Funds have become more extensive than Open Pension Funds. According to the Ministry of Social Security and Assistance, Closed Pension Funds' assets (U.S.$77.821 billion) represented 10.1 percent of GDP in December 1998, while Open Pension Funds' assets only represented 0.9 percent (U.S.$6.898 billion), for a combined total of 11.1 percent of GDP. There are a number of obstacles to market extension including

- low wages and incomes in Brazil,
- rudimentary enterprise structures which resent difficulties in organizing pension funds or in negotiating complementary benefits with other enterprises, and
- costly benefit plans that cannot be financed exclusively by employees.

Since the 1980s, Open Pension Funds have been of secondary importance in comparison with Closed Pension Funds. While the latter hold 90 percent of the private pension market, the former has never surpassed 10 percent and has maintained this share for the past 15 years.

### Open Pension Funds

Information on Open Pension Funds is rather scarce. Nothing is known about the portfolio distribution of their assets, the types of plans each one adopts (whether defined-benefits or defined-contributions), the number of affiliates, the geographic location of the entities, the value and types of benefits paid or population coverage. There are three types of Open Pension Funds:

- Insurance companies, which account for 73.4 percent of the existing market assets. A significant number of insurance companies in Brazil belong to enterprise groups, led by commercial banks (including investment banks) and leasing companies.
- Specifically constituted for-profit organizations, which account for 13.4 percent of the market.
- Specifically constituted non-profit organizations, which account for 13.2 percent of the market.

### Closed Pension Funds

Closed Pension Funds may also be classified according to the role played by employers in their constitution and management. In order to identify the main features of each segment, it is important to observe the profile of sponsoring enterprises in terms of sources of capital.

In Table 4.3, Closed Pension Funds are classified as either public (affiliated to public enterprises) or private (affiliated to private enterprises). Public Closed Pension Funds have more assets and a larger number of benefits. This occurs because they have existed for a longer period and are thus more numerous and have wider coverage. The growth of Private Closed Pension Funds, however, suggests that they will acquire a leading market position in the future.

In spite of the unstable performance of the Brazilian economy, the Closed Pension Funds have presented high average rates of return, which are noticeably higher than GDP growth rates (averaging 10 percent a year from 1987 until 1996). Nevertheless, the Closed Pension Funds do vary in financial performance.

Table 4.3
Brazil: Private Closed Pension Funds—General Indicators

| General Indicators | Public Enterprises Number/Values | Percent | Private Enterprises Number/Values | Percent |
|---|---|---|---|---|
| Number of Closed Pension Funds | 95 | 27 | 257 | 73 |
| Total assets (U.S.$, December 1998) | 54 billion | 69 | 24 billion | 31 |
| Insured population | 3.2 million | 50 | 3.2 million | 50 |
| Beneficiaries | 292,503 | 58 | 209,238 | 42 |

*Source*: Secretaria de Previdência Complementar, 1999.

According to recent data (World Bank, 1995: 86), real average rates of return achieved by Public Closed Pension Funds were 14.5 percent a year between 1986 and 1992, against 12.2 percent a year by Private Closed Pension Funds.

In recent years, the actuarial situation of the Closed Pension Funds has not been as healthy, given the deficit shown in December 1998. Public Closed Pension Funds revealed an aggregate deficit of 6.4 percent of the total actuarially required reserves while Private Closed Pension Funds revealed deficits of merely 0.2 percent. The comparatively better situation of private sector funds is probably due to the greater presence of mixed contribution plans whose contractual reposition rates are lower than those of the more rigorous defined-benefit plans. To a large extent, actuarial problems arise from two factors:

- insufficient contributions to cover the obligations to affiliated employees who had been promised integral salary complements at the inception of the plans, even if the contributions paid on their behalf fell short of what was necessary (the enterprises would contribute for them throughout the years until time of retirement); and
- overly generous benefit plans, with high levels of benefit payouts and early retirement (age 55 or less, in the case of employees who affiliated before the Law 6,435 of 1977 was promulgated).

## THE CRISIS OF THE SOCIAL SECURITY SYSTEM: CURRENT DIAGNOSES

Endogenous and exogenous factors may be identified as components of the crisis of social security in Brazil. Among the former are historical financial and

**Table 4.4**
**Social Security Financial Balances: General and Special Regimes for Civil Servants, by Level of Government (U.S.$ Millions)**

| Types | 1997 | 1998 | 1999 Projection |
|---|---|---|---|
| I. General Regime | (2,329) | (6,512) | (9,089) |
| II. Civil Servants Special Regimes | (26,702) | (28,728) | (32,345) |
| Federal | (14,268) | (15,284) | (18,471) |
| States | (10,491) | (11,344) | (11,699) |
| Municipalities | (1,943) | (2,101) | (2,174) |
| Total | (29,031) | (35,241) | (41,433) |

*Source*: Secretaria de Acompanhamento Econômico, 1999.

funding difficulties, the high costs of benefit plans and the administrative problems. Exogenous factors include demographic trends, economic circumstances and labor market problems. Because they affect the social security system's performance in decisive ways, exogenous factors are part of the actuarial projections necessary for long-term management.

Each of the components above will be briefly considered in order to show the critical features of the system.

## The Problems of Public Social Security Finances in Brazil

Although various factors contribute to the crisis—especially the low coverage of the system and the inequalities in pension values—the financial dimension is undeniable since resources captured have been insufficient to cover benefit obligations. The resulting deficit is high and recent reforms have not led to its elimination, although they have been able to reduce its size, as suggested by Table 4.4.

In addition to the growing deficit, Table 4.4 also shows the significant financed imbalances of civil servants' regimes. In a period of strong fiscal adjustments, social security reform has become a strategic issue in the public agenda and in the government's reformist program.

With respect to resources, the current diagnoses of the financial structure of social security have emphasized the excessive weight of contributions on enterprises' payrolls, even though many benefits are not explicitly contribution related. This has resulted in high contribution rates, which may reach a total of

29 to 34 percent of payroll costs (including both the urban employees' and employers' shares of the contributions in the General Regime). Many analysts argue that this inhibits the competitiveness of Brazilian products in foreign markets. It is also considered unjust, since a very small segment of the population bears the burden for a system that is designed to benefit all citizens.

Proposals for a reduction of contribution rates have been frequently presented, especially by business groups, under the argument that it would both increase competitiveness and encourage an increase in the number of contributors. In fact, another critical factor influencing the system is the limited base of contributors since only 43.1 percent of the employees, or 40.5 percent of the economically active population, are insured.

The 1988 Constitution diversified the financial sources for public social security to include contributions from gross revenues, financial transactions and net profit. However, contributions based on the first two sources affect several stages of production and increase the tax burden, especially on exportable products. As a consequence, this form of financing penalizes the competitiveness of Brazilian products in foreign markets, worsening the balance of payments deficit and aggravating economic problems, as many critics of the current tax system have pointed out. The tax burden also encourages evasion and concealment, even beyond the unacceptably high current levels. In 1992, evasion rates were estimated as 76 percent of total contributions based on gross revenues and 98 percent of potential net profits (Beltrão et al., 1993).

Thus, besides unfairly burdening a small segment of society that is responsible for financing a universal system of benefits, the new sources for financing public social security also proved to be inefficient and unproductive as a basis of tax contributions, unjustifiably combining contributive and distributive principles.

But economic factors should not be overlooked in the analysis of the public social security system's performance. The recent economic context of monetary stability, fiscal adjustment, increasing unemployment and open imports has negatively affected the social security system. Until the mid-1970s, economic growth and high rates of employment benefited the system's early stages by allowing for a high contributor/beneficiary ratio. In the 1990s, however, the realignment of pension payments and enforcement of constitutional measures was accompanied by modest rates of economic growth, a reduction of formal employment rates and increases in unemployment. This has highlighted and reinforced the fragile and dire situation of the public social security system.

### The High Costs of Benefit Plans in the Public Social Security System

Due to the absence of minimum-age requirements in entitlement rules—as in the case of the length-of-employment pensions—and high replacement rates of active salaries—up to 100 percent of final salary—most analysts consider Brazilian public pension benefits to be generous. Retired employees may continue in the labor market and accumulate additional pension benefits; and, of the total number of beneficiaries with length of employment pensions in 1995, 32 percent were age 49 or less at the moment of retirement and 67 percent were age 54 or less.

The available information shows that persons retiring under length-of-employment or other special pensions have higher life expectancy upon retirement than those retiring due to old age. On the other hand, although they are only 37 percent of the total volume of pensions, the special and length-of-employment persons represent 61 percent of the expenditures. In spite of resistance from some sectors, the introduction of minimum-age requirements and the elimination of length-of-employment pensions were almost consensual in recent reform proposals.

## Management Problems of Public Social Security

In 1998, the administration of the public social security system accounted for 7.9 percent of the total benefit expenditure. Many observers consider this to be unacceptable. In addition, in spite of improvements—the average time for processing retirement applications has decreased from 160 to 22 days since 1992—the quality of services remains inadequate. Tax evasion and concealment is still high, representing nearly 22 percent of the total value of potential contributions in 1996 (excluding those who do not contribute). The proportion of canceled benefits as a result of fraud auditing procedures is currently 3.2 percent of the total number of benefits but reached 14.3 percent in 1993 when special auditing was carried out in order to combat frauds. These frauds or inefficiencies occur during medical exams or in the bureaucratic processing of pension applications.

Finally, the system has not been completely computerized and a registry of contributors has only been available since 1997, which only recently made possible greater prevention of fictitious estimates of length of employment which could occur previously, for example, through false statements from employers or fellow employees.

## Public Social Security and Demographic Trends

These financial imbalances have also been exacerbated by recent demographic trends. In addition to the increase in the proportion of the population aged 60 or more, life expectancy at birth continues to climb, as does life expectancy after retirement, which directly impacts social security. Between 1980 and 1997, the number of active contributors for each beneficiary fell from 3.2 to 2.1. This is similar to dependency ratios in countries with older age structures, such as Japan, the United States of America, France and Germany. Projections indicate this ratio may reach 1.2 or less by 2020 unless formal employment rates increase or benefit entitlement rules do not change rapidly (Além and Giambiagi, 1997).

## Labor Market and Public Social Security: A Brief Analysis

Labor market factors merit a specific analysis. Although the current dependency ratio is 2.1 contributors per beneficiary, this would change to 6.8 if the entire employed population were required to contribute (based on 1997 data). The slowing economy, growing unemployment and a decrease in formal employment have reduced the pool of contributors to the system. The economic recovery that began in 1993 did not increase formal employment (in terms of number of contributors in the public social security system). While wages represented 36.4 percent of the functional distribution of income in 1990, they fell to 28.8 percent in 1997. Informal employment did not absorb the difference, as its participation varied between 6.92 percent and 5.7 percent during this period.

Eight out of 10 jobs created were in the informal labor market, according to Baltar (1998), reflecting the increasingly fragile labor market in Brazil. The unemployment rate reached 8.15 percent by March 1999. The economic crisis, the obstacles to reforming the state apparatus and its control instruments and the competitive barriers in the world market have also aggravated the situation. It is impossible to anticipate exactly what the short and long-term results of these trends will be. However, under current eligibility rules, if solutions are not found soon, they may create insurmountable actuarial problems which may reinforce the social exclusion that has been a permanent feature of Brazilian society.

## THE MAIN PROPOSALS FOR REFORM

A range of proposals has been developed to address the crisis of the public social security system.

### Proposals to Restructure Benefit Plans

For analysts more closely identified with private-sector interests, as well as for many who defend the public nature of the system, benefits should be planned according to more rigorous actuarial criteria.

#### *Public Retirement Pension Reform*

For retirement pensions, this means the elimination of length-of-employment criteria and the need for a minimum retirement age requirement—generally advocated to be within the 60 to 65 age-range—both of which are considered central to the system's future viability. There is greater consensus about a minimum contribution period being set between 15 and 20 years. Opinions differ, however, with respect to the permanence of rural and welfare benefits in the social security system even though there is agreement on their tax funding. There is also general agreement that women should have a shorter contribution period than men—usually five years less—although some recent proposals defend equal periods.

### Work-Injury Benefits Reform

Work injuries are seen as a function of the degree of supervision of working conditions, which should be strengthened.

## Proposals to Restructure Finances

Among the most important proposals being debated are those related to the restructuring of social security finances, upon which there is not a consensus. Although most analysts consider contribution rates to be high in comparison to other countries, very few propose any rate reduction, any limiting of the base to employees' salaries, or any exempting of employers from their contribution responsibility as has been the case in Chile since 1981. Indeed, those who defend workers' interests consider that high employer contributions are necessary in view of the low prevailing wage levels. As argued also by analysts linked to the public sector, given the state's feeble controls, reduced employer contribution rates would mean lower tax revenues without effectively generating additional formal employment. The defenders of the private interests consider this to be a feasible alternative.

## Proposals to Restructure Public Social Security Institutions

The strongest proposals for change focus on the legal-administrative aspects of public social security provision. Both public and private sector interest groups believe that a reduction of the ceiling of General Regime benefits, and the transfer of special civil servants' regimes to that regime, would reduce benefit disparities while, at the same time making room for private complementary pension funds under an individual capitalization regime. Most of these proposals defend a defined contribution regime and the predominance of the private sector in social security provision. Within this model, the social security regime would rest on two pillars: compulsory adherence to the General Regime and optional affiliation to private complementary pension funds.

The discussion regarding the transition from the current to a future regime has occupied a significant part of the debates. Among the alternatives discussed, one posits pecuniary incentives to the lower-income insured (those earning less than 10 times the minimum wage) through an accumulation equivalent to the total amount of past contributions, which would receive actuarially estimated interest rates and which would be transferred to the new complementary pension fund system. The insured could also remain in the previous regime as long as they paid actuarially determined contributions. This mechanism would imply a significant reduction in tax revenue as it would increase tax deductions on salaries for contribution expenditure.

The state would regulate and exercise fiscal control over those complimentary pension funds as well as participate directly, in many cases, through benefit plans created by state banks. These banks would compete with the private sector and receive tax exemptions similar to those already in effect. Such measures would be accompanied by a gradual elimination of the earlier described fraud and management problems present in the public social security system.

Although advocates of employees' interests do not agree with proposals to lower ceilings in benefits and contributions, they tend to accept uniform rules for all systems which would allow for the introduction of complementary benefits for those insured under the civil servants schemes.

### The Probable Costs of Proposed Reforms of the Public Social Security System

Several actuarial studies have been made to predict the future of the Brazilian public social security system. Recent simulations by the Ministry of Social Security project three scenarios based on the following assumptions: the imposition of minimum-age requirements; the lowering of minimum pension benefits (from 1 to 0.5 times minimum wages); the elimination of shorter contribution periods for women and rural workers; and the lowering of ceilings for both contributions and benefits (but not the elimination of the employer contribution rates or changes in the current income-replacement rates). Several exogenous variables are also introduced in the model, such as changes in GDP, gross revenues, undistributed profits, per capita income and average minimum wages.

The best scenario results from a public–private partnership with private sector predominance, as all the variables in the model reveal increases (Scenario 1, assuming an annual GDP growth rate of 4 percent). On the other hand, a public–private partnership with public sector predominance, under the assumption of state success in resolving the financial problems (through higher tax revenues and a reduction in the budget deficit), reveals lower increases in all variables (Scenario 2, assuming an annual GDP growth rate of 4.5 percent). Finally, the third set of projections portrays a social security system in crisis scenario and predicts low or negative variation in all the variables (scenario 3, assuming an annual GDP growth rate of 4 percent).

The introduction of a minimum-age requirement ranging from age 60 to 65, similar to those observed in most OECD countries, would considerably reduce the potential deficit. If such a change were accompanied by the elimination of gender differences in that requirement, expenditure reduction would be even more pronounced. Only a significant reduction in benefit ceilings would result in substantial deficit reduction: not even a reduction from 10 to 3 times the minimum wage would have perceptible effects on the deficit, especially in view of the risks of individual capitalization schemes. In the short run, until 2005, such changes would even tend to aggravate public finances. Only in 2030 would benefit reductions show a limited favorable impact on the financial balance. The

**Table 4.5**
**The Brazilian Social Security System: Financial Needs in 2005 and 2030 under Different Ceilings and Scenarios (as a Percentage of GDP)**

| Scenarios by Year | | Without Minimum Age (present situation) | | | Ages 60 (women) and 65 (men) | | | Age 65 (both women and men) | | |
|---|---|---|---|---|---|---|---|---|---|---|
| | | 3 times min. wages | 5 times min. wages | 10 times min. wages | 3 times min. wages | 5 times min. wages | 10 times min. wages | 3 times min. wages | 5 times min. wages | 10 times min. wages |
| 1 | 2005 | 1.04 | 1.36 | 1.06 | 0.56 | 0.56 | 0.23 | 0.46 | 0.45 | 0.12 |
|   | 2030 | 5.05 | 6.46 | 6.21 | 2.70 | 3.30 | 2.96 | 2.25 | 2.08 | 2.44 |
| 2 | 2005 | 0.77 | 1.19 | 0.80 | 0.43 | 0.37 | +0.04 | 0.31 | 0.24 | +0.18 |
|   | 2030 | 5.30 | 6.63 | 6.27 | 2.86 | 3.38 | 2.93 | 2.30 | 2.77 | 2.30 |
| 3 | 2005 | 1.62 | 1.98 | 1.58 | 0.81 | 0.83 | 0.40 | 0.67 | 0.68 | 0.24 |
|   | 2030 | 7.43 | 9.59 | 9.25 | 3.95 | 4.88 | 4.43 | 3.33 | 4.18 | 3.71 |

*Source*: Oliveira, Beltrão and Marsillac, 1995.

major differences seem to occur in a crisis scenario. In the case of market-oriented readjustment, the maintenance of a ceiling ten times the minimum wage would lead to the best results, as is the case with public sector readjustment. Finally, a reduction in benefit ceilings to 0.5 times minimum wages has a positive impact on public social security finances under all of the scenarios considered: reduction in expenditures would be 1 percent (scenarios 1 and 3) to 2.2 percent of GDP (scenario 2) by the year 2030. Table 4.5 shows these impacts in the three scenarios considered.

## THE REFORM OF 1998 AND THE NEW PERSPECTIVES FOR THE PUBLIC SOCIAL SECURITY SYSTEM

After a long period of discussion, and as a result of four years of intense parliamentary debates, the reform of Brazilian social security was approved at the end of 1998, opening the way for new perspectives and future scenarios.

### The Recent Social Security Reform in Brazil

The reform of the Brazilian social security system gathered pace in April 1995 during the Fernando Henrique Cardoso administration. Emphasis was placed on amending the constitutional nature of many of the social security principles and on improving the balance between contributions and benefits. It was pointed out during the policy debate and discourse that, under existing conditions, the insured with low wages were bearing the financial burden of those with higher incomes, an unjust situation creating system imbalances. The government's main reform objectives were to increase the contribution base and period and to reduce the value and length of benefits.

The parliamentary proceedings on the government's reform proposal, which occurred between 1995 and 1998, were long and arduous, but a partial reform of the system was finally approved in 1998. Among the most important changes introduced were

- Changes to the benefits: abolished were the length-of-employment pension; the proportional pensions (granted five years before stipulated years of employment with a 30 percent reduction in the value of full pension benefits); and the special pension for certain occupational categories (except those for elementary and secondary school teachers and for workers in unsanitary occupations).
- Changes to eligibility criteria: specified were minimum-age requirements of 60 for men, and 55 for women and for civil servants; minimum periods of public employment of 10 years and 5 years in the same job in order to receive full pension benefits; the prohibition of cumulative pensions, except for physicians and teachers.
- Changes to special regimes and social assistance benefits: different special civil servants' regimes in the three levels of government were merged, and state and municipal governments were prohibited from creating their own regimes; social assistance benefits (such as birth assistance, funerary assistance and lifetime monthly income) under the General Regime's benefit plans were discontinued.
- Changes to private complementary pension funds: Public Closed Pension Funds were prohibited from absorbing expenditures above 50 percent of total contributions; Closed Pension Funds' benefit plans were required to permit portability of funds and anticipated withdrawals.

A limited consensus exists in support of these reforms. Although the measures have significant implications for public finances (particularly fiscal deficit reduction), the government considers them insufficient to overcome the financial problems in the public sector. Partly as a result of these limitations, further revisions were undertaken immediately after approval of the reform, including increasing the contribution rates of higher-income insured and the introduction of contribution rates for higher-income groups. The estimated financial impact of both sets of measures—those included in the reform and those adopted in later revisions, through normal legislation—are shown in Table 4.6.

Although important, the medium-term effects of these reforms are modest and tend to reintroduce policy discussions and public debate about a new wave of changes in the public social security system.

**New Perspectives for Social Security Reform in Brazil**

To a certain extent, the limited reforms introduced in 1998 reflect ill-conceived policy strategies, whether from the government or from the groups opposing reform.

**Table 4.6**
**Estimated Impacts of 1998 Social Security Reform and Fiscal Adjustments on Budgetary Savings**

| Results | 1999 U.S.$ billion | 1999 % GDP | 2000 U.S.$ billion | 2000 % GDP | 2001 U.S.$ billion | 2001 % GDP |
|---|---|---|---|---|---|---|
| General Results of Structural and Temporary Reforms | 4.66 | 61 | 8.59 | 108 | 11.10 | 131 |
| Social Security Reform—Structural | 2.53 | 33 | 5.00 | 63 | 7.38 | 87 |
| Fiscal Adjustment—Civil Servants— Temporary | 2.13 | 28 | 3.59 | 45 | 3.70 | 44 |

*Source*: Oliveira, Beltrão and Marsillac, 1995.

The government's strategy actually presented social security reform as a gradual, incremental process. In Brazil, as in other countries undertaking social security reforms within a democratic context, this process mobilizes the entire society—all interest groups—and, therefore, tended to involve protracted, conflict-laden negotiations.

Nevertheless, in the Brazilian case, the process that transpired between 1995 and 1998 was off-track, sluggish and mishandled by the federal executive branch. This highlighted the absence of a coherent explanation of the general importance of either the set of measures or the resulting profile of the social security system underlying them. Moreover, improved benefits were not even promised.

In fact, the government's strategy in presenting its reform proposal was to adopt a low profile and to defend each measure separately, in a fragmented manner, rather than as part of coherent totality. Although this strategy had some advantages, as it allowed for separate negotiations regarding each measure or groups of measures, the disadvantages were significant, including the loss of both coherence and the assurance that the measures would result in sustained system balance.

Due to their ambiguous stance in relation to delicate and difficult issues, the political actors opposing reform were disappointing, as they vetoed morally and socially preferable measures and supported socially regressive and unjust positions. Consequently, the opposition lost a valuable opportunity to separate the issues which the reformists had strategically combined: control of the public deficit, generated by factors more important than social security, and the importance of social security reform itself because of the need for its long-term financial balance and because of the distortions and inequities which it contains.

The ensuing political vulnerability may be disastrous, as new rounds of social security reforms are being announced. By April 1999, the government had presented Congress with a legislative proposal which contained several new measures: the creation of individual social security accounts earning 3 percent annual interest rates forming the basis for personal provision and the gradual increase in the number of months of earnings used to determine benefit entitlement from 36 to 120 months. According to the social security officials, the General Regime would, therefore, move from the present risk pooling, defined-benefit social insurance system to a defined-contribution, individual capitalization system which will, ultimately, be fully self-funding. Funding sources would include the INNS contributions collected and the accumulated future reserves, including the government's active debt. The current system would be maintained up to a ceiling of U.S.$1,002. Nevertheless, resources would continue to be directed to cover benefit expenditures without the creation of reserves. Such procedure is necessary since Brazil could not support the high costs of a transition from a simple defined-benefit social insurance regime to a defined-contribution, individual capitalization system without a transition period lasting several years.

Since many insured retired before reaching age 55, it is expected that final benefits will fall under a defined-contribution, individual capitalization system. This would open the way for a greater presence of a private complementary pension system since the difference between the social security benefit provided and the final salary would be much larger than it is currently. Although current proposals do not guarantee the immediate constitution of a more significant individual capitalization system, as in neighboring countries, they would open the way for those initiatives in the future. The central problem of such proposals is the abrupt imposition of real losses on a more complex society.

## Perspectives of the Dimension of the Private Complementary Insurance Market

Projections of the accumulation of assets of private complementary pension funds in Brazil have not been very successful. In addition to the problems normally involved in actuarial projections, expectations regarding the future structure of the public social security system will determine the market opportunities available for exploitation by private institutions. Obstacles to reform increase the uncertainties in estimating the size of the future market.

An example of these difficulties may be observed in the forecast by *Associação Brasileira de Entidades Fechadas de Previdência Privada* (the Brazilian Association of Closed Pension Funds (ABRAPP)). It estimated that Pension Funds will increase their share of GDP from 11 percent in 1999 to 18 percent by the year 2000. It is difficult to imagine a 63 percent increase can be achieved in a single year, but it does reflect the magnitude of the expected decrease in the public-sector participation in social security that will follow the ongoing reforms and the subsequent market entry of a large number of private insurance firms.

Subsequent projections that take into account recent social security reforms indicate significant asset growth in the private complementary insurance market. Of all Latin American countries with privatized systems, Brazil's continue to hold the largest volume of pension fund assets although their share of GDP is more modest. Privatized provision will continue, therefore, to be important in the Brazilian and in the Latin American context more generally, although projections show a reduction in the participation of private financial assets from the current 60 percent to 46.7 percent in the year 2015.

## FINAL OBSERVATIONS: SOME LESSONS FROM THE RECENT BRAZILIAN EXPERIENCE

The three main trends observed in the recent movement toward social security reform in Brazil have been the search for financial balance in the public system, the exclusive or enlarged participation of the private sector in the complementary pension market, and the development of a new regulatory framework. As this chapter has demonstrated, most of the reform proposals, and the recently approved reform measures, involve the de-monopolization of benefit provision, involving a move toward the creation of a partially competitive social security market. In that sense, the Brazilian case is similar to those of its Latin American neighbors.

However, the Brazilian system has several specific distinguishing features. Although its public social security system has been experiencing growing financial difficulties and problems, it has fulfilled its financial obligations without going bankrupt. As a consequence, many of the reform proposals would impose greater losses on the insured than they have experienced in the past due to inflation, or even at present, since the major problems have not manifested themselves through abrupt decreases in pension entitlements or discontinued payments. Therefore, pension reform tends to be perceived by the insured as involving only immediate short-term losses in expectation of possible long-term future benefits. This view reinforces opposition to the reform. However, current expenditure projections show that the public system will encounter, at least in the medium-term, serious problems. Under present conditions, just in the Federal Regime, the projected deficit in 2030 will vary between 6.2 percent and 9.3 percent of GDP, the equivalent of 20 percent to 30 percent of current tax revenues! Financial deficits of these magnitudes could hardly be absorbed without a deterioration of social security provision, especially in terms of reduced real pension entitlements. In addition to this dire public deficit situation, retired employees are facing a high medium-term risk of increased income insecurity as a result of dependence on public provision.

Recent reforms have not yet been able to alter this negative scenario. But it is similarly wrong to imagine that the privatization model, by itself, would correct these imbalances. Projections based on the parameters of the radically privatized Chilean model indicate that privatization in Brazil would immediately increase the system-wide deficit by an amount equal to 6.5 percent of GDP and would increase the public system deficit by amounts varying between 8 percent and 8.5 percent of GDP—a level of imbalance that could hardly be met by public finances in Brazil.

The private sector of the system also has its distinctive features that seem to resist the Chilean-type radical privatization solutions. The private sector has a long history, as it is surely the oldest and most powerful private social insurance sector in Latin America, and is large in terms of volume of financial assets. It is closer in form to the United States model of pension funds than to the Chilean one, insofar as it is financed by both employers and employees rather than only by individual employees purchasing defined-contribution benefits managed only by private institutions. This view is reinforced by the weak performance of Open Pension Funds in comparison to the predominant Closed Pension Funds as a result of the prohibitive costs of funds operating without employer contributions.

Therefore, the perspective of a Chilean-style radical privatization does not seem promising, indicated by the recent regulatory project of civil servants' pension funds (federal, state and municipal) submitted to the National Congress in April 1999, which proposed a Closed Pension Fund, rather than an Open Pension Fund, format.

However, it is undeniable that a more pronounced market orientation, compatible with a public social security system, complementing and supplementing each other, may contribute to overcome the difficulties encountered by the latter. In fact, this is the point of view of most proposals and tendencies of public opinion. Among other conditions, this requires a growing private sector and measures that would make it compatible with the design and characteristics of the General Regime.

The systemic factors restricting the attraction of private pension funds and, therefore, the broader market orientation of the system are not trivial. The high income-replacement rates in the General Regime and full income replacement for civil servants tend to reduce the need for complementary pensions, especially in the context of stability created by the Real Plan, since 1994.

Although it is true that current reforms raise the issue of complementary pensions in the perspectives of the insured and of future beneficiaries, the uncertainties and contradictory tendencies of the reform process, and its future, prevent a fully stable regulation of this sector. This situation inhibits the entrance of new insured persons and institutions into the still stagnated voluntary private pension market.

It is important to mention that the paths and rhythms of the market orientation of the Brazilian social security system will probably express the solutions of the regulatory framework and, in general terms, of the reform of the state.

Many of the obstacles still inhibiting the accelerated development of the private social insurance sector today are of a regulatory nature. Inadequate system rules and distortions, such as the requirement of minimum levels of portfolio investments in stocks and public securities, are seen as factors which contribute to lower rates of return of funds and inhibit the action of private managers.

However, the limited capacity to control fraudulent funds, as occurred in the

1970s, and the sluggish recuperation of resulting losses through the courts, instill a lack of confidence in potential affiliates and thus inhibit the growth of this sector.

Finally, the obstacles regarding vesting and portability also inhibit the extension of the private system to potential employees. The new bill of April 1999 dealing with the private pensions treats portability in a more incisive manner. But the structure and nature of the future institution of re-insurance is still unclear, especially with respect to the protection of insured from possible inept and fraudulent management, as it exists in other countries.

**REFERENCES**

Além, A.C.D. and Giambiagi, F. 1997. *Despesa Previdenciária: Análise da sua Composição, Efeitos da Inflação e Bases para uma Alternativa Intermediária de Reforma*. Rio de Janeiro: Departamento de Economia da PUC-RJ, Texto para Discussão, setembro.

Baltar, P.E.A. 1998. *Emprego e Informalidade das Ocupações Urbanas no Brasil dos Anos 90*. Caxambú: Anais do XI Encontro Nacional da ABEP.

Beltrão, K. I., Oliveira, F.E.B. de, Lustosa, B. J. and Marsillac, M.T.P. 1993. Fontes de Financiamento da Seguridade Social Brasileira. In *A Previdência Social e a Reforma Constitucional*. Brasília: MPAS/CEPAL.

Ministério da Previdência e Assistência Social (MPAS). 1997. *Anuário Estatístico*. Brasília: MPAS.

Oliveira, F.E.B. de, Beltrão, K. I. and Marsillac, M.T.P. 1995. *Análise Atuarial dos Benefícios da Previdência Social*. Brasília: MPAS.

Secretaria de Acompanhamento Econômico. 1999. *Boletim Macroeconômico*. Brasília: Ministério da Fazenda.

Secretaria de Previdência Complementar. 1999. *Boletim das EFPP*. Brasília: MPAS, março.

Superintendência de Seguros Privados. 1998. *Boletim das EAPP*. Brasília: Ministério da Fazenda.

World Bank. 1996. *Social Insurance and Private Pensions 1995* (Country Report). Washington, DC: World Bank.

*Chapter 5*

# Marketization of Sickness and Disability Insurance in the Netherlands: A Review of the Polder Route

Ruud Muffels and Henk-Jan Dirven

## INTRODUCTION

The evolution of the Dutch social security system after the Second World War can be divided into two main stages: a period of expansion until 1977 followed by a period of contraction and reform afterward. After the war, particularly in the late 1960s and 1970s, the social security system saw a rapid expansion that brought the level of social security among the highest in Western Europe. The expansion of the welfare state, particularly the evolution of the social insurance programs, had some typical corporatist features because of the traditional pillar-structure of the socio-economic institutions. Christians, Protestants, socialists and liberals were organized separately at the industry branch level (within industrial insurance boards). The representatives of these pillars used their influence and power in the decisive tripartite social and political bodies, notably, *Sociaal-Economische Raad* (the Socio-Economic Council), and *Stichting van de Arbeid* (the Foundation of Labor), to affect the form and content of the welfare state. This pillar-structure characterized the Dutch welfare state up to the early 1980s.

The social security system evolved into a mixed system embodying elements of various ideal types of welfare states such as the Bismarckian model, the Beveridgian model, and even, in some sense, the liberal model (Engbersen et al., 1993). Social insurance programs, notably the employee benefit programs, were of the Bismarckian type: they were organized through industrial organizations ruled by public law and controlled by the state. They are employment-based (employee insurance or *werknemersverzekeringen*) and based on compulsory contributions levied of the Beveridgian type, providing universal flat-rate benefits financed by compulsory contributions levied on every adult (general insurance or *volksverzekeringen*) or through general taxes. The National Assistance Act (1965) was inspired by views about the role of the state as being a "provider of last resort," when other social security programs fail to guarantee income security. Social assistance benefits are financed out of general taxes. The amounts are generally means tested but at a uniform rate, although different to household type (singles, one-parent families, couples) and at a minimum level. This kind of benefit resembles the typical features of a liberal welfare system. Notwithstanding the mixed character of the institutional design of the Dutch system, we might reach a different conclusion when it comes to the outcomes of the social security system. With respect to the tightness of conditions and the generosity of the benefit levels, we might conclude that the Dutch system belongs to the social-democratic type (Goodin et al., 1999).

The 1970–1977 period saw the completion of the post-war social security system. The center-left government headed by Joop den Uyl reacted upon the first oil crisis by raising the minimum benefit levels in order to maintain effective demand. Moreover, the government believed that social security was not meant only to compensate for income losses due to social risks but that it should also aim at the redistribution of income based on equity or "solidarity" principles. The General Disability Benefits Act (1976) is usually considered as the finishing touch of the building up of the social security system during the previous post-war period. It closed the remaining gap in coverage of the income loss due to disability by the self-employed and the non-working population (Netherlands, Social and Cultural Planning Office, 1998).

The 1978–1998 period was characterized by major reforms of the social security system. The main reasons for reforming the system were based on the worsening of the economic situation in the second half of the 1970s. The government responded by retrenchment measures and cuts in public expenditures. In these years, social security was among the major government sectors that suffered as a result of these cutbacks.

The early 1980s were a turning point. A prioritization shift occurred with respect to the competing social security goals: before, the goals focused on broadening the range of social risks addressed and population coverage; after, the prevailing economic conditions required the government to restrict the number of beneficiaries and to slow down the growth in social security expenditures. This re-focusing thus meant that the principle of efficiency was set on even par with the principles of equity and fairness. As a result of this shift toward efficiency, policy measures aimed at tightening the conditions for entitlement (reducing the inflow) or at activation and re-integration into the labor market (increasing the outflow) became more popular.

This fundamental social security policy shift was induced and led by market-driven policies of three coalition governments, operating from 1981 to 1993, headed by the Christian-Democratic leader Ruud Lubbers. In the early 1990s this resulted in the introduction of elements of privatization and marketization. The first so-called purple coalition government (a coalition of Social Democrats,

Liberals and Social Liberals) headed by the Social-Democrat Wim Kok from 1994 to 1998 made the maintenance and creation of jobs and the marketization of public sector activities his government's primary policy goals.

With reference to the measures taken to achieve these goals, the 1978–1998 period can be subdivided into three main stages (see Netherlands, Social and Cultural Planning Office, 1998: 425–26). These stages differ with respect to the emphasis placed on measures affecting the social security financing, the level and duration of benefits, and the conditions for entitlement, respectively:

- 1978–1982: ad hoc measures were adopted with an emphasis on safeguarding the funding of the system;
- 1983–1989: the first reform of the system took place (*stelselherziening*) with an emphasis on reducing benefit levels and the duration of entitlement; and
- 1990–1998: major reforms of the system were instituted with an emphasis on further tightening the conditions for benefit entitlement, on entry and re-entry into the labor market and on the privatization of some social security programs, particularly the sickness and disability programs, which constituted a fundamental shift in the political perspectives and ideological values underlying extant institutional arrangements.

The final stage of the expansion of the Dutch social security system, and the period of contraction and reform afterwards, may be characterized by their impact on the number of benefit-years—the average number of benefits paid during one calendar year. Between 1970 and 1985, the number of benefit-years increased strongly by 61 percent (Table 5.1). Thereafter, the growth was much more moderate. In the same period, the population grew by only 21 percent. Huge increases in benefit-years occurred in the social assistance, unemployment and long-term disability programs in particular. The expansion of the other programs was much less dramatic. In recent years, there is a tendency for the number of benefit-years to decrease somewhat. This is the combined effect of the aforementioned retrenchment policies and, especially, the growth of employment because of which the inflow is marginally lower and the outflow marginally higher. This occurs within all social security sectors, including sickness and disability, but with the exception of old age (see Tables 5.1 and 5.2).

Internationally, the Dutch welfare state is often pictured as having one of the most equitable, generous and comprehensive social security systems, comparable with social security systems in the Scandinavian countries, particularly Sweden and Denmark, which produce a high degree of income equality. Social security expenditure as a percentage of gross domestic product (GDP) is among the highest in the European Union (Table 5.3). Social security expenditure per capita is also quite high (16 percent higher than the European Union average in 1996), especially with respect to long-term disability programs which represent 15 percent of social security expenditure, almost twice the European Union average.

Large numbers of the non-working population in the Netherlands are receiving sickness or disability benefits. As a pecentage of the Dutch labor force, the

Table 5.1
The Expansion of the Dutch Social Security System, 1970–1998 (× 1,000 benefit-years[a])

|  | 1970 | 1975 | 1980 | 1985 | 1990 | 1995 | 1997 | 1998[b] |
|---|---|---|---|---|---|---|---|---|
| Old age | 1,028 | 1,159 | 1,280 | 1,781 | 1,956 | 2,079 | 2,127 | 2,150 |
| Widowhood and orphanhood | 151 | 162 | 168 | 171 | 187 | 191 | 182 | 149 |
| Long-term disability | 196 | 312 | 608 | 698 | 778 | 752 | 742 | 646 |
| Sickness and short-term disability[c] | 234 | 280 | 306 | 257 | 346 | 306 | 295 | 307 |
| Unemployment[d] | 58 | 197 | 235 | 652 | 537 | 675 | 293 | 262 |
| Social assistance[e,f] | 70 | 117 | 112 | 180 | 176 | 164 | 463 | 429 |
| Family allowances[g] | 1,927 | 2,100 | 2,174 | 2,165 | 1,809 | 1,814 | 1,809 | 1,805 |
| Total (excl. Family allowances) | 1,737 | 2,227 | 2,709 | 3,739 | 3,980 | 4,167 | 4,102 | 3,943 |
| Index (1970 = 100) | 100 | 128 | 156 | 215 | 229 | 240 | 231 | 227 |
| Total (incl. Family allowances) | 3,664 | 4,327 | 4,883 | 5,904 | 5,789 | 5,981 | 5,911 | 5,748 |
| Index (1970 = 100) | 100 | 118 | 133 | 161 | 158 | 163 | 161 | 157 |
| Population (x 1 million) | 13 | 14 | 14 | 15 | 15 | 15 | 16 | 16 |
| Index (1970 = 100) | 100 | 105 | 108 | 112 | 115 | 118 | 121 | 122 |

a. The number of benefit-years is defined as the number of benefit-days cumulated over one calendar year divided by the number of days in that year. Each day for which a benefit is provided, is counted as a benefit-day.
b. Estimated figures for 1998. See Social Report 1999: 153–54.
c. Benefit-days divided by 261.
d. Including unemployment assistance until 1995.
e. Persons below 65 years of age not living in institutions.
f. The 1997 and 1998 figures include beneficiaries formerly receiving unemployment assistance.
g. Number of households.
*Sources*: Netherlands, Social and Cultural Planning Office, 1998: 499; Netherlands, Second Chamber, 1998: 151–54.

**Table 5.2**
**Sickness and Disability Beneficiaries as a Percentage of the Total Population, 1990 and 1995**

|  | Sickness |  | Disability |  | Total |  |
|---|---|---|---|---|---|---|
|  | **1990** | **1995** | **1990** | **1995** | **1990** | **1995** |
| Netherlands | 7.1 | 5.2 | 8.9 | 8.0 | 16.0 | 13.2 |
| Belgium | 3.8 | 3.3 | 4.2 | 4.4 | 8.0 | 7.7 |
| Sweden | 6.1 | 3.8 | 3.5 | 3.9 | 9.6 | 7.6 |
| Denmark | 4.4 | 6.0 | 3.8 | 4.2 | 8.2 | 10.1 |
| Germany | 5.0 | 4.5 | 3.3 | 3.1 | 8.3 | 7.6 |
| United Kingdom | 2.6 | 3.4 | 3.5 | 4.9 | 6.1 | 8.3 |

*Source*: Ministry of Social Affairs and Employment, Report 1999.

proportion receiving such benefits was 13 percent in 1995, down from 16 percent in 1990. In terms of benefit-years, the receipt of sickness and disability benefits is even more striking internationally than the receipt of unemployment benefits. In 1997, protection for sickness and disability amounted to 1 million benefit-years, compared to less than 300,000 benefit-years for unemployment protection. Both, however, have shown a strong decrease since 1990. Long-term disability program expenditure was 12 percent of social security expenditure in 1996, rather higher than unemployment program expenditure (see Table 5.3).

Elements of marketization and privatization were mainly introduced in the 1990s, which is the focus of this chapter, although the foundations for these changes were laid in the 1980s. The 1990s are particularly characterized by the reform of the sickness and disability programs, which involved a tightening of the conditions for entitlement in order to downsize the inflow into sickness and disability; by the development of new workforce entry and re-entry policies to increase the outflow; and by the adoption of privatization measures, which might be conceived as the search for a policy route toward a new public-private balance within the social security system. This policy route, whether purposely aimed at or not, was set in motion in the 1990s, and new legislation will most likely come into force in the near future. Its direction and scope are, however, hard to predict, given the absence of clearly stated political goals about the future of social security. Although a debate on the future of social security was anticipated during the first "purple coalition" period of government in the mid-1990s, it never took place because of lack of political will on the part of the

**Table 5.3**
**Social Security Expenditure in the Netherlands and the European Union, 1996**

|  | Netherlands[a] | European Union (EU-15) |
| --- | --- | --- |
| Social security expenditure |  |  |
| % of GDP | 30.9 | 28.7 |
| Per head (PPS) | 5,952 | 5,120[b] |
|  |  |  |
| Social benefits (% of total expenditure) |  |  |
| Sickness/health care | 28.3 | 27.0 |
| Disability | 15.3 | 8.5 |
| Old age | 32.9 | 39.2 |
| Survivors | 5.5 | 5.4 |
| Family/children | 4.4 | 8.0 |
| Unemployment | 12.0 | 8.4 |
| Housing | 1.2 | 2.0 |
| Social exclusion not elsewhere classified | 0.4 | 1.5 |

a. Provisional data.
b. Estimated data.
*Source*: European Communities, 1999.

three coalition partners. In the meantime the government was preparing new measures aimed at reforming the labor market and social security institutions. The agendas under which these new measures were proposed and defended were, again, privatization, work activation and re-integration of disabled people into the labor market.

## Socio-economic Conditions

The upturn of the economy in the second half of the 1990s followed the downturn during the first half. In 1998, the economic growth was almost 4 percent of GDP. Over the last 20 years, this growth rate was only surpassed in 1989 and 1990, which were well above 4 percent. The recession was at its bottom in the year 1993, when economic growth was below 1 percent (Netherlands, Statistics Netherlands, 1999).

Internationally, the Netherlands has built up an outstanding economic record.

Over the last three years the average real growth rate of Dutch GDP was more than one percentage point higher than the average real growth rate of European GDP (Donders, 1999). At the same time, the annual inflation rate has been rather low at 1.8 percent in 1998, which is, however, among the highest in the European Union (Netherlands, Statistics Netherlands, 1999).

The current favorable economic conditions are reflected in the ratio of non-working to working population. In the first half of the 1980s, the ratio increased strongly and then remained at a rather stable level of about 83 non-working people to every 100 workers until 1995. In recent years, it has fallen considerably to 76 in 1998. Although much higher than in the United States, the Dutch experience compares rather favorably to other Western European countries (Netherlands, Second Chamber, 1998: 102). The decline of the ratio is a result of rising employment levels, on the one hand, and a falling number of people on sickness and disability benefits, on the other. The decline in the levels of disability, however, is expected to be temporary because currently the number of people on disability benefit has begun increasing again (Netherlands, Social and Cultural Planning Office, 1998: 453).

During the 1990s, employment grew both absolutely and as a proportion of the working age population. It was, however, strongly affected by the increase in part-time and flexible jobs. In 1990, 61 percent of the working age population was employed compared to 68 percent in 1997. The latter was 8 percentage points *above* the European Union's average. In full-time equivalents, the increase in the net participation rate was much smaller: from 50 to 52 percent, which is *below* the European Union's average, due mainly to many women working part-time. This difference, however, has become smaller (Netherlands, Second Chamber, 1998: 96–97). Only recently has the number of new full-time jobs surpassed the number of new part-time and flexible jobs.

The unemployment rates mirrored the up- and downturns of the economic cycle. They increased during the first half of the decade and decreased in recent years. Long-term unemployment, which was at a rather high level in the Netherlands in the 1980s and early 1990s, remained at that level in the late 1990s. In 1998, the unemployment rate was 4.1 percent. This was 1 percentage point below the level at the start of the decade. Currently, the Dutch unemployment rate is half the average of the European Union as a whole (Netherlands, Second Chamber, 1998: 100). Long-term unemployment (over one year) is high in the Netherlands. During the period 1992–1998, long-term unemployment was steadily around 50 percent of overall unemployment. In 1997 and 1998 unemployment went further down whereas long-term unemployment increased slightly to 52 percent in 1997 and 54 percent in 1998.

**Political Factors and Ideological Values**

The political context of the Netherlands is characterized by a long tradition of coalition governments. The 1990s saw three coalitions. Firstly, the center-left

Lubbers III government (1989–1994) consisted of Christian Democrats and Social Democrats. This government was the third coalition directed by Christian-Democrat Ruud Lubbers, who had been Prime Minister since 1982. It was followed by the first "purple coalition" (Kok I government 1994–1998) of Social-Democratic, Liberal and Social-Liberal Parties under the direction of the Social-Democrat Prime Minister, Wim Kok. For the first time since the Second World War, the Christian Democrats were excluded from government. The "purple coalition" was continued after the elections of 1998 (the Kok II government 1998-).

Alarmed by the growing numbers of recipients of disability benefits, Prime Minister Ruud Lubbers stated in 1990 that the Netherlands might be viewed as a sick country. The Lubbers III government therefore launched a variety of measures aimed at lowering the benefit levels and tightening of the conditions for entitlement of the sickness and disability benefits. The government also introduced measures for marketization of the sickness and disability programs. Their primary goal was to reduce the current numbers of sickness and disability recipients to the 1989 level of 844,000 recipients.

The measures were reluctantly supported by the Social-Democratic Coalition Party and continued by the purple coalition. The rationale for the Social Democrats was that adjustment of the disability program was a precondition for the maintenance of benefit levels in the long run. However, the decisions of the Lubbers III government with respect to disability were strongly opposed by the unions and the organizations of beneficiaries and, eventually, led Social-Democrat Secretary of State Elske ter Veld to resign in 1989.

The main goal of the Kok I government was to create jobs in order to reduce the high ratio of non-working to working population, which was considered to be mainly due to benefit entitlements that achieve high income-replacement rates, little incentives to search for a job, and high levels of taxation. Active labor market policies were already instituted by the Lubbers III government and were intensified during this government by the Minister of Social Affairs and Employment, Ad Melkert. Apart from restructuring the sickness and disability programs, the policies of the Lubbers III government were also aimed at the introduction of a conditional linkage mechanism because of which annual increases in benefit levels were not automatically linked to the contract wage index but were dependent on the socio-economic conditions. The annual increases of the minimum social assistance benefits and the minimum wage depend on the ratio of non-working to working population. This makes the social partners (employers' and employees' organizations) co-responsible for the success of employment measures and the decentralization of the Employment Offices. The Kok I government did not change this policy. Moreover, the government put more efforts into making these employment policies more successfully implemented. These included the Job Pool Program, the Youth Employment Guarantee Program, work experience jobs and four types of so-called Melkert jobs (after the Minister of Social Affairs and Employment, Ad Melkert). Wage restraint, the functioning of the labor market, reducing inflow into the social security system and reinforcing labor market re-integration of social security beneficiaries are also high on the agenda of the Kok I government.

The recent economic and social successes of the Dutch "polder model" may be attributed to the consensus building in the policy tripartite—government, employers and employees—playing a certain role (Netherlands, Social and Cultural Planning Office, 1998: 103–4). These parties were committed to a coherent program of wage restraint, increasing labor market flexibility, the downsizing and reorganization of the government, the reform of social security legislation and the creation of employment programs. In recent years, the legitimacy of this program has strengthened through the achievement of high economic growth rates, increasing numbers of jobs and decreasing unemployment rates. The favorable economic conditions render further support for the policy route of marketization and privatization of social security arrangements of the current government.

## THE MARKET-DRIVEN APPROACH OF SOCIAL SECURITY IN THE NETHERLANDS

### The 1993 Report of the Parliamentary Inquiry Committee on Social Security

The first step on the route to privatization was set after the issuing in 1993 of the report of the parliamentary inquiry committee on social security, chaired by Flip Buurmeier—an elder Social Democrat and Member of Parliament. The Buurmeier Committee discussed the role of the various controlling, advisory and supervising bodies within the social security system. The report was very critical and mentioned extensively the failure of these bodies to downsize the increase in social security expenditures and the rising number of recipients and particularly the rising number of disabled people (Netherlands, Second Chamber, 1993). In general, Buurmeier criticized the corporatist features of the Dutch social insurance because of which in his view the gate watchers of the social security system failed in the execution of their controlling and supervising tasks. He therefore proposed rather drastic changes in the institutional arrangements. Buurmeier criticized the bipartite composition of the supervisory body, the Social Insurance Council (SVR), and a more independent supervision of the social security system was proposed. This new body became the Committee for the Supervision of the Social Insurance Institutions (the Ctsv). At the same time Buurmeier criticized the lack of managerial competence of the industrial insurance boards to execute the Disability Insurance Act. These boards were again ruled by the bipartite organization of employers and employees. He therefore recommended the transfer of this responsibility to the National Institute for Social Insurance (Lisv).

Buurmeier also recommended the transfer of the managerial responsibilities of the Unemployment Insurance Act, which were also in the hands of these malfunctioning industrial insurance boards, to the Regional Bureaus for the Labor Market Provisions (RBAs). The main corporatist players in the field of social security therefore had to transfer their responsibilities to new bodies not ruled by the two main social parties only but from then on by the state and independent professionals. The role of the main corporatist bodies, under public law operating industrial insurance boards, was replaced and transferred to social insurance agencies being private social insurance institutions (the Uvi) (Aarts et al., 1998). Apart from these institutional changes, Buurmeier also proposed to increase the financial incentives, particularly within the Sickness Benefits and Disability Insurance Acts, by letting the contribution rates vary according to the disability risks. Other proposals were the abolishment of the Sickness Benefits Act and the mandatory continuation of the wage payment by the employer in the case of sickness. The Sickness Benefits Act proposals certainly marked the road to privatization set in motion by the government in the 1990s.

## Opting-Out

The proposals of the Buurmeier Committee implied a fundamental reform of the social security institutions and a radical move away from the corporatist arrangements of the old social security system. Although the committee did not seek to introduce market elements into the system, its proposals meant a radical break away from the state dominance. Evidence for this might be found in the transfer of the implementation of employee benefits to private agencies as well as in the transfer of the responsibility for coverage of the sickness and disability risks to the employers. Thus employers could either opt out of the public system, and thus shift the disability and sickness risk away from the public system, or they could also stay within the public system and pay industry-differentiated contributions.

## Controlled Liberalization

The marketization of social security programs does not necessarily imply that the state has withdrawn entirely from their operation. On the contrary, the Buurmeier Committee's proposals implied the introduction of market elements and, simultaneously, the transfer of the responsibilities and authority from the social partners to the state. Therefore, it implied also a stronger role for the government with respect to the control and supervision of the management of the administrative bodies responsible for the execution of social security laws. Most of these proposals were adopted by the government in the years to follow and were transformed into new legislation. Therefore the actual social security privatization measures that came into force after 1992, can best be understood as a controlled liberalization of the social security market (Van der Veen, 1999). A sketch of these reforms is given below.

## The Reforms of the Social Insurance System during the 1990s

### Disability and Sickness Program Reforms

On March 1, 1992, an act came into force aimed at the reduction of the number of people drawing disability benefits. Its aim was primarily to increase the financial incentives for both employers and employees to reduce the incidence and duration of sickness and disability benefits.

The reward–penalty or bonus–*malus* system was introduced within the Disability Insurance Act. Employers were obliged to pay a penalty for each worker who became disabled, and similarly they received a bonus—a wage subsidy—for each disabled person hired on the labor market. This system was abolished in 1995 because of criticism made by the employers and employees organizations and after quite some public debate in the media. The main reasons for its abolition were that for small employers the burden of the wage penalty endangered the employment of the other employees and worsened the labor market position of handicapped persons, since employers because of the penalty, preferred not to hire employees with a high disability risk. In the same spirit, employees' organizations argued that the re-integration objectives of the government measures could be frustrated by the penalty system. The reward for hiring a disabled person could not counterbalance the risk for a penalty, because of which employers were very reluctant to hire people with impairments.

On January 1, 1993, differential sickness contributions were introduced under the Sickness Benefits Act. From then on, the contribution rates differ according to the sickness incidence achieved by the employer compared to the average level in its branch of industry. Moreover, on August 1, 1993, an additional Act was introduced aimed at a reduction of the claimants of disability benefits. First, the degree of disability was no longer related to the working capacity, now being more strictly defined in medical terms. This meant that fewer people were considered to be totally disabled and, therefore, fewer would receive the maximum income-replacement rate of 70 percent. More people would have some residual earnings capacity because of which they were deemed only partially disabled. For the remainder, those who were not covered by the disability insurance had to apply for unemployment insurance or a social assistance benefit, which are either shorter in duration or at a lower benefit level.

Second, the duration and level of disability benefits became related to age and the insured wage level. The disability benefit was split into two separate benefit regimes: the earnings-related wage replacement benefit for people aged 33 years and older (which is 70 percent of the previous earnings) and the prolonged disability benefit at minimum wage level. On top of the prolonged minimum benefit, an additional allowance may be received equal to 2 percent of the difference between the actual wage and the minimum wage times the number of years that the person was older than 15 years on the first day of his/her disability period. For the whole disability period it meant that the benefit levels became more strongly related to age. For younger age beneficiaries the level and duration of the disability benefit was reduced, whereas for older age beneficiaries (those aged 50 years and older) the benefit level remained the same although the length of the payment period was extended. This implied that, on average, the income-replacement rate diminished because the higher the insured wage level, the lower the disability allowance. These measures, it must be understood, apply only to new recipients, whereas existing disability benefit recipients retained their existing rights. Nevertheless, it appears that compared to the previous situation, some workers became underinsured and were confronted with a so-called disability insurance hole. At the end of 1997, 61 percent of the firms and 82 percent of all workers appeared capable of reducing their under-insurance due to the withdrawal of the government by making semi-collective occupational or private arrangements.

Third, a large re-examination of all recipients below 50 years of age had to take place in conjunction with the examination at regular time intervals of the right to draw on disability benefits. This re-examination testing was especially directed at new recipients, thereby stressing the temporary nature of disability benefits.

Fourth, the revision of the formal definition of "a suitable job" to which a handicapped person had to apply was a very important reform element. The notion of a "suitable job," which had previously been rather strictly defined according to experience level, level of education, and pay, gained a broader interpretation. To assess this the private social security institution looks for three suitable functions on the labor market with which the insured can earn the highest income and where all functions jointly represent at least 30 job vacancies. It is irrelevant whether the insured gets that job or not. In the assessment procedure, the level of pay of the function in the middle category is assumed to represent at best the earnings capacity of the insured disabled person. The reduced benefit levels under the Disability Insurance Act induced employees to establish private arrangements as part of the outcomes of the collective bargaining process to surmount the "gap" in public coverage of the disability risk. Generally, this led to the rise of private insurance that reduced the disability insurance gap. Overall, the impact of these measures was much larger than had been expected.

The Acts aimed at reducing sick leave and at enhancing occupational health and safety practice came into force on January 1, 1994. These were designed both to raise the involvement of the social partners for preventive measures and to address the rising sickness incidence. In co-operation with a commercial occupational health and safety service, employers were obliged to examine their disability patterns and to develop preventive measures. Moreover, in order to increase the incentives for the employers to limit the costs of sickness leave, part of the responsibility for the coverage of the sickness risks was shifted to the employer. During the initial period of disability (two weeks for small companies and six weeks for larger companies), the sickness benefit entitlements, which previously were determined by the industrial insurance board, were abolished. Employers then became obliged to pay their salary at the income-replacement rate of 70 percent during this sickness benefit waiting period, provided it was pay not less than the legal minimum wage. The employers were allowed to reinsure the risk for short-term sickness leaves with private insurance companies. For extended periods of sickness leaves beyond the three-month period, the employer became obliged to develop an employment re-integration plan for the disabled employee.

### Administrative Reforms

In 1995, a new Act on the organization of the social insurance programs was enacted. Under this Act, the Buurmeier Committee's recommendations were implemented, based on the premise that the social partners should be held responsible for the dramatic increase in sickness and disability benefit recipients. The reform proposals involved the installation of an independent Supervisory Committee with authority to oversee the execution of social insurance programs (the Ctsv). This institute replaced the former bipartite Social Insurance Board (the SVR). Moreover, according to this Act the employers and employees became less directly involved in the implementation of the social insurance programs. Previously, the execution of the sickness and disability insurance was the responsibility of the industrial insurance boards, and all employers within a specific branch of industry were obliged to be affiliated to one of these boards. All employees working for these employers were then collectively insured with one of these industry branch insurance boards. Now there has been a contracting-out of the administration tasks the bipartite industrial insurance boards formerly had to specially constituted private social security institutions (the Uvi). This was meant to foster an independent and business-like relationship between the insurance boards, on the one hand, and the private social security institutions, on the other hand. It was also meant to contribute to increased marketization. The idea of contracting-out was aimed at fostering competition. However, because it was agreed that, until the year 2001, the industrial insurance boards would sign a contract with their former social insurance agencies, the contracting-out option has hardly been of any real significance.

### The Rise of Oligopolies in Social Insurance

The prospect of increased competition induced the specially constituted private social security institutions to merge with other players in the same market in order to profit from economies of scale. The number of private social security institutions decreased from ten in 1989 to only four in 1998 endangering therewith the ideal of a large competitive market. Moreover, many private social security institutions searched for private partners such as commercial insurance companies and banks. Some critics fear the rise of conglomerates operating as oligopolies in the social security marketplace. In the Netherlands there are many examples of these types of mergers between the private social security institutions, the insurance companies and the banks which may support this view. In such a malfunctioning market the economic rent is being extracted because of imperfect competition. The consumer of a social insurance product thus pays too high a price for too low a quality of service.

Due to the intertwining of the operation of the public and private providers and to the fear of inadequate competition, these specially constituted private social security institutions (holdings) were subjected to a tight market-entry test, according to which the public and private activities were examined in terms of their market competitiveness. This created two separate sections within the holdings: the first deals with the assessment and judgement of benefit claims and the provision of the benefits (the so-called public A-leg), the other carries out commercial activities such as private insurance and re-integration activities (the so-called private B-leg).

On January 1, 1996, the Act for the Privatization of the General Civilian Pension Fund came into force. It was decided that the civil servants would be brought under the employee insurance as of January 1, 1998. The Act requires that the civil servants become subject to the same contribution regime as the private sector employees, although the institutional arrangements remain unchanged.

On March 1, 1996, short-term disability that used to be covered by the Sickness Benefits Act was privatized. The Act was purposefully aimed at extending the obligation of the employer to pay wages during periods of sickness leave. The risk period covered by the employer was extended to 52 weeks. In reality, this obligation meant that most employees receive a minimum income replacement of 70 percent during any sickness. Employers may decide to contract with a private insurance company to cover this sickness risk, but they could alternatively opt for staying in the public domain. In real practice, about 80 percent of all employers did opt to insure with a private insurance company and to increase the sickness benefit to 100 percent of previous wages. The Sickness Benefits Act has thus become a safety net program for specific categories of employees only, such as temporary workers. Because sickness benefits were financed through unemployment insurance and the program has virtually been abolished, the differential contributions that were introduced in 1993 were also abolished.

In March 1997, a new Act for the organization of social insurance came into force. It introduced new institutional arrangements for the implementation of the social insurances, specifically

- greater room for the marketization of the implementation of the social insurances (administrative contracting-out, differentiation of contributions, opportunities to reinsure social security risks with private insurance companies);
- independent judgement of market-entry requests by any organization wanting to become acknowledged as a private social security institution;

- independent supervision of the social security practices; and
- execution at regional level and integration of case treatment.

As a result of this legislation (Haak and Koemans, 1996), the tripartite composed National Institute for Social Insurance, was created to become responsible at the national level for the execution of the social insurance programs and the private social security institutions operating at the regional level. The industrial insurance boards were transformed into the private Sector Councils, comprising employer and employee representatives. These have to advise to the National Institute for Social Insurance, which has as its main task the re-integration of disabled people into the labor market. To achieve this goal, the National Institute for Social Insurance requires the social security institutions to operate in their market and to improve their co-operation with both other private social security institutions and with the labor mediating agencies (such as the regional employment offices and the municipalities). The implementation of the social insurance programs is the responsibility of the specially constituted private social security institutions. The 1997 Act has been heavily criticized, since it was clear from the start that it did not offer a clear view on the future of the organization of the social security system. The Supervisory Committee (Ctsv) complained about its lack of clarity on the steps to be taken to attain full marketization. Particularly, it was unclear how to demarcate the public A-leg and the private B-leg, either within the holding or between the public principal (the National Institute for Social Security) and the private contractors (the specially-constituted private social security institutions).

In January 1998, the Act allowing for the differentiation of the disability contributions across industry sectors and the marketization of the employee's disability insurance (the so-called Pemba Act) came into effect. This caused a profound adjustment to the funding system used to finance disability insurance. Previously, contributions were paid jointly by employees and employers, but with Pemba all contributions have to be paid by the employer. Moreover, contributions became related to the disability incidence within the company or the industry sector. Employers could decide to insure through one of the private social insurance institutions or to self-insure. In the latter case, they would only pay a flat-rate contribution at a much lower level. For the individual firm, such behavior is rational only when the firm's disability incidence is below average, and the employer is at least as efficient in the execution of the disability insurance as the social security institution would be.

As of January 1, 1998, the public disability benefit program (AAW), which guaranteed a minimum disability benefit for the early handicapped and the self-employed, has been replaced by two separate programs. These are the WAZ for the self-employed and the WAJONG for young early handicapped, both of which were part of the general social assistance program. The creation of these two programs, and their placement under the General Social Assistance

Act, appears purposefully aimed at making a clear division of responsibilities between the public and private domain in the disability sector. The public domain was made responsible for the implementation of the universal, flat-rated minimum disability benefit programs. The private domain was made responsible for all supplementary selective and earnings-related disability benefit arrangements.

### *The Market for Disability Insurance: Is It a Real Market?*

Although the Buurmeier Committee in 1993 paved the way for the market reform of the social security system over the following five years, the social security system has yet to function as a market. First, it is not a market of producers and end-users. The end-users take no part in the marketization process because the responsibility for the insurance against sickness and disability risks rests entirely with employers. The mandatory contributions are therefore paid entirely by the employer. The overall providers of social security—the specially constituted private social security institutions—do not necessarily carry out the actual implementation of all the various arrangements. Employers operating at the regional level may contract out sickness and disability programs to private organizations. Contrary to the situation in a competitive market where there are numerous suppliers, actually there is only one, the National Institute for Social Insurance, which from 1997 operates as the principal or supervisor for the private social security institutions. After the enactment of the new Organization Act 2001, which currently is in preparation, the situation might change and the private social security institutions might become more competitive. According to this new Act, the numerous decentralized contracting-out agencies will constitute a real market for disability insurance.

### *The Splitting of Public and Private Activities*

Another critical issue is the demarcating of the public and private activities of the private social security institutions, which operate in a tightly regulated social security market. Thus their costs are higher and their competitive power is less than it would be if they operated in a fully competitive market environment. The principal restriction is that if they want to combine public and private tasks in a "holding," they must make a clear distinction between their public and private spheres (Algemene Rekenkamer, 1997 and 1998). The implementation of mandatory social insurance (the so-called A-leg) and the non-mandatory complementary social security benefits or other commercial products (the B-leg) must be strictly separated. Although the government proposals are aimed at relaxing the criteria for market-entry, the government's concern for the efficient and legitimate use of public money will require it to establish a robust set of regulations for the social insurance market, once the new proposals come into force. Whether the millennium year 2000 will mark a real change in the regulatory practice remains, therefore, to be seen.

The social security institutions are currently also subject to a very strict market-entry test administered by the National Institute for Social Insurance. It carefully examines whether the proposed private social security institution can fulfill the criteria set by law. These criteria restrict the private social security institution's private management domain, because of which the profitability and attractiveness of operating in this market is substantially mitigated. These restrictions will be relaxed according to the proposals in the new Organization Act 2001. One might expect that especially in the domain of the internal organization and business operation of the social security institution the government will withdraw to give greater room to the social security institution.

Further, employers are currently obliged to affiliate with particular private social security institutions operating in their industry, as they are forced to insure with them. A competitive market would imply that there is competition within the social security market in getting contracts for any sector. In the new proposals, the social security institutions may indeed compete with each other for contracts in any industry.

## Labor Market Participation and Re-integration Proposals

Another major policy development in the 1990s was the shift to labor market participation and re-integration policies in order to prevent people becoming dependent on public social security. One part of the Buurmeier Committee's recommendations in 1993 was devoted to the improvement of the labor market participation and re-integration measures in order to lower the inflow into, and to raise the outflow from, the sickness and disability programs. The idea was that a more efficient treatment of clients could be attained by the integration of implementing bodies and labor market mediation services into one service desk, where the client is informed about the full package of social services and labor market provisions. These activities, the Buurmeier Committee considered, should be combined into one organization, the Regional Centers for Work and Income (the Cwi), responsible to the National Institute for Work and Income (the Liwi). The Cwi/Liwi proposals play a very central role in the current debate about the extent to which the implementation of the disability insurance should be private or public. Some argue that the making of judgements on disability benefits claims, based on an assessment of the seriousness of the disability as an impediment to the applicant's remaining in the past occupation, should remain of public concern to be carried out by the Cwi/Liwi. Others, however, prefer the transfer of all implementation responsibilities to private social insurance agencies.

### *The Proposals for New Legislation*

The problems experienced with the privatization of the Sickness Benefits and Disability Insurance Acts, particularly the artificial separation of a public A-leg and a private B-leg, rendered new ground for the debate on the public–private interplay in the domain of social security and labor mediation. In 1998 the government asked the advice of the Socio-Economic Council (SER) on the future organization and implementation of the employee insurances. A more client-oriented approach became more important, an approach that aimed not only to give a better service to the client but also, at the same time, to improve measures that enhance re-integration into the labor market. In the government's request to the SER for an advisory report, it stressed the need to keep the disability benefit claim determination within the public domain. At the same time, the government recognized the need to relax the social security market entry conditions that permit a social security institution to be registered with the Supervisory Committee. The very tight market-entry criteria meant, in reality, that few new private organizations could enter the social security market. Therefore, the conditions necessary for a contestable market did not exist. The government also wanted to give greater room to the social security institutions to use the contracting-out formula or to implement market-like activities and to operate in accordance with market forces.

On June 19, 1998, the SER (Sociaal-Economische Raad, 1999) issued its advice to the government. It argued that benefit claims determination should be part of the work task of an independent non-profit unit within the private social security institutions (or the holdings). The SER distanced itself from the government's view that separate public organizations—the Regional Centers for Work and Income—should be given the responsibility to carry out benefit determination. However, the government maintained its view that benefit determination should be a public concern to be carried out by employees of the Regional Centers for Work and Income, working as a pilot or *bargee* with private social security institutions. In this *bargee* model, the medical practitioners and the labor market experts fulfill their tasks at the private social security institutions as employees of Regional Centers for Work and Income/the National Institute for Work and Income, which thus retains full responsibility for the execution. This model hinges upon the notion that the management of the disability re-assessment practices could best be done at the central level by the National Institute for Work and Income, which is considered best equipped to collect the information for the improvement of the directives and the protocols to be used in the implementation practice.

### *The Road to Full Marketization of Disability Provision*

In view of the government's wish to extend the marketization of the social insurances, a new organization act is in preparation which should be enacted in 2001. To date the contours of this new Act are not fully sketched out, but the government has let it be known that it will opt for one of the two following models: (1) the Regional Centers for Work and Income (Cwi)-plus model, under which a limited number (15 to 18) so-called Cwi-plus offices would perform the disability retests; or (2) the *bargee* model, under which initially the disability tests will be performed by the private social security institutions with the secondary disability re-testing for the prolonged benefits also undertaken by the private social security institutions. In the first model the public responsibility for the disability judgement is better reflected, whereas in the second model integration of the labor market re-entry and disability re-examination activities are better structured. The *bargee* (or *loods* model) was proposed by the Nyfer Institute in 1998 to avoid the principal–agent problem that might arise when private social security institutions have the authority for the claim judgement and therefore have more interest in making a strict than a rightful judgement of the benefit claim (Bomhoff et al., 1997). Under the alternative approach suggested by the National Institute for Social Insurance, the Foundation of Labor (*Stichting van de Arbeid*) and the National Institute for Work and Income, the private social security institutions would have primary and full responsibility for making disability judgements. However, the assessment would be submitted to the Regional Centers for Work and Income for a second examination and for a final determination. The government's view has been that such a model would give too little room for public interference. But, apart from that, the government has argued that a model in which the private social security institutions bear a substantial responsibility, but with the Regional Centers for Work and Income having the formal responsibility, might easily lead to a diffuse distribution of responsibilities with all the risks on malfunction involved (Netherlands, Second Chamber, 1999). The government seems to consider the *bargee* model as very attractive because of the clear distribution of responsibilities between the public and private players in the field.

### The SUWI-Report of Spring 1999

In the government sponsored report on a new organizational structure on the execution of work and income arrangements (the so-called SUWI report), issued in spring 1999, the government responded to past criticisms and paved the way for a further marketization of the disability insurance market (Netherlands, Second Chamber, 1999). First, the role of principal, which was previously held by the National Institute for Social Insurance, would be decentralized to Sector Councils of employers and employees. The compulsory linkage of the employer with the industry-based private social security institutions would be abolished, and employers would be free to choose any supplier. If the negotiations between the principal and the social security institution do not lead to agreement, the standard contract of the National Institute for Work and Income, which offers a basic insurance service package, should be accepted by both sides. Each private social security institution should formally be obliged to accept any employer meeting this standard contract.

Competition should further be improved, according to these proposals, by letting the specially constituted private security institutions compete with each other for the provision of disability insurance. To improve the scope for market activities, the very tight market-entry criteria governing access to the disability insurance market would be relaxed. Also the private social security institutions would no longer need to hold part of their profits, as well as part of their financial assets (shares), with the National Institute for Social Insurance. They would also become free to contract-out part of their disability insurance administration. No limitations would be set on the mixture of public and private activities, provided the private social security institution did not violate privacy or fair competition regulations and provided it accepted external supervision. Compared to the previous situation, this proposal should be considered a major change in government policy toward privatization. The transfer of the disability claim determination responsibilities to the public domain (Regional Centers for Work and Income) meant that the strict distinction between the public and private leg within the private social security institutions' holdings would be abolished. This is important because as they operate in the market, all that matters is the marginal profit derived from an investment in any activity of the firm, whether in the public or the private domain.

To improve market transparency, the private social security institutions would become obliged to disclose their financial results, details of their insurance products and data on the outcome of their re-integration efforts. The scope for private initiative by the private social security institutions would expand further because the SUWI-report proposals gave them administrative responsibility not only for disability benefits but also for contribution calculation and collection.

The government, however, still claims the right to test whether the private social security institutions would meet their statutory or regulatory obligations. The assessment criteria proposed relate to the quality of the administration (that is, the internal organization and the demands for certification of the contracts entered into with the principals). The certification itself has been considered a private task that can be done by the market. Other criteria proposed relate to the use of personal data records, the integrity of the board members, the separation of the contributions revenue and benefits expenditure from administration expenditure and insurance-related revenues, such as re-integration, and the supervision by the Supervisory Committee.

The major changes proposed in the SUWI-report are first, the transfer of the disability benefit claim determination to the Regional Centers for Work and Income, which suggests that full privatization of disability insurance is unexpected. Second, the proposed abolition of the compulsory linkage of the employer with the industry-based private social security institutions is likely to make the market for disability insurance more competitive, yet the public control of the social insurance sector is to be retained. The government would therefore retain its control on the disability benefit claim judgements on abuse and fraud and on the supervision of social security institutions. For these reasons the privatization process can best be qualified as controlled or regulated liberalization.

In June 1999, the Socio-Economic Council (SER, 1999) issued a new advisory report on the institutional arrangements for social insurance. In this report the Council criticized the way the government wanted to transfer the power to make disability claim judgements from the private social security institutions to the Regional Centers for Work and Income, because the social partners had already agreed that the private social security institutions should gain full responsibility for the disability claim judgement. In their view, the Regional Centers for Work and Income should have a supervisory responsibility and thus use samples of cases decided by the private social security institutions to review and monitor the appropriateness of their practices. For the implementation of the social insurances, the creation of the Regional Centers for Work and Income would, in the view of the Council, lead to another bureaucratic layer in the already complex administrative structure and, therefore, would not contribute to the administrative targets being more client-oriented and more efficient. The clients would be confronted with quite a number of so-called transfer moments when they have to move from the counters of the private social security institutions to the counters of the Regional Centers for Work and Income and back again, perhaps repeatedly. The report therefore requested the postponement of the implementation of the SUWI-proposals. It also called for greater scope in initiatives to be taken at the local level for collaboration between the existing labor market institutions and the private social security institutions. The Council, however, endorsed the proposals for the integration of the National Institute for Social Insurance and the National Board for the Labor Market Provision (CBA) into a new tripartite institute called the National Institute for Work and Income (Liwi). The Council particularly stressed the need for the creation of a more coordinated regional labor market policy framework that should also be directed at the elaboration of industry sector policies, which it argued is an issue that the government has paid too little attention to.

Soon after the Council's release of its report, the parliamentary debate on the SUWI-report took place in June 1999. It was criticized notably by the opposition parties (the Christian, Green and Left Parties) but also by some of the coalition partners of the cabinet (Labor and the Social-Liberal Parties). Their critique particularly addressed the privatization proposals, involving the selling of shares in the specially constituted private social security institutions on the stock market, which, they argued, reflected no clear view on the results and outcomes of the privatization process envisaged. They therefore asked for postponement of the introduction of these privatization proposals. This postponement would also mean that the private social security institutions would remain as they are and that there was no need to shift responsibilities to the Regional Centers for Work and Income. The outcome of the debate in the Second Chamber was that the government agreed to postpone the implementation of the SUWI-proposals a few weeks, until the end of summer, so that more information could be gathered on the effects of these privatization proposals. At that stage we stated that: "the outcome of this political process remains to be seen, but one might guess that the purple coalition will choose for a more gradual and step-wise approach to the marketization of social insurance and the integration of labor market and social security institutions. The public control and impact of the social security system on the marketization process is thus likely to be strengthened as a result." The truth of this observation was borne out a few months later in the fall of

1999 when the government issued a new plan on the future implementation of the social insurance.

## The Government Proposal of November 1999

This latest proposal marks an essential break with the former proposals since it is proposed that the execution of the social insurance would again become a public domain responsibility. The implementation of the social insurance should be carried out by public agencies (the so-called agencies for the implementation of the employees' insurance (the UWV)). These agencies will also act as the principals for the disability re-integration activities, which would remain, however, in the private domain (the former A-leg of the private social security institutions). This also means that the disability benefit claim determination would remain in the public domain, especially the administrative and social insurance related activities. The role of the social partners in the implementation practices would be strongly mitigated and restricted to being members of a tripartite national advisory board on labor market issues. The role they had in the Sector Councils would vanish since the activities of these councils in the previous proposal were to act as the principals for the private social security institutions, over which they would have no authority. For that reason the social partners (employers' and employees' organizations) mounted through the media and within the tripartite national consultation a strong campaign in opposition to this proposal. The chairman of the SER, Herman Wijffels, and even the chairman of the Board of the National Institute of Social Insurance, Flip Buurmeier, also reacted negatively to the proposal. They expressed their support for the views of the social partners who wanted to retain their co-determining power in the implementation practices of the social insurance. The ensuing policy debate on the role of the social partners in the social insurance has elicited from the labor unions a strong position of support for the new proposals, which in turn has been interpreted by the media as a sign of the crumbling of the consensus-building practices in Dutch labor relations, the so-called polder model.

## THE PERFORMANCE OF THE MARKET-DRIVEN ROUTE OF SOCIAL SECURITY

### The Reasons for Privatization

The government started down the road to marketization of the social security system for three reasons. The first, and most important, was to reduce public social security expenditures and particularly sickness and disability expenditures. The second reason was to improve administrative efficiency by engaging the market in the provision of services and providing appropriate financial incentives for social insurance agencies, employers and employees. The third reason was to prevent people from becoming dependent on social security by paying more attention to labor market entry and re-integration by beneficiaries.

To what extent, then, has the marketization of the social insurances been successful? To an economist the question should perhaps be phrased in reverse terms, since private provision is presumed to be superior to public provision. Public social security provision can, however, be defended because of market failure caused by adverse selection and moral hazard (Bekkering, 1994). For low risk groups, insurance could lead to a welfare loss because the average risk premium determined by the insurer who has no information whatsoever on the distribution of risks across the insured population would be too high given their risk profile. High risk groups, on the other hand, would experience a welfare gain because the average risk premium would be too low given their risk profile. For these reasons a negative selection process will occur that will lead to an unprofitable, self-destructing market. Moral hazard arises when insurance leads to more risky behavior than without it. Since insurers have no prior information on the extent of moral hazard among the insured population, they will not take it into account. But also the risk-avoiding customers do not take moral hazard into account when buying insurance products; therefore, they will buy less than they really need given their risk profile (Aarts, Burkhause, and de Jong, 1996; Aarts and de Jong, 1999; Teulings et al., 1997).

Public provision can also be defended on equity and merit-good grounds if market failures would lead to unfair outcomes or the underconsumption of valuable social goods (Hoogerwerf, 1995). In such cases government intervention can be rational and enhance society's welfare. Public provision can also be made more efficient if the government creates a public monopoly by extending insurance coverage, by introducing universal pay-as-you-go systems or by creating a collective system with mandatory payment. The fixed costs would then be covered by a much larger number of insured persons, for which reason they are much lower than those of a private insurer (Teulings, 1997). The cost containment advantages are significant when moral hazards are low, as where the insured risk can be simply and objectively assessed (as with old-age pensions) (Aarts and de Jong, 1999).

Why then does government opt for marketization? If we assume that governments operate rationally, the obvious reason should be that the government expects efficiency gains from privatization. This means that a rational government would expect the welfare losses due to government failures to be larger than the welfare losses due to market failures (Hessel et al., 1998). In other words, the efficiency losses due to government intervention should be considered larger than those due to market failure. But is there any evidence that this assumption is true? If it is not true, then other reasons must apply, perhaps political ones, which might well explain the positions taken during the privatization processes.

*Adverse Selection*

The privatization of sickness and disability benefits has shifted their cost burden from the state to employers. The employers were first required to cover the cost of the first two to six weeks of sickness; then they were expected to cover the cost of the first whole year of sickness; and finally they had to pay sickness costs for the five years following the first year of the disability spell. This is thus an employer obligation, whether the employer self-insures or participates in a collective agreement. Due to the Pemba Act bringing on the differentiation of disability contributions across industry sectors and the marketization of the employee's disability insurance, they might also be confronted with an increased disability insurance cost if their disability risk is above average. Up to now there is some considerable evidence that the Pemba Act has induced risk-averse employers to be more reluctant to hire workers with health impairments. A survey among employers at the end of 1997 indicates that about 60 percent of all employers state that they have changed their personnel selection practices by taking more notice of the disability risk of future employees (Berendsen et al., 1998). If that were to happen on a broader scale, it is likely that the people with low disability risks would be covered by private disability insurance, while those with a high disability risk would be covered by the public system. The public sector share would thus be growing at the cost of the private sector share. In this scenario, the privatization policy could be deemed to have failed and, a posteriori, we might conclude that we would have been better off had privatization not been initiated in the first place. Privatization may have pay-offs in terms of efficiency gains, but it also incurs costs in terms of equity losses due to adverse selection and welfare losses due to moral hazard (Berkouwer and Hoogerwerf, 1996; Donner, 1998; Garner, 1997; Kotlikov and Sachs, 1998; Kotlikov et al., 1998; Steuerle and Bakija, 1997). The way privatization has been implemented in the Netherlands means there is a real danger that this worst-case scenario will be realized.

### *Privatization and Re-integration Efforts*

The Pemba Act was also meant to increase the financial incentives for employers to devote more attention to disability prevention and re-integration of disabled employees into work. Evidence from the United States indicates quite clearly that differentiation of contributions increases the prevention and re-integration efforts of employers (Aarts and de Jong, 1996). At the same time, it has appeared that employers have little interest in increasing their re-integration efforts when the cost of re-integration is large and the returns rather insecure. The Supervisory Committte's (Ctsv) 1997 employer survey shows that 50 percent of employers overall, and an even higher percentage of small and medium sized employers, agreed that the differentiation of contributions required by the Pemba Act provides an incentive for them to do more about disability prevention and re-integration of disabled workers. We might then say that in this respect the Pemba Act seems to have been successful. Many employers, however, cast doubt on the presumption that preventive measures will lead to a strong reduction of disablement. They point out that a major part of the inflow in disability is not work related but associated with risky lifestyles.

## Privatization and the Prospect of a Two-Tier Healthcare System

An unanticipated employers' response to the Pemba Act has been to demand more efficient treatment of workers by the healthcare system. They believe that the Pemba Act has shown that there is a need to shorten the waiting list for treatment because the longer the waiting time, the more time needed for recovery, and the more difficult recovery will be. This will lead to increased inflow into disability and, thus, higher costs for the employer. Because of this, employers' organizations have requested special priority treatment of workers by the healthcare system. To avoid the existence of a two-tier healthcare system with better access to health care for the well-to-do, the time and capacity needed for the special treatment of employees should be in addition to the existing capacity and be carried out in specialized healthcare centers. There is ample debate in the media about how to guarantee employee priority treatment without detriment to the non-working sick. The current situation is that when certain conditions are met, the Minister of Health Care will approve the creation of special services for the workers. These conditions are, first, that the priority treatment must be additional and not interfere with the treatment of ordinary care requests; second, that the waiting times for treatment in the care sector must be reduced to normal length; and finally, that public and private expenditures must be clearly separated.

## Adverse Selection by Choosing a Particular Private Social Security Institution

Adverse selection may also arise when the principals (industry councils) enter into contracts with a very strict private social security institution, one of those that very strictly apply the legal eligibility criteria when determining a disability benefit claim. This means that those employers would have an incentive to select only healthy personnel because it would be less attractive (more costly) to employ people with high disability risks. To avoid this adverse selection, a minimum standards contract is required that will guarantee that the less healthy will be covered by a disability insurance, which ensures a level of risk pooling that compensates for the coverage of bad risks with the coverage of good risks. It is for this reason that the government decided to allow only firms with 100 workers or more to self-insure. Another solution would be for small firms to jointly contract at the industry level (Teulings, 1997).

## Moral Hazard in Practice

To what extent moral hazard exists in the Netherlands is hard to say, for there is lack of evidence on this issue. To avoid moral hazard, the government decided to increase the financial incentives for both employers and employees. This was pursued first by the establishment of the Act on the re-integration of disabled people (REA), which came into force in July 1998. According to this act employers who hire a disabled person might be rewarded in the form of a tax deduction or a wage subsidy. For the employee, new opportunities were created by providing additional allowances that make it more attractive for them to accept a job. The government also pursued this goal by penalizing risky and unwanted behavior by employers through a monitoring system and the imposition of sanctions. The success or failure of this reward/penalty system is hard to assess. In general, however, there is little evidence of positive effects from this system on the behavior of employers. The implementation of the Act also has yet to produce any evidence the reward/penalty system has any impact on re-employment probabilities.

*Incentive Effects*

There is some evidence available on the impact of the existing penalty regimes on the behavior of social security beneficiaries. This evidence suggests that financial sanctions may be at least a partially efficient tool to achieve the desired behavioral changes. The findings of two recent research projects on social assistance (1998) and unemployment benefits (1996), provide some indications that financial penalties have a rather strong positive impact on the re-employment probability of the beneficiaries (Abbring et al., 1996; Berg et al., 1998). It appears, however, that the observed effect is strongly determined by the research methodology. Only if the selectivity of the sanction process is itself taken into account (corrected for differences in work motivation) could these effects be found. Otherwise, no effect, or even a reverse effect, was found. From earlier studies in which no account was taken of the selectivity process, it appeared that the penalty system had little effect on the outflow from the unemployment programs (In 't Groen and Koehler, 1996). With the Disability Act we doubt whether the effects will be as strong as with the unemployment programs because the labor market opportunities for disabled people are much worse, partly because of the handicap and partly because of their older age. If there are few opportunities in the labor market, the likelihood of return will be very low, and thus the sanctions will have little effect. A recent empirical study indeed shows that the labor market opportunities for disabled people are rather bad, and worse the longer they are disabled (Koehler and Spijkerboer, 1999). For this reason we might expect that the measures to raise the incentives for employees and employers might have a small but positive effect on the outflow from disability programs.

In Table 5.4 some evidence on the inflow and outflow of short- and long-term disability is presented for the period 1993 to 1998. Although employment grew during this period, the inflow as well as the outflow for long-term disability remained stable. Moreover, the average length of a disability spell became even longer, at least up to 1998. The incidence of sickness leave is likely to be less affected by the changes in incentive structure than by the changes in the legislation itself. The percentage of recovered sick people appears to vary markedly across the 1990s, probably because of the series of radical reforms of the Sickness Act. It emerges that there is a strong decline in the number of sick, not

*Marketization of Sickness and Disability Insurance in the Netherlands*   113

Table 5.4
Administration Costs and Flow Percentages for Sickness and Long-Term Disability Insurance for the Netherlands, 1993–1998

|  | 1993 | 1994 | 1995 | 1996 | 1997 | 1998 |
|---|---|---|---|---|---|---|
| **Sickness** | | | | | | |
| Administration costs (x 1,000,000 Dfl.) | 917 | 643 | 483 | 331 | 201 | 245 |
| Costs per benefit-year | 2,659 | 2,989 | 2,193 | 2,446 | 2,070 | 2,358 |
| Incidence | 6.2% | 4.9% | 4.9% | 4.6% | 4.6% | 4.7% |
| Recovery | 27.5% | 39.2% | 49.8% | 34.2% | 64.0% | 72.1% |
| **Disability** | | | | | | |
| Administration costs (x 1,000,000 Dfl.) | 1,334 | 1,344 | 1,402 | 1,355 | 1,497 | 1,476 |
| Costs per benefit-year | 1,657 | 1,706 | 1,864 | 1,832 | 2,018 | 1,895 |
| Incidence | 11.0% | 10.5% | 9.9% | 9.8% | 9.7% | 9.8% |
| Inflow in % of insured population | n.a | 1.2% | 1.1% | 1.3% | 1.4% | 1.4% |
| Outflow in % of disabled population | 9.2% | 10.5% | 11.0% | 9.4% | 8.6% | 8.7% |
| Average length of spell (no. years) | 2.4 | 2.2 | 3.6 | 3.7 | 3.3 | 2.5 |

*Sources*: Kras and Mangolnkarso, 1997; Berendsen et al., 1998; Landelÿk Instituut Sociale Verzekeringen, 1999.

because of the incentive structure but simply because when employers took over the full responsibility for the sickness insurance the number of insured under the sickness insurance declined. The changing composition of the sick population from 1997 on might also be responsible for the increase in the proportion of recovered sick people. This evidence provides us with some but not many clues about the likely impact of incentives built into the Dutch system, which would appear not to be very substantial with respect to short- and long-term disability.

*Administrative Costs*

Part of the expected efficiency gain of privatization is a reduction in the administration costs. In Table 5.4 some evidence on administration cost is given for the period 1993 to 1998, specifically total administration costs and the average costs per allowance paid (expressed in benefit-years). The evidence sug-

**Table 5.5**
**Incidence of Sickness Leave by Insurance Type, 1998**

| Insurance Type | Sickness Leave in Percent of Total Working Time |
|---|---|
| Executioner at own risk | 5.3% |
| Sickness partially reinsured (stop-loss) with insurance company | 4.4% |
| Sickness fully reinsured with insurance company | 3.6% |

*Source*: Berendsen et al., 1998.

gests that while the total administration cost for short-term disability (Sickness Act) was indeed reduced, the cost of long-term disability increased. The reduction in the cost of sickness insurance can be attributed to the administrative shift from the government to employers. The rise in administration costs for long-term disability can be explained by reference to the increased labor market participation and re-integration efforts, which were taken up by the so-called private Arbo-services (labor conditions services), operating on behalf of the private social security institutions. The picture becomes even more unfavorable if we look at the costs per allowance (benefit-year). We find that only in 1994 were the costs significantly reduced, which has to be attributed to the shift in responsibility for very short periods of sickness (the first two to six weeks) to the employer. These very short-term periods of sickness leave constituted a large fraction of the sick and therefore a substantial smaller number appeared from then on in the files of the industrial insurance boards ("Bedrijfsverenigingen"). From 1995 to 1998 the costs per benefit-year remained rather stable, which is remarkable given the large drop in sickness cases due, again, to a further shift in responsibility from the government to employers in 1996 (Kras and Mangoenkarso, 1997). The reasons for the administration costs not falling might well be that private firms have higher administration costs for marketing, advertisement and for investment as compared with the public sector. A further reason might be that their costs are higher because of their tendency to be selective which reduces the number of insured, thus reducing their capacity to achieve economies of scale. Since, however, privatization was only partial and there was a mandatory payment requirement, it is hard to believe that this is the main reason for the administration costs not falling. A more important reason is likely that the government did not specify the requirements for a more efficient treatment of the social security clientele.

If we consider the evidence in Table 5.5, we find that, contrary to what we might expect, the sickness leave incidence is higher for employers who self-insure and lower for firms who fully reinsured their sickness risk with an insurance company. We would have expected that for firms with lower than average disability risks it might be interesting not to reinsure with an insurance company, because they then pay the average risk premium, but to self-insure and to pay below average contributions.

We might therefore conclude that firms with a higher than average risk do not want to pay the higher contributions and thus self-insure to reduce the incidence of sickness leaves.

### *Labor Market Participation and Re-integration Measures*

From Table 5.4 it is evident that the success of the labor market participation and re-integration measures has yet to be proven, given the incidence and outflow figures on disability have remained stable. It might well be, of course, that if the government had maintained its previous policy, employers would be even more unfavorable, but this is hard to prove. We have little reason to assume that these new measures will change employer behavior, despite employers asserting that they now have more interest in adopting appropriate policies. This likely small positive effect must be balanced against the somewhat larger negative effect of increased discrimination against the disabled at the entrance gate.

## THE LESSONS TO BE LEARNED FROM THE DUTCH EXPERIENCES WITH MARKETIZATION

### A New Road to Social Security?

The government proposals for an institutional reform of the social insurance system during the period 1992 to 1998 has been characterized as a new road to privatization of the social security system. It became clear that the privatization decisions were taken without having any clear notion about the future design of the social security system. Maybe that is also the reason why it went wrong, why a new deadlock appeared and why in the fall of 1999 a completely new plan was formulated causing again a radical break with the previous proposals. Probably the most important lesson to be learned from the Dutch experience is that to start privatization and to reform social security administration drastically without a clear vision creates the necessary conditions for serious problems that might reverse the reform timeline by 10 or more years.

The 1990s did stimulate a rethinking of our social security system, which was much needed in terms of its efficiency and effectiveness at addressing issues such as globalization, flexibilization, individualization and the aging of the population. Quite a number of new Acts came into force in this period that changed the public–private social security nexus considerably, particularly for social insurance. To speak of complete marketization as the government did before the release of the November 1999 plan is concealing what really has happened. First, privatization was incomplete since long-term disability for spells of five years or longer remained within the public domain and since significant administrative practices remained in the public domain, particularly disability claim determination and the premium calculation for most of the firms (Geleijnse, 1995). Second, the government has kept a watchful eye on what happened in the social insurance sector so as to minimize benefit fraud or avoid inefficient private practices (Keuzenkamp, 1997). The government also feared negative publicity in the media which could have endangered the policy route adhered to before. For all these reasons, it is more justified to speak of regulated private provision, with maintenance of significant state control with respect to defining criteria for access of the implementation agency, to defining protocols, and to certifying contracts between the National Institute for the Social Insurance and the implementation agencies at the regional level.

The reform of the Dutch social security system was said by the government to be in a transitional stage which was due to be completed by the end of 2001 with the creation of the new Organization Act on the Social Insurance (OSV-2001), which was intended to replace the Organization Act of 1997. By the time the government finished arguing about its desired policy, the specially constituted private social security institutions had had sufficient time to change their role from direct provision in the public domain to regulators of private provision. At the same time, they had been able to adjust to the prospect of competing among themselves for social security contracts with the private firms. By 2002 the new legislation would have opened the door to complete marketization of social insurance. This could have happened were it not that in November 1999 the government launched a new plan, completely different from the previous one, implying an essential retreat from the path of privatization. The plan actually proposed to revert almost entirely to state regulation for the implementation of social insurance. Although retaining some of the privatization proposals with respect to the re-integration activities, the plan represents an essential retreat from the route to full marketization of social insurance to a system dominated by public intervention, because the implementation bodies were again placed under full public control.

This plan, still in debate, will probably be implemented, although it may still be amended to acknowledge the important role of the unions and the employers' organizations in the implementation of social insurance.

**The Evaluation of the Polder Route to Marketization**

In summary, it is rather difficult to come to a positive conclusion about the Dutch privatization route. There are two main reasons for this: the emergence of a hybrid structure and the lack of a fundamental political debate on the future of social security.

*The Emergence of a Hybrid Structure*

The hybrid structure of social insurance (the mixture of public and private activities in the same organization) that has emerged has had a detrimental impact on the goals of increasing efficiency, of downsizing disability incidence and of providing a more client-friendly administrative process. None of these goals have been attained by means of privatization. Moreover, privatization was enacted without much consideration being given to the risks of adverse selection, the increasing gaps in disability coverage and heightened administration costs. The government chose neither complete private provision nor complete public provision. The lesson that can be learned is that privatization policy design must avoid ambiguity and hybrid characteristics. The government should clearly decide which road it wants to follow: private provision with public regulation or public provision with some contracting-out of significant administrative responsibilities.

The result achieved in the Netherlands is an ambivalent endeavor to give greater room to privatization, without setting the necessary conditions for competitive provision by the private social security institutions. In fear of the government losing public control, this outcome is the product of a compromise within the first "purple government," between Social Democrats and Liberals. The main problem was that the political actors had no clear vision about the future of social security and had not anticipated the implementation obstacles. Thus the privatization proposals came into force without the government having any clear perception how employers and employees would react and without having a clear idea about where the reform proposals would end up. Thus the recent parliamentary debate (June 1999) resulted in a new deadlock since the government, under pressure of the Second Chamber, had to defer the privatization proposals and had to bring the benefit claim determination activities of the private social security institutions under public control. However, not all proposals were deferred. The Second Chamber accepted the proposals for the integration of labor market and social security institutions, which will be implemented in the years to come. That the November 1999 proposals, although much clearer and more transparent, were completely the opposite of the earlier plans indicates that the debate is governed by opportune political considerations and disputes.

## *The Need for a Fundamental Debate about the Future of Social Security*

The government refused to initiate a fundamental and public debate about the future of the social security system. It wanted to leave the level of benefits out of the political debate because of its controversial nature. For that reason the focus shifted to the creation of a more efficient and less bureaucratic system based on modern management practices. However, the route to privatization set in motion in 1993 by the parliamentary inquiry (the Buurmeier Committee) and followed up by a series of privatization measures, marked the road to a new social security system, one that reflects increasingly neoliberal values. The November 1999 proposal might be seen as a step aside on the road to privatization, returning again to public control of the implementation bodies of social insurance but with maintenance of significant private parts.

## CONCLUSION

It is certainly true, as many commentators have argued, that a modern social security system in the twenty-first century should be very different from the one that was built on the working conditions and lifestyles of the twentieth century (Lazar and Stoyko, 1998). The new system should not only be more efficient and less bureaucratic, it should also be better equipped to deal with the changes in work (working times, work contracts, work location) and changes in household composition, earners' capacity, and lifestyles. A sustainable system needs to be much more flexible to cope with the fundamental trends and challenges of the next century related to globalization, flexibilization, population ageing and individualization (WRR, 1997).

The Dutch social security system has evolved into a three-pillar system: flat-rate social assistance benefits operating as a safety net for the un(der)insured; earnings-related occupational programs for employees and private provision for those who can afford it. In the Dutch pension system this distribution of responsibilities between the state and its citizens has nearly been realized, but less so in the social insurance and healthcare systems. But such a clear-cut division of responsibilities between the public and the private domains—leaving the state just to provide a safety net for the poor—might be the best option for the pension system but not necessarily for the social security system as a whole. It resolves neither the adverse selection problem nor the moral hazard issue, since low income earners will opt to overinsure because it makes no sense for them to bear a high social security risk when the burden of the income loss is almost entirely covered by the government (Teulings, 1997). It is clear that a privatized system cannot work efficiently and equitably without public intervention. The debate on the most appropriate public-private mix in the Netherlands, therefore, has not ended with the new proposal for a larger role of public agencies operating at the regional level. New impulses are therefore required which may come from a new state committee, in the same vein as the "Van Rijn" Committee in 1948 that after the Second World War was assigned by the government with the task to design a new social security system. This committee should be tasked with designing the contours of a modern, flexible and sustainable social security system and initiating a debate about the future of the welfare state and its administrative arrangements in the new millennium.

## REFERENCES

Aarts, L., Jong, P. de, Teulings, C. and Veen, R. van der. 1998. Vijf jaar na Buurmeier [Five years after Buurmeier]. *Economisch Statistische Berichten* 83 (4157): 472–80.

Aarts, L.J.M., Burkhause, R. V. and Jong, P. R. de. 1996. *Curing the Dutch Disease: An International Perspective on Disability Policy Reform.* Aldershot: Avebury.

Aarts, L.J.M. and Jong, P. R. de. 1996. *Private voorziening van sociale zekerheid in de praktijk. Een empirische studie naar de verdeling van private en publieke verantwoordelijkheden in de verzekering van het risico van beroepsgebonden arbeidsongeschiktheid in de Verenigde Staten* [Private social security provisions in practice. An empirical study into the distribution of responsibilities within the occupational disability insurance in the United States]. The Hague: VUGA Publishers.

Aarts, L.J.M. and Jong, P. R. de. 1999. *Private sociale zekerheid* [Private social security]. The Hague: Aarts & de Jong.

Abbring, J. H., Berg, G. J. van den, Mullenders, P. and Ours, J. van. 1996. Sancties in de WW: een werkend perspectief [Penalties in the unemployment act: a working perspective]. *Economisch Statistische Berichten* 81 (4072): 750–57.

Algemene Rekenkamer. 1997. *Ontvlechting en marktwerking in de sociale zekerheid* [The disentanglement and entanglement in the social security]. The Hague: Sdu Publishers.

Algemene Rekenkamer. 1998. *Toezicht op uitvoering publieke taken* [Supervision on the execution of public tasks]. The Hague: Sdu Publishers.

Bekkering. J. M. 1994. *Private verzekering van sociale risico's* [Private insurance of social risks]. WRR. Voorstudies en achtergronden V84. The Hague: Sdu Publishers.

Berendsen, L., Burger, J., Koehler, J. and Spijkerboer, P. 1998. *Augustusrapportage arbeidsongeschiktheidsverzekeringen 1998* [August report on the disability insurance 1998]. Zoetermee: College Toezicht Sociale Verzekeringen.

Berg, G. J. van den, Klaauw, B. van der and Ours, J. van. 1998. Sancties in de bijstand vergroten kans op werk [Penalties in the social assistance programs result in better work opportunities]. *Economisch Statistische Berichten* 83 (4161): 556–65.

Berkouwer, J. and Hoogerwerf, A. 1996. *Markt. ongelijkheid. solidariteit: op zoek naar een herkenbare PvdA* [Market, inequality and solidarity: On search for a identifiable labor party]. Tilburg: Syntax Publishers.

Bomhoff, E. J., Koopmans, I. and Lageweg, I. M. 1997. De herziening van de sociale zekerheid [The reform of the social security]. *Economisch Statistische Berichten* 82, 4133: 981–88.

Doeschot, R. 1998. *Evaluating Social Security Reforms: Seven Questions* (mimeo). The Hague: College Toezicht Sociale Verzekeringen.

Donders, J. 1999. The Dutch Economy, *CPB-report*, 99 (1): 9–13.

Donner, J.P.H. 1998. *Staat in Beweging* [State in movement]. WRR. Voorstudies en achtergronden. V100. The Hague: Sdu Publishers.

Engbersen, G., Schuyt, K., Timmer, J. and Waarden, F. van. 1993. *Cultures of Unemployment.* Boulder, CO: Westview Press.

European Communities. 1999. *Social Protection Expenditure and Receipts: European Union, Iceland and Norway. Data 1980–1996.* Luxembourg: Office for Official Publications of the European Communities.

Garner, C. A. 1997. Social Security Privatization: Balancing Efficiency and Fairness. *Review. FED of Kansas City* 82 (3): 21–36.

Geleijnse, L. 1995. *Publieke en private sociale zekerheid. Theorie en illustratie ervan aan de hand van recent sociale-zekerheidsbeleid* [Public and private social security. Theory and illustration of it with reference to recent public policy measures]. The Hague: Tilburg University/TISSER VUGA Publishers.

Goodin, B., Headey, B., Muffe, R. and Dirven, H. J. 1999. *The Real Worlds of Welfare Capitalism*. Cambridge: Cambridge University Press.

Haak, H. A. van den and Koemans, J. A. 1996. *De ontvlechting en vervlechting. Rapportage over de reorganisatie in de uitvoering van de sociale verzekeringen ten gevolge van de invoering van de nieuwe organisatiewet* [The disentanglement and entanglement. Report on the reorganization of the execution of the social insurances due to the enactment of the new Organization Act 1997]. Zoetermeer: CTSV.

Hessel, B., Schippers, J. and Siegers, J. 1998. *Market Efficiciency versus Equity. Balancing the Welfare State*. Amsterdam: AWSB/Thesis Publishers.

Hoogerwerf, A. 1995. *Politiek als evenwichtskunst: dilemma's rond overheid en markt* [Politics as the art of balance: Dilemmas around government and market]. Alphen aan de Rijn: Samson H. D. Tjeenk willink.

In 't Groen, A.J.B.A. and Koehler, J.B.I. 1996. *De regels van het spel. De toepassing van sancties in de WW door bedrijfsverenigingen* [The rules of the game. The application of penalties in the WW by the industrial insurance boards]. The Hague: VUGA Publishers.

Keuzenkamp. H. A. 1997. Marktwerking in de sociale zekerheid [Marketization in the social security system]. *Economisch Statistische Berichten* 82: 4133.

Koehler, J.B.I. and Spijkerboer, P. M. 1999. *Augustusrapportage arbeidsongeschiktheidsverzekeringen 1999* [August report on the disability insurance 1999]. Zoetermeer College Toezicht Sociale Verzekeringen.

Kotlikoff, L., Kent, J., Smetters, A. and Walliser, J. 1998. Social Security: Privatization and Progressivity. *The American Economic Review* 88 (2): 137–41.

Kotlikoff, L. J. and Sachs, J. A. 1998. The Personal Security System: A Framework for Reforming Social Security. *Federal Reserve Bank of Cleveland Review* 80 (2): 11–13.

Kras, J. and Mangoenkarso, P. P. 1997. *Voortgangsrapportage uitvoeringskosten 1990–1997* [Progress report administration costs 1990–1997]. Zoetermeer: College Toezicht Sociale.

Landelijk Instituut Sociale Verzekeringen. 1999. *Kroniek van de sociale verzekeringen 1999* [Chronicle of the Social Insurances 1999]. Amsterdam: Landelijk Instituut Sociale Verzekeringen.

Lazar, H. and Stoyko, P. 1998. The Future of the Welfare State. *International Social Security Review* 51 (3): 3–36.

Netherlands, Second Chamber. 1993. *Parlementaire enquête uitvoeringsorganen sociale verzekeringen. Rapport van de Commissie* [Parliamentary inquiry social insurance institutions. Report from the committee 1992–1993]. 22730: 7–8.

Netherlands, Second Chamber. 1998. *Sociale Nota 1999* [Social Report 1999]. The Hague: Sdu Publishers.

Netherlands, Second Chamber. 1999. *Toekomstige structuur van de uitvoering werk en inkomen [SUWI]* [Future structure of the execution of work and income]. 26448: 1. The Hague: Sdu Publishers.

Netherlands, Social and Cultural Planning Office. 1998. *Sociaal en cultureel rapport 1998* [Social and Cultural Report 1998]. Rijswijk: Social and Cultural Planning Office.

Netherlands, Statistics Netherlands. 1999. *Het Jaar 1998 in Cijfers* [The year 1998 in figures]. Voorburg/Heerlen: Statistics Netherlands.

Sociaal-Economische Raad (SER). 1999. *Ontwerpadvies structuur uitvoering werk en inkomen* [Draft advice on the structure of work and income]. The Hague: Sociaal-Economische Raad.

Steuerle, C. E. and Bakija, J. M. 1997. Retooling Social Security for the 21st Century. *Social Security Bulletin* 60 (2): 37–60.

Teulings, C., Veen, R. van der and Trommel, W. 1997. *Dilemma's van sociale zekerheid: een analyse van 10 jaar herziening van het stelsel van sociale zekerheid* [Dilemmas of social security: an analysis of 10 years of reform of the social security system]. The Hague: VUGA Publishers.

Teulings, C. N. 1997. Keuzevrijheid versus solidariteit [Free choice versus solidarity]. *Economisch Statistische Berichten* 4133: 961–70.

Veen, R. van der. 1999. Het trilemma van sociaal beleid [The twofold dilemma of social policy]. *Economisch Statistische Berichten, Dossier* 4201: D26–29.

WRR. 1997. *Van verdelen naar verdienen; afwegingen voor de sociale zekerheid in de 21e eeuw* [From distributing to earning. Considerations for the social security in the 21st century]. The Hague: Sdu Publishers.

*Chapter 6*

# The Forms of Privatization of Social Security in Britain

## Carol Walker

Very considerable steps have been taken to increase the role of the private sector in both the provision and administration of social security in Britain in the last 20 years. This move toward privatization has been driven, first and foremost, by a growing concern about the cost of the social security system. As Walker (1984: 36) bluntly argued, "privatization is a euphemism for cuts in the total amount of public expenditure devoted to the social services." But privatization of social security in Britain has also been driven by an ideological commitment toward reducing state intervention to support people in times of adversity by, instead, making individuals more responsible for the financial security of themselves and their families and by a presumption that the private sector is, de facto, more efficient than the public sector in delivering services. The main architects of privatization were the successive Conservative governments between 1979 and 1997 under the Prime Ministerial leadership of Margaret Thatcher and then John Major. However, the social security policy of the new Blair Labour government elected in 1997 reflects many of the same values that underpinned its predecessors' strategy.

This chapter will describe briefly the reasons for the growth in social security in the last two decades and consider the different ways in which privatization has been applied to shift both the burden of responsibility and the financial costs away from the state toward the individual and the private sector.

## PRIVATIZING SOCIAL SECURITY

Privatization within the British social security system can be separated into four main types. First, the encouragement by government for individuals to use the private sector as a means of securing future financial security and the encouragement of the private sector to provide benefits for a wider range of people. This development has occurred particularly, but not exclusively, in the field of pensions. Second, the devolvement of benefits administration from the Department of Social Security to employers, local authorities, autonomous agencies and to claimants themselves. Third, and despite the seemingly inexorable growth in the social security budget, the very significant cuts made both in the level of social security benefits and in their scope and coverage: benefits are less generous than in the past and they reach fewer people. Fourth, by both reducing the efficacy of the benefits system and by putting greater onus on claimants and potential claimants for obtaining their due entitlement, the family and individuals are expected to be more self-sufficient, whether or not they are able or willing to do so. Privatization in British social security thus goes beyond merely transferring responsibility for benefits provision or administration to the private sector to incorporating the values of the private sector into public sector provision (Walker, 1984).

## THE BEVERIDGE LEGACY

The British social security system is founded on the legacy of the Beveridge Report (1942) on Social Insurance and Allied Services. Published during the Second World War, it formed the basis of income maintenance policy throughout the post-war period. Even as successive governments have begun to backtrack from Beveridge's underlying principles, they have sought justification for their own developments and reforms in his report. The significance and uniqueness of the Beveridge Report was two-fold: first, it was the result of a thorough rethinking of the aims and goals of state income maintenance policy; and, second, it set out to provide a comprehensive plan to both prevent and alleviate poverty. Subsequent reviews of the social security system in Britain have set much more limited goals of an administrative or financial nature (Walker, 1993; U.K., DSS, 1998), within the context of a system with the more modest goal, at best, of poverty alleviation.

The bulwark of Beveridge's proposals was the social insurance system: in return for contributions made while they were in work, contributors would receive benefits when they could not support themselves during sickness, unemployment or retirement. Two other strands underpinned his proposals for social insurance: means-tested social assistance for the few (and, he thought, diminishing number of) people who were not able to contribute; and voluntary insurance, which would be used to top up subsistence level benefits. Beveridge's goal was an adequate benefits system but not one that stifled personal initiative.

In Social Insurance and Allied Services, Beveridge stressed that the state National Insurance (NI) system should provide benefits that were adequate both in amount and in duration. Neither of these goals was implemented in the initial or subsequent legislation. From the outset in 1948, the flat-rate NI benefit rates fell short of providing an unambiguous national minimum (Atkinson, 1991).

Subsequent governments throughout the post-war period, favored the cheaper alternative of increasing social assistance rather than NI benefits, with the result that a gap developed and expanded between the two types of benefits. As a result, for the majority of people, NI benefit rates have been lower than means-tested benefits. Furthermore, short-term NI benefits, such as for sickness and unemployment, have always been limited in duration. As a consequence the majority of unemployed are not eligible for NI benefit (formerly unemployment benefit, now replaced by contributory job seeker's allowance) and either claim means-tested job seeker's allowance or have no benefit entitlement. Since 1979 expenditure on means-tested benefits has increased much faster than for other benefits, from 17 percent of all benefits in 1978–1979 to over 30 percent in 1998–1999 (Piachaud, 1997).

From the 1960s onwards, a number of government and independent reports were published that concluded that, despite its national income maintenance policies, poverty persisted in Britain. Benefits were not high enough to lift people out of poverty, and many poor people, in work and out of work, fell outside the scope of the social security system. Paradoxically, the political debate around social security shifted, between the 1970s and the 1980s, from a concern for poverty and the efficacy of the social security system in alleviating it, to a discussion of its costs and the viability of maintaining its high levels of expenditure. Other emerging and growing concerns included the complexity of the benefits system, especially with the implications this had for staffing, and the level of fraud and abuse within the system. The 1980s became the decade of the "dependency culture." Proponents of this thesis, which included the then Prime Minister, Margaret Thatcher, and her senior Cabinet colleagues, maintained that people were encouraged to remain dependent on the state by the very policies which had been put in place to assist them (Moore, 1987). The views underlying this philosophy can be seen in the treatment of various groups of claimants during this period. No group was spared close government scrutiny.

First, and most obvious, was the treatment of the unemployed. Although the 1980s saw a peak in the (manipulated) official unemployment statistics, the government increasingly introduced punitive measures against the victims of the economic downturn and major industrial restructuring which was occurring in traditional heavy industries like coal and steel. The political debate began to center, not on the lack of jobs or on poverty among unemployed people and their families, but on whether unemployment people were "genuinely" unemployed and making sufficiently strenuous efforts to find work. A series of measures to cut and restrict benefits to the unemployed were introduced. Eventually, in the 1990s, NI unemployment benefit was abolished and replaced by Job Seekers Allowance. This reduced NI benefit entitlement to six months and made payment of even the contributory part of this benefit conditional on meeting tougher rules regarding job search.

The next group to receive attention was older people. During the 1960s, poverty had been seen primarily as a "pensioners' problem" (Abel-Smith and Townsend, 1965; Hall et al., 1975) and policies were pursued aimed at improving their take-up of benefits. However, the 1980s saw the emergence of a new group, the so-called "WOOPIES" (well-off older people). Originally identified by the marketing industry as a new target group for advertising, the concept was seized upon by the government as a justification for re-examining provision for people over retirement age. Ministers began to talk increasingly of the growing numbers of affluent retirement pensioners and of the rising proportion of people retiring with an occupational pension. Both these trends were highlighted in the debate, discussed below, on the future financing of pensions outside the state sector.

Another group singled out for special consideration was young people. In the face of rising numbers of unemployed young people leaving home in the 1980s, the government sought to prevent those on social assistance from living in commercial board and lodging accommodation. After several false starts, it was eventually successful and this type of accommodation was closed to young people on benefit. Withdrawal of income support as a right of 16 and 17 year-olds in 1988, and less generous housing benefit rules for these young people, made it virtually impossible for them to live independently. The result was increased poverty and homelessness among young people (Kirk et al., 1991).

During the 1980s, the number of lone-parent families claiming means-tested benefit rose, making them a target group for critical appraisal. While this was largely a result of increased unemployment levels, the Conservative government concentrated its concern on the level of support absent parents (normally fathers) were providing for their children. In 1990, legislation was introduced to increase the amount of support obtained from fathers after separation and to increase official powers to collect this money through the Child Support Agency. The impact of this legislation on both first and second families is discussed below. Before losing office, the Conservatives framed legislation to abolish those benefits that were targeted specifically at lone parents. This was one of the first social security measures to be implemented by their new Labour Party successors.

Finally, in the 1990s, it was the turn of people with long-term illness and disability (Hyde, 2000). The main NI benefit for this group—invalidity benefit—was replaced by incapacity benefit, which had much tighter rules regarding eligibility and assessment. In 1999 the new Labour government continued to reduce benefit entitlement for this group in its own reforms to incapacity benefit which, while providing more help to some severely disabled people, reduced entitlement of many who had paid into the NI system.

All these initiatives have had the same end result. Whether they present unemployed people as being unwilling rather than unable to work, pensioners as not really being poor, parents as not taking responsibility for their young people, or fathers as not taking responsibility for their children, the promulgation of such arguments is designed to reduce pressure on government for improved state support for the poor. By making subtle, and sometimes less than subtle, attacks on people living on social security benefits, successive governments and politicians have deliberately sought to undermine the credibility of these people. Do they really deserve the cutting of benefits to promote an ideology that makes individuals more responsible for their own welfare, either by making family members take responsibility for each other or by compelling individuals to provide for their own future financial security by buying from the private sector?

## SOCIAL SECURITY PROVISION AND THE PRIVATE SECTOR

The Conservative government explored several ways in which private insurance might have a greater role to play in the provision of traditional state benefits. The opportunities for some individuals to take out private insurance were developed in relation to pensions, sickness benefits and, to a more limited extent, to cover other contingencies such as unemployment. Not only has it been argued that further privatization could increase private provision, perhaps to the point that it could replace state provision of certain benefits, but also that the scope is limited for the private sector to provide cover for the non-insurance elements of the British social security system.

Research already indicates that those living on low incomes or in insecure employment are unlikely to be adequately covered by any private insurance system (NACAB, 1995; Howard and Thompson, 1995). A private insurance model for social security is therefore unlikely to meet the goal of protecting against the risk of poverty for all and would favor some individuals over others, for example, those distinguished on the basis of their working patterns. The most vulnerable, and at greatest risk, would be the group most likely to lose out. (Harker, 1997: 256)

Notwithstanding the potential inefficiencies and the inevitable inequalities inherent in promoting private insurance to meet income maintenance needs, the Conservative government took several significant steps along this road, a road that has since also been trodden by the Blair Labour government. The greatest impact has been on long-term pensions; other examples include changes made to sickness benefits and to the financial assistance available to those with mortgages. Proposals concerning the financing of long-term care of older people are still under consideration. The Conservative government had begun to explore the possibilities of introducing private unemployment insurance before they lost office in 1997 (Barr, 1994).

### The Privatization of Public Retirement Pensions

By far the most significant involvement of the private sector, both in terms of population coverage and finances, is with respect to long-term pension provision. Public pensions not only represent the largest element in the British social security budget, but they also generate the greatest number of recipients.

With demographic aging, more people are living longer, and thus drawing pensions longer after retirement. The trend of population aging, sadly, has been greeted not as a cause for celebration by policy makers, but as a major cause for concern, both now and, particularly, for the future.

State age pensioners were attacked, over the course of the 1980s, as part of the general onslaught on public spending. The specter of the economic burden of old age was used more and more openly to justify restraint, first, in social security expenditures and, subsequently, in health and social services spending (Walker, 1993: 26).

The cuts in state old-age provision were deemed essential because of the rising cost of pensions and justified because more people were retiring with occupational or personal pensions, the promotion of which had been financially supported by the state through tax concessions. The Conservative government attacked state pensions provision in the 1980s. First, the value of the state retirement pension began to fall after 1980 following the introduction of less favorable uprating rules. Second, the government saw the State Earnings Related Pensions System (SERPS), which had been introduced in 1976 with an all-party agreement in Parliament, as the mechanism that would end pensioner poverty. The program was due to come fully on stream in 2003, although partial benefits began to come through sooner.

The intention was severely to curtail and possibly to abolish the (SERP) system and to encourage the growth of private and occupational pensions in its place. This part of the campaign began quietly and took the covert form of several official statements highlighting the future cost of pensions. Then, in 1983, ... an inquiry was announced into provision for retirement.... This inquiry provided a focus for public discussion of the pension issue, and as far as the government was concerned, this meant the rising cost "burden" of pensions ... the government portrayed state pensions as a "burden" and a threat to Britain's future economic performance. In contrast, the income needs of pensioners were discussed only summarily. (Walker, 1993: 26)

When a government report on pensions reform was published in 1985 (U.K., DHSS, 1985a: 18), government concern went beyond the level of current expenditure to the implications of the future costs of pensions:

Our belief in One Nation means recognizing our responsibilities to all the generations represented within it.... It would be an abdication of responsibility to hand down obligations to our children which we believe they cannot fulfil.

The government's initial proposal was to phase out SERPS and thus

achieve a steady transition from the present dependence on state provision to a position in which we as individuals are contributing directly to our own additional pensions and in which we can exercise greater choice in the sort of pension provision we make. (U.K., DHSS, 1985b: 6)

Despite widespread opposition to these proposals from interests as diverse as the Confederation of British Industry (CBI) and the pensions industry to trades unions and pensioners' groups, the pensions issue did not adversely affect the Conservative Party's success in the intervening 1987 election. This enabled them to be even bolder on the pension reform issue in their third term. The main emphasis, at that stage, was to encourage and facilitate a growing role for the private sector by giving generous additional tax incentives for the purchase of personal or occupational pension plans that allowed employees to contract out of SERPS before 1993. The Department of Health and Social Security (now the Department of Social Security) estimated that half a million people would take out a personal pension (Deacon, 1991). However, the generosity of the taxation incentives, together with the poor long-term pessimistic prognosis for the value of the state pension and a massive advertising campaign by the private pensions industry led 4 million people to opt out of SERPS by April 1990. While tax relief was not given to those who stayed in SERPS, NI contribution rebates were given to those contracting out of SERPS. A 2 percent rebate on NI contributions was given to those taking out personal pension plans or an employers' money purchase (or defined-contribution) pension, with an extra contribution of 2 percent of earnings paid into occupational pension plans for the first year (six years for personal pension plans). By 1997 the Exchequer had lost £16 billion in tax relief given with respect to personal pensions. Six million contributors to SERPS or to occupational pension plans transferred into personal pension plans, with only 17 percent of the workforce remaining in SERPS. The misrepresentation of the benefits that would flow from personal pension plans in Britain in the 1980s, mainly, but not exclusively, to public sector employees, is now one of the great scandals of the British financial markets. It is estimated that as many as 3.5 million people would have been better off staying in SERPS (Walker, 1997). Several of the major private pension providers were implicated in this pension mis-selling scandal and the majority of people affected have yet to get their money back.

The cuts in the state NI retirement pension and in benefits under SERPS means that both current and future pensioners will lose out. Those current pensioners who do not have a second pension funded through their employer or through a private pension plan have seen the value of their retirement income fall. The only compensation has been some slight increase in means-tested income support for the poorest pensioners, an improved fuel subsidy and, from April 2000, free television licenses for the over 75s. The prosperity of future pensioners will depend on the extent to which they are willing and able to invest in their own pensions. Those who do not have a full employment record or who are in low paid work, insecure work or casual work are unlikely to be able to provide adequately for their future. And yet this significant pensions policy shift toward privatization has not provided the promised budgetary savings, for it has merely converted public pensions expenditure into tax revenue foregone through the provision of increasingly generous tax concessions. Since the late 1980s the cost of tax concessions to non-state pensioners began to outstrip social assistance provision for pensioners (Sinfield, 1993). The policy of privatizing pensions has meant that there has been a switch of resources away from poor pensioners to the rich and from today's pensioners to tomorrow's:

> The distributional outcome is a net transfer of resources away from current generations of pensioners (with the biggest impact on the 900,000-plus not claiming income support), a significant proportion of which has gone to subsidize the private pensions of future generations and the high administrative costs of such schemes (up to 25p for every £1 invested compared with 1.1p for every £1 paid out from NI. (Walker, 1997: 8)

The new Labour government published its own, delayed, proposals for pension reform in 1998. Its policy Green Paper, *Partnership in Pensions*, pays little attention to the needs of today's pensioners (Hyde, Dixon and Joyner, 1999). Proposals are confined to the introduction of the minimum income guarantee (MIG)—means-tested income support for those over retirement age, extra help with fuel bills and measures to increase the take-up of the MIG by pensioners because older people are the most resistant of all eligible beneficiaries to taking up means-tested benefits. The Green Paper departs from the election manifesto, which referred to increasing the basic pension "at least in line with prices," and instead affirms that "we will raise it in line with prices." In other words the basic pension will continue to decline relative to both average earnings, because real average earnings are increasing, and the value of the pensioner's price index, because inflation differentially impacts on pensioners.

The Green Paper recommends the final abolition of SERPS (even the Conservatives backtracked from this and merely drastically reduced its value and scope). A State Second Pension—the so-called citizenship pensions—will replace SERPS, but as a flat-rate pension for low-paid workers not covered by occupational schemes and for whom "private second pensions are not an option." Although superficially this second pension would yield substantial benefits for low-paid workers, these gains will be undermined by the continued erosion of the basic NI retirement pension that will continue to fall in value relative to average earnings. An example of the two pensions combined provided in the Green Paper, shows that a person retiring in 2050 on average earnings would expect a replacement rate of around 25 percent—one of the lowest rates in the European Union.

For those earning more than half the national average, the only state provision will be the NI retirement pension. Therefore, their retirement income will be almost entirely derived from whatever savings they have been able to make through occupational, personal or the proposed voluntary stakeholder plans—privately administered, defined-contribution plans that are subject to tight state regulation—none of which are as secure as SERPS: a certainty has definitely been replaced by a lottery (Atkinson, 1998). The Green Paper says that the government rejects the extreme alternative of increased privatization (in favor of the stakeholder pension). But the inadequacy of the new system will mean that pension coverage will increasingly be privatized, either because people will be forced to provide for themselves, where they can, because of the paucity of state provision, or because those individuals who were probably most vulnerable to poverty during their working lives will have to bear the cost of inadequate state pensions. The government's pensions proposals do not offer a "partnership in pensions" but a residual role for state provision, focusing on the poorest, with the private sector taking responsibility for the rest. By contrast the original SERP system provided a genuine partnership between the state and occupational pension schemes in which the state promoted good quality schemes and protected the position of those employees that contracted out.

The increased emphasis on the private sector for pensions has several implications for both poor people and the poorer pensioners. Those who had limited or no access to the labor market during their working lives, the majority of whom are women, will not be able to benefit from the private pensions sector. Those who are on low wages, which remains a major cause of poverty in Britain, will have similar difficulty in providing for their own old age. The social division between public and private pensioners has been a long-term feature of the British social security system, but the residualization of public pensions and the subsidization of the private pensions sector will widen this division still further in the future. Reliance on personal pensions means that future pensioners' incomes will depend, not just on government policy or on prices and earnings, but also on the vagaries of the financial markets. The complexities of the private pensions sector make it difficult, even for well-educated people, to make informed choices: "If users of a service lack relevant technical or other information ... then this will permit monopoly exploitation by private providers" (Le Grand and Robinson, 1984: 8). The truth of this was revealed in the massive pensions mis-selling scandal of the 1980s.

The increasing privatization of pensions mainly benefits affluent workers who will become affluent pensioners. It benefits those who are in secure and, in particular, well-paid, employment, and who can thus afford to contribute to occupational and private pension plans. "Private pensions provide high benefits for high life-time earners but do very little for the life-time poor, and they are necessarily less redistributive than public pensions" (Johnson and Falkingham, 1994: 9). In the short term, the poverty of many current retirees can only be relieved by redistributing to them a greater share of public revenue, and this requires either higher NI contributions or more means-testing. "Privatization cannot work magic; it cannot deliver higher pensions out of a fixed or shrinking contributions pot" (Johnson and Falkingham, 1994: 9).

## The Privatization of Public Sickness Benefits

In the 1985 Green Paper on the Reform of Social Security (U.K., DHSS, 1985a), which was based on the review of social security initiated by the then

Conservative Secretary of State for Social Security, provision was made to draw together employer-based sickness benefit schemes with state provision: "the overlap between state and private occupation provision has been rationalized by the new statutory sick pay system" (p. 86). It was argued that as the majority of people were already covered by their employer's voluntary sick pay schemes, changes in state provision would affect relatively few people. In fact only about half of all private firms offered even short-term sickness benefits at the time. Those most likely to have no coverage were those in part-time, unskilled, low-paid and insecure employment. NI sickness benefit was abolished for the first eight weeks of sickness (this was later extended to 28 weeks) and replaced by statutory sick pay (SSP) paid by the employer. Three rates (later reduced to two) were payable which related to the level of earnings not to NI contributions (though beneficiaries had to be earning over the lower NI contributions floor limit). No dependants' allowances were payable.

There were several advantages of this change for the government: £400 million in benefit savings; a reduction in the size of the civil service, as employers were responsible for the payment of benefits; and, for the first time, over 90 percent of sickness payments were taxed. By bringing together employer and state benefits, the government also achieved its goal of reducing the overlap between the two sectors on the principle that "The state should, wherever possible, disengage itself from activities which firms and individuals can perform perfectly well for themselves" (Andrews and Jacobs, 1990: 104). In order to placate objections by employers, the government agreed to reimburse employers for the costs of the benefits paid out (though this was subsequently changed) and to reduce employers' NI contributions to compensate for the extra costs of administration. Organizations representing people with disabilities, such as the Disability Alliance, reported that these changes had created a pattern of "private insecurity," with some employees being forced onto means-tested benefits, with some firms refusing to operate the system or to pay some workers, and with other workers being sacked or being encouraged to declare themselves self-employed" (Baloo et al., 1986). In the first year of the system, employees lost £155 million, the DHSS saved £90 million and employers gained £95 million (Howard, 1997). That the government regarded this as a success was confirmed by its decision to put NI-based maternity benefits on the same footing in 1987.

A relatively minor, but highly significant, change toward the abolition of mortgage repayment relief subsidies for new income support claimants was made in 1995, even though early evidence on private mortgage protection policies had revealed their very serious shortcomings. Many people who thought they had mortgage insurance coverage found that they did not meet the conditions of the small print when they eventually found themselves out of work and tried to draw on their policies (Burchardt and Hills, 1997). Nevertheless, income-support claimants who have mortgages can get no mortgage repayment relief subsidies for a considerable time after qualifying for income support.

### The Privatization of Long-Term Care

Long-term care is another area where private insurance has been considered as a likely way forward by both major political parties. Although in its discussions the House of Commons Social Security Select Committee rejected private insurance as the best mechanism for meeting the costs of long-term care of older people, the Blair Labour government has not acted on the findings of the Royal Commission on Long Term Care it set up soon after gaining office—because the issue was so urgent—in part, it is feared, because they are not happy at the Commission's rejection of the private insurance option.

## PRIVATIZATION AND THE ADMINISTRATION OF SOCIAL SECURITY

An important element in government policy on social security has been to remove responsibility for the administration of key benefits away from government. This privatization of administration is now an established element in social security policy. This has been done in a series of steps that have gradually disassociated government from the everyday administration of some benefits.

### The Privatization of Housing Benefit Administration

The first step occurred with the introduction of housing benefit in 1982–1983. The responsibility for paying all rent and rate rebates was passed from the relevant government department (first the Department of Health and Social Security now the Department of Social Security) to local authorities. Local authorities saw this change as a way of reducing their arrears (because housing benefits to local authority tenants were paid directly to the local authority treasury not to the tenant). The introduction of housing benefit has been described as the "largest administrative shambles of the post-war welfare state" (Weir, 1984: 21). Government introduced regulations too late in the planning process for local authorities to get their computer systems up and running. Gradually legislation removed from local authorities any flexibility they had to vary housing benefit payments to reflect local conditions and needs. They also lost the subsidy originally paid to cover the costs of housing benefit administration. Housing benefit, one of the three major means-tested social security benefits in Britain, has thus been removed, administratively, from the purview of the responsible Secretary of State to local authorities who are left with the responsibility for its administration while losing all power or authority on the level or scope of the benefits paid to recipients.

## The Privatization of Sickness and Family Benefit Administration

The Conservative government moved toward greater privatization in the administration of the benefits system by co-opting employers, who were usually reluctant, into social security administration. First it was in the administration of statutory sick pay. In 1983 employers took over responsibility for this system with severe adverse consequences to themselves—because of the complexity of the rules—and, most significantly, for those off work because of ill health (Baloo et al., 1986). Second, the Conservative government sought to transfer the administration of family credit (a top-up benefit paid to working families with children) to employers. While the most vocal opposition came from key pressure groups working on behalf of poor families, the most influential opposition came from the Small Employers' Federation which argued that its members simply could not cope with the additional administrative burden.

The transfer of administration from central government to employers, and to the local authorities, enabled the relevant government department, now called the Department of Social Security, to cut its staffing and thus its administrative costs. Of course, much of the savings to the public purse is illusory. Employers were reimbursed for their costs and housing benefits administration, whether paid for by local or national government, is still a public charge. Hills (1987: 92) has argued that such changes amount to no more than "creative accounting":

A large chunk of what had been sickness benefit was handed over to employers, who deducted the cost from what they would otherwise have had to pay in tax. This magically reduced the level of public spending, even though it made little difference to the overall balance of the government's finances.

Shifting responsibility for administration away from central government departments places an intermediary between the claimant and the state. An employee may be reluctant to pursue problems over SSP with the employer. In addition, blame for problems with this provision may fall on the employer or the local authority rather than on central government.

## The Corporatization of National Social Security Administration

The final and conclusive step in the de facto privatization of social security administration—separating it from direct political control—was taken in the Next Steps initiative in 1991. This split the policy function of the Department of Social Security from its operational arm. A number of corporatized agencies were created to administer different aspects of the benefits system: the Contributions Agency, the Benefits Agency, the Child Support Agency and the War Pensions Agency. A Chief Executive was appointed to head up each of the agencies which were to be managed along business lines, none of which was accountable to Parliament. The Secretary of State for Social Security no longer answers many of the Parliamentary questions asked about the administration (or maladministration) of benefits on the grounds that this is the responsibility of the relevant agency. Officially, the new agencies have no control over policy. The first chief executive of the Benefits Agency pointed out soon after taking office that he was responsible only for the operation of the system:

It's no good saying we can change policy. We have a role in ensuring policy takes account of operational issues, but at the end of the day policy issues remain with ministers. We may not be able to improve the level of benefits our customers think they need, but we can improve the way they're delivered. (Lunn, 1990: 20)

However, the impartiality of the new Benefits Agency was called into question when it was revealed that it had played a key role in effecting an important policy change in 1991. A letter from the Chief Executive, which was leaked to a Labour MP, suggested that the agency had actively campaigned for a change in policy. In the light of a Social Security Commissioner's decision that would have allowed some 50,000 people with learning difficulties to claim benefit arrears going as far back as 1948, the Benefits Agency responded: "to the views of, and pressure on, local services faced with mounting requests for review following take-up campaigns" (*The Guardian*, September 5, 1991) by lobbying the policy group of the DSS to have the appropriate law changed. This was duly done in August 1991. Thus, in a situation where the legitimate rights of claimants conflicted with the interests of the Benefits Agency, operating along business lines, the Agency will endeavor to influence policy where it conflicts with the organizational goals of the agency. All agencies have to operate within fixed targets, and with diminishing resources, it would not be credible to assume they would not seek policy change to make that task easier.

It has been argued that the private administration or provision of social security benefits is unlikely to replace the state social security system entirely. As Harker (1997: 256) notes:

The administration of complex benefits is unlikely to be attractive to the private sector and their complexity could not be compromised without jeopardizing their effectiveness in meeting needs. It is hard to image how those benefits which are less complex—such as child benefit, where two percent of expenditure goes towards administration—could be delivered more effectively by the private sector. The cost of administration is connected to the complexity of the benefit concerned, not the administrative system itself.

Nevertheless, further steps have been taken to privatize some aspects of provision.

In 1991 the Conservative government published a policy statement (White Paper), *Competing for Quality*, in which it outlined plans for "market testing" in the public sector. In a speech in spring 1993, the then Citizen's Charter

Minister, William Waldegrave, set out how the Conservative government would expose the public sector to the rigors of the market.

In brief, he explained, public services should be carefully scrutinized to determine whether they should be provided at all. If a public service survived this test then ideally it should be sold to the private sector. If this was not feasible, then the service should be further scrutinized to see if it could be contracted out directly. The alternative to direct external contracting-out is the creation of internal markets by inviting in-house tenders for particular services. It is this last form which is referred to as "market testing" (Sainsbury and Kennedy, 1994: 12).

## FROM THE STATE TO THE INDIVIDUAL

A more pervasive and invidious method of administrative divestiture has been the transfer of responsibility from the social security system to claimants themselves. In order to cut staff, new administrative procedures were introduced which placed more onus on claimants to identify their own needs, to find out about help which might be available, to obtain any appropriate forms and to fill them in correctly. The introduction of postal claiming and the policy of radically reducing the number of home visits meant that there were fewer opportunities through the formal administration for claimants' needs to be identified and met. Before losing office in 1979, the Conservative government had proposed delaying the date of payment of benefit from the date of claim to the date the claimant had submitted all necessary documentation. Given the complexity, especially of the means-tested benefit system, this would have meant that many claimants would have lost several weeks' benefit entitlement.

## THE PRIVATIZATION OF POVERTY

Social security spending in Britain accounts for over one-third of all public expenditure. It is by far the largest public spending program. One of the most punitive ways in which social security has been privatized has been the many cuts that have been made in the last two decades. In the 1970s the Labour government began to cut benefits covertly and rather shame-facedly. There was no such reticence by the Conservative Thatcher and Major administrations. The Blair Labour government, elected to office in 1997, has used more positive language but has continued to make significant cuts in benefit and to increase the role of means testing, despite very considerable opposition from a significant minority of its own backbenchers and the House of Lords. The greatest savings in benefit expenditure was yielded by the 1980 change in the annual benefit indexing formula. Instead of increasing each year in line with prices *or* earnings, whichever had risen faster, benefits are now uprated only in line with prices. The cumulative result over the ensuing 20 years of this change in policy is that the state NI pension is 25 percent lower at the end of the twentieth century than it otherwise would have been. This pension already fails to offer protection against poverty to Britain's pensioners. The assumption is that it will, in the words of one prominent Conservative minister at the time, be worth a "nugatory" amount in the future. The fall in value of benefits means that current benefit recipients have standards of living which are falling further and further behind the rest of society and that people need to take out private pension arrangements if they want to protect themselves against poverty in their older age or, indeed, at other times when they are unable to support themselves.

One of the features of social security reform over the last 20 years has been to encourage "self-reliance" and "independence." However, while pursuing these goals may mean less dependence on some state benefits, it will increase private dependence on the family, especially for women and young people. It will also lead to much greater hardship. For example, the growth of homelessness among 16 and 17 year-olds is closely tied to the removal of their right to social assistance in 1988. Similarly, the abolition of a number of grants available under the social assistance program up until 1988, which were inadequately replaced by discretionary means-tested loans from the Social Fund, led to more families turning to charities and voluntary organizations for help.

As well as rates of benefit being lower, the state social security system is also providing support to fewer people because more and more people are falling outside the government's restricted definition of those in need. One way of excluding people from benefits has been to tighten up eligibility criteria for contributory, non-contributory and means-tested benefits. Many young people, students, and others whose incomes take them just over social assistance level have been removed completely from eligibility for some benefits. Originally, entitlement to NI unemployment benefit was dependent only upon an adequate contributions record and proof of availability for work. This rule was first tightened in 1980 with administrative changes requiring the completion of a questionnaire upon initial claim and every six months afterwards. From 1989, claimants were also required to show that they were actively seeking work as well as being available for it. In October 1996, unemployment benefit was replaced by a Jobseeker's Allowance which is paid on a contributory basis for the first six months and on a means-test basis thereafter. Eligibility is reliant not only on an adequate contribution record but also on signing a Jobseeker's agreement that details job search activities. Failure to comply with this agreement can lead to sanctions and ultimately the withdrawal of benefit.

Strenuous steps were also taken to reduce the number of people claiming benefit on the grounds of long-term illness or disability. Despite steps taken in 1995 to try to curb the three-fold increase in claimants of invalidity benefit between 1979 and 1995 by tighter administration, the Conservative government replaced this benefit with an incapacity benefit, the eligibility conditions for which were much more limited. It was estimated that the tighter criteria would generate substantial savings to the Treasury. The new Labour government later enacted further tightening up of eligibility for incapacity benefit, which ends the entitlement of many disabled people who have paid into the NI system and means-tests this benefit for the first time. In 1990, unemployment benefit and means-tested benefits were withdrawn entirely from full-time students in favor of means-tested student loans.

One of the most punitive areas of cutbacks in eligibility refers to refugees and asylum seekers. An habitual residence test was introduced in 1994 disqualifying recent entrants to Britain, including British citizens, from means-tested benefits. A report by the National Association of Citizen's Advice Bureaux (1996) found that five times as many people as expected, including 5,000 British citizens, failed the new residency test. Even more draconian rules were introduced in early 1996 to prevent asylum-seekers receiving a range of benefits unless they had declared themselves as such at the port of entry, which many do not do for fear of jeopardizing their entry into the country. This development led to the Red Cross distributing food parcels to destitute asylum-seekers in London, the first time they had undertaken such action in this country (*The Guardian*, December 19, 1996).

Cuts in benefits have been facilitated by the highly provocative stance taken by governments on the issue of benefit fraud. Successive Secretaries of State maintained a very high profile, anti-fraud rhetoric at the same time as the mainstream benefits system was being criticized for inefficiencies and inaccuracies. Growing numbers of people have been denied benefit as a result of these policies (Sainsbury, 1998; Rowlingson and Whyley, 1998).

## FROM STATE TO THE FAMILY

A result of the state gradually making social security provision less generous and less comprehensive is that the cost of poverty lies where it falls: with the family or the individual. Need becomes privatized. The Conservative government defended its decision to deny 16 and 17 year-olds the right to benefit in the 1986 Social Security Act by arguing that most lived with families whose responsibility it was to continue to support them. However, evidence showed that the majority lived in poor families (Walker, 1993). A growth in the number of lone parents claiming means-tested benefits in the 1980s led to increased concern about their cost and, in particular, the role that absent fathers should have in supporting their children. The intention of the Child Support Agency (CSA) was to "ensure that parents honor their legal and moral responsibility to maintain their own children whenever they can afford to do so" (Howard, 1997). In practice, critics could be forgiven for thinking it was only concerned with reducing the cost of lone-parent support to the Treasury. While the duty to pay child maintenance applies to all absent parents, the legal requirement placed on parents with care to give their permission to pursue maintenance applies only to those in receipt of income support, family credit and disability working allowance. These groups formed 97 percent of the cases dealt with by the CSA in its first year (Knights, 1994). Pursuing maintenance only for those parents with care (usually mothers) who were claiming means-tested benefits guaranteed that few would be better off because any money awarded would be deducted from their mother's benefit. The only people to benefit would be those "small numbers" (Knights, 1994: 30) who managed to get off benefit and into work.

## CONCLUSION

Privatization is now an inherent part of the social security system in Britain. The private sector is playing an increasing role in the provision of benefits, especially with regard to the largest segment of the benefits system, namely long-term pensions. Administration of social security has increasingly been moved away from the Department of Social Security to autonomous agencies, employers and local authorities, though the government has removed any discretion from administering authorities, notably local authorities, to vary benefits payments in favor of their local citizens. Social security administration is also increasingly being run on business principles with an emphasis on efficiency and targets, but with less attention to effectiveness in meeting individual need. The pressure to reduce public spending has meant that the social security system is less generous and less comprehensive so that individuals are forced to make alternative provision in the private sector for their future financial security. Those who are unable to do so face poverty. The cost of a less adequate public social security system means that poverty is privatized with its cost falling to the individual and his or her family.

There were two paradoxes in the Conservative governments' policy to privatize social security, both of which remain on the Blair Labour government's policy agenda. First, privatization emphasizes the responsibility of the family in providing for the financial security of its members. However, families do so at a time when it is becoming increasingly difficult for a large section of the community to achieve financial security. The goal of full employment has been abandoned. Workers are being told by the government that they must be flexible and expect to change jobs or careers several times during their working lives. Low pay remains a major cause of poverty in Britain. Unemployment, low pay, part-time work, casualized employment and contract employment are all elements of intractable problems within the current labor market which make it difficult for many people to meet their current consumption expenses, let alone set aside sufficient and regular savings for the future.

Second, while governments have focussed on the need to cut spending on public welfare, the Conservative government in particular committed enormous sums to underpin private provision (such as for pensions and long-term care) either through tax incentives or public subsidies. Some public expenditure "savings" have merely been movement of resources from one budget line item to another. Thus, the cuts in housing subsidies provision—the area where Conservative administrations were most effective in reducing the headline spending figure—partly reappeared under social security spending. The increase in housing benefit from £1.54 billion in 1983–1984 to over £10 billion in 1994–1995 was caused by the growing number of claimants and higher rents resulting from de-regulation, forcing the government to re-impose controls on "exceptionally high" rents in 1994. Similarly, the growth in private residential care in the early 1980s was subsidized almost entirely by the social security system, which, again, forced the government to impose ceilings on the level of residential and care costs which could be met. As a consequence, an increasing number of older or disabled people, or their families, have had to top up the cost of private residential and nursing care, sometimes from very low incomes, and some nursing homes are closing down because, they claim, levels of state support are too low.

Britain's social security system was devised to provide "security" at times of need, on a "social" basis because many individuals were unable to buy the financial security they needed from the private sector. The move toward both market principles and the private market, in various aspects of the benefits, is socially divisive. Those who are well paid will buy themselves better pensions. Those in well-paid, secure employment will also receive good occupational benefits. Those in low-paid employment, those who are unemployed and those unable to work through ill health or caring responsibilities will have no alternative but to depend on a state residual benefits system, providing help to the poorest primarily on a means-tested basis.

**REFERENCES**

Abel-Smith, B. and Townsend, P. 1965. *The Poor and the Poorest*. London: Bell.
Andrews, K. and Jacobs, J. 1990. *Punishing the Poor: Poverty under Thatcher*. London: Macmillan.
Atkinson, A. B. 1991. A National Minimum? A History of Ambiguity in the Determination of Benefit Scales in Britain. In Wilson, T. and Wilson, D. (eds.), *The State and Social Welfare: The Objectives of Policy*. London: Harlow.
Atkinson, A. B. 1998. *Incomes and the Welfare State*. Oxford: Oxford University Press.
Baloo, S., McMaster, I. and Sutton, K. 1986. *Statutory Sick Pay: The Failure of Privatization in Social Security*. Leicester: Leicester City Council/Disability Alliance Education and Research Association.
Barr, N. 1994. Private Unemployment Insurance: Myths and Realities. *Benefits* 10: 1–4.
Beveridge, W. 1942. *Social Insurance and Allied Services*. Cmnd 6404. London: HMSO.
Burchardt, T. and Hills, J. 1997. *Private Welfare Insurance and Social Security: Pushing the Boundaries*. York: Joseph Rowntree Foundation.
Deacon, A. 1991. The Retreat from State Welfare. In Becker, S. (ed.), *Windows of Opportunity: Public Policy and the Poor*. London: Child Poverty Action Group.
Hall, P., Land, H., Parker, R. and Webb, A. 1975. *Change, Choice and Conflict in Social Policy*. London: Heinemann.
Harker, L. 1997. New Paths for Social Security. In Walker, A. and Walker, C. (eds.), *Divided Britain: the Growth of Social Exclusion in the 1980s and 1990s*. London: Child Poverty Action Group.

Hills, J. 1987. What Happened to Spending on the Welfare State? In Walker, A. and Walker, C. (eds.), *The Growing Divide: A Social Audit 1979–87*. London: Child Poverty Action Group.

Howard, M. 1997. Cutting Social Security. In Walker, A. and Walker, C. (eds.), *Divided Britain: The Growth of Social Exclusion in the 1980s and 1990s*. London: Child Poverty Action Group.

Howard, M. and Thompson, P. 1995. *There May Be Trouble Ahead*. London: Disability Alliance and the Disablement Income Group.

Hyde, M. 2000. From Welfare to Work? Social Policy for Disabled People of Working Age in the United Kingdom in the 1990s. *Disability & Society* 15 (2): 327–41.

Hyde, M., Dixon, J. and Joyner, M. 1999. "Work for Those That Can, Security for Those That Cannot": The United Kingdom's New Social Security Reform Agenda. *International Social Security Review* 52 (4): 69–86.

Johnson, P. and Falkingham, J. 1994. Privatization and Pensions. *Benefits* 10: 5–10.

Kirk, D., Nelson, S., Sinfield, A. and Sinfield, D. 1991. *Excluding Youth: Poverty among Young People Living Away from Home*. Edinburgh: Bridges Project/Edinburgh CSWR.

Knights, E. 1994. The Truth about Child Support: CPAG's Monitoring of the Child Support Agency. *Benefits* 11: 29–31.

Le Grand, J. and Robinson, R. (eds.). 1984. *Privatisation and the Welfare State*. London: George Allen and Unwin.

Loney, M. 1987. A War on Poverty or the Poor? In Walker, A. and Walker, C. (eds.), *The Growing Divide: A Social Audit 1979–87*. London: Child Poverty Action Group.

Lunn, T. 1990. This Customer Business. *Community Care* 16 (August): 23–25.

Moore, J. 1987. *The Future of the Welfare State*. Mimeo, September 26.

National Association of Citizen's Advice Bureaux. 1995. *Security at Risk: CAB Evidence on Payment Protection Insurance for Public Policy*. London: National Association of Citizen's Advice Bureaux.

National Association of Citizen's Advice Bureaux. 1996. *Failing the Test: CAB Clients' Experiences of the HRT in Social Security*. London: National Association of Citizen's Advice Bureaux.

Piachaud, D. 1997. The Growth of Means-testing. In Walker, A. and Walker, C. (eds.), *Divided Britain: The Growth of Social Exclusion in the 1980s and 1990s*. London: Child Poverty Action Group.

Rowlingson, K. and Whyley, C. 1998. The Right Amount to the Right People? Reducing Fraud, Error and Non-Take-Up of Benefit. *Benefits* 21: 7–11.

Sainsbury, R. 1998. Putting Fraud into Perspective. Benefits 21: 2–7.

Sainsbury, R. and Kennedy, S. 1994. Flogging Social Security: Market Testing and Benefit Administration. *Benefits* 10: 10–15.

Sinfield, R. A. (ed.). 1993. *Poverty, Inequality and Justice*. Edinburgh: New Waverley Papers.

United Kingdom. Department of Health and Social Security (DHSS). 1985a. *Reform of Social Security: Programme for Change*. Cmnd 9517. London: HMSO.

United Kingdom. Department of Health and Social Security (DHSS). 1985b. *Reform of Social Security: Programme for Change*. Cmnd 9518. London: HMSO.

United Kingdom. Department of Social Security (DSS). 1998. *A New Contract for Welfare: Principles into Practice*. London: The Stationery Office.

United Kingdom. Her Majesty's Treasury. 1979. *The Government's Expenditure Plans, 1980–81*. London: HMSO.

Walker, A. 1984. The Political Economy of Privatization. In Le Grand, J. and Robinson, R. (eds.), *Privatization and the Welfare State*. London: George Allen and Unwin.

Walker, A. 1993. Thatcherism and the New Politics of Old Age. In Myles, J. and Quadagno, J. (eds.), *States, Labor Markets, and the Future of Old-Age Policy*. Philadelphia: Temple University Press.

Walker, A. 1997. The Social Division of Welfare Revisited. In Robertson, A. (ed.), *Unemployment, Social Security and the Social Division of Welfare*. Edinburgh: New Waverley Papers.

Walker, A. and Walker, C. (eds.). 1987. *The Growing Divide: A Social Audit 1979–87*. London: Child Poverty Action Group.

Walker, A. and Walker, C. (eds.). 1997. *Britain Divided: The Growth of Social Exclusion in the 1980s and 1990s*. London: Child Poverty Action Group.

Walker, C. 1993. *Managing Poverty: The Limits of Social Assistance*. London: Routledge.

Weir, S. 1984. Housing Nightmare. *New Society* 27 (January): 11–13.

*Chapter 7*

# A Hydra-Like Creature? The Marketization of Social Security in New Zealand

## Michael O'Brien

**INTRODUCTION**

New Zealand has long prided itself on the comprehensive nature of its social security system. In large part, this is because of the early introduction of state-provided income support for a range of income deficits arising from social security contingencies of age, sickness and industrial injury, care of children, unemployment and widowhood, which began in the 1890s. In her recent book, McClure (1998) demonstrates that this pride is at best only partially justified, going on to argue that the belief about the comprehensiveness of coverage has acted as an impediment to the subsequent development of social security. Changes in the social security system over the last 15 years in New Zealand lend some support to her claim. Indeed, those changes represent a marked deterioration in the living standards for those dependent on the various components of "income support" (the term used to define what was formerly called social security, which has been used since the creation of the Income Support Service in 1993). It is a term which in itself is ideologically and politically significant in representing and symbolizing the official discourse surrounding the nature of social security, or more accurately "social insecurity" (Cheyne et al., 1997). This chapter will review aspects of those changes insofar as they represent the particular New Zealand approach to marketization.

Marketization of social security in New Zealand/Aotearoa (the latter being the Maori name for New Zealand) can be described as a hybrid process, with four quite distinct income-support components. The first component encompasses categorical assistance benefits for lone parents, the unemployed, widows, the sick and disabled. Marketization processes for this group are different from those that have been applied to retirement pension provision, which is the second component. Both of these marketization approaches are different again from those that have operated in relation to housing assistance and wage subsidies, which is the third component. Different yet again are the elements of marketization adopted with respect to accident compensation coverage, which is the fourth component. Quite different processes of change have occurred in each of these components, and the current provision in each area reflects both these different processes and the outcome of different political and ideological struggles. It should be noted that there is little discussion of disability benefit provision within this chapter because of the complexities of provision for this group arising from the distinction drawn between those disabled as a result of sickness and those disabled as a result of an accident.

The discussion of these four income-support components forms the substantive part of the chapter. Each of the four components begins with a discussion of the key historical shifts, a discussion that is necessarily brief. From here the key distinguishing features of marketization for each component are considered. The discussion of each component concludes with reflections on outcomes, both already known and anticipated. The discussion on outcomes focuses primarily on the effects for the most vulnerable. Other dimensions, such as the cost to the state, the quality of service delivery, and gendered and ethnic differences, could also have been highlighted, but the critical dimension is the impact on the most vulnerable because this is a major role for social security. The chapter concludes with a discussion of the lessons and implications of the New Zealand experience of marketization.

A superficial review of the components of marketization could easily lead to the conclusion that state income-support provision is an example of a benevolent institution. Such an argument is not being advanced in this chapter. A range of material clearly demonstrates that any comprehensive analysis of the state action with respect to income support requires a much more sophisticated and analytic approach, if those actions are to be adequately understood. What is critical is that the actions of the state have been shaped in significant ways by the experience of the failures of the market.

The complexities of marketization and its multiple forms within social security mean that there is no simple manifestation of marketization. Rather, the impacts and development of marketization reflect a mixture of historical, ideological and political forces, a mixture that varies across the different income-support components identified. While many of the changes were defended and promoted on the basis that they were necessary to contain both increasing numbers of recipients and increasing costs, these issues were only one influence on the changes. The forms of marketization and the marketization processes utilized were the result of a mix of ideological, political and historical forces rather than the result of some inexorable fiscal and demographic factors.

## THE STRUCTURE OF SOCIAL SECURITY IN NEW ZEALAND

The New Zealand social security marketization framework has multiple components, which can be categorized as follows: the "political market," the "failed market," the "subisdized market" or the "renewed market." It should be noted, however, that some components are included within more than one marketization category, which reflects the multiple functions that the different components fulfill and their role in the overall structure of social security:

- The "political market": the marketization efforts made with respect to tax-funded (a) categorical, flat-rate benefits for lone parents—the Domestic Purposes Benefits (DPB)—widows, the unemployed, and people who are sick or disabled as invalids; (b) safety net programs, namely the Special Needs Grants (SNG) and Special Benefits (SB), which, while included here, are safety net programs that have links in varying ways to all four market components.
- The "failed market": the marketization efforts made with respect to tax-funded, universal, flat-rate retirement pension to all those who reach the qualifying age (currently increasing gradually to age 65 by 2001).
- The "subsidized market": the marketization efforts made with respect to tax-funded, flat-rate assistance to those in paid work whose incomes are considered to be inadequate for family needs, including housing costs and the costs of childcare. The major wage subsidy programs are the Guaranteed Minimum Family Income (GMFI), Independent Family Tax Credit (IFTC), and Family Support, which is also paid to those with children who are in receipt of one of the categorical benefits. Housing costs are subsidized through the Accommodation Supplement (AS), which is available to both beneficiaries and to those in paid work, for which eligibility is established irrespective of whether the recipient is renting or paying a mortgage. Childcare costs are subsidized for those in work or training that meet the eligibility criteria.
- The "renewed market": the marketization efforts made with respect to income support for those who have incurred income loss as a result of an accident. This is provided by the Accident Rehabilitation and Compensation Insurance Corporation (commonly, the ACC), which, uniquely, operates on a contributory insurance basis. Eligibility is not dependant upon past contribution record, and benefits are related to previous levels of earnings, with the income replacement rate set at 80 percent, subject to an earnings ceiling of NZ$1,277.18.

Table 7.1 illustrates some of this complexity in that the elements of social security cut across these four market forms.

It should be noted too that the various ingredients of income support identified here do not represent the totality of income for recipients. Some of those receiving income under the first three components above have additional earned income, albeit limited in most instances. For example, approximately 75 percent of those receiving retirement benefits are located in the bottom two household-equivalent, disposable-income quintiles (New Zealand, Statistics New Zealand,

Table 7.1
Framework of Social Security in New Zealand

| Ingredient | Groups Covered | Marketization Form | How Funded and Delivered | Range of Coverage |
| --- | --- | --- | --- | --- |
| Categorical Benefit | Lone parents, unemployed, sick and disabled, widows. | Political Market | Funded by taxation. Delivered through central government department. | Flat-rate weekly benefits, income tested. Variable rate for different categories and different age groups with range of possible supplements. |
| Superannuation | Persons over age 63. | Failed Market | Funded by taxation. Delivered through central government department. | Weekly benefit paid to all on reaching eligible age. |
| Supplementary Payments | Eligible beneficiaries and wage earners. | Political Market, Subsidized Market | Funded by taxation. Delivered through central government department. | Variable payments (dependent on income and expenditure) to cover such matters as housing costs, disability payments, child care costs. |

| | | | |
|---|---|---|---|
| Guaranteed Minimum Family Income/ Family Support/ Independent Family Tax Credit | Eligible low wage earners and beneficiaries (Family Support only). | Political Market, Subsidized Market | Funded by taxation. Delivered through central government department. | Variable weekly payments payable on basis of earnings and family size. Income tested. |
| Safety Net Programs | Eligible beneficiaries and wage earners. | Political Market | Funded by taxation. Delivered through central government department. | Variable payments (dependent on income and expenditure) to cover such matters as inadequate income and emergencies. Income and asset tested. |
| Accident Compensation | All those suffering loss of income as a result of accident, irrespective of cause. | Failed Market | Funded by levy on workers, employers and motor vehicle owners. | Weekly payment related to previous earnings with supplements to meet rehabilitation costs. |

1999). Of course, white males are more likely to have such income than women, Maori and ethnic minorities (Else and St. John, 1998; Periodic Report Group, 1997). Furthermore, some ACC recipients may also be receiving some income, albeit limited, from paid work. Finally, there are significant differences in the income received by different income support recipient groups (see Table 7.2). The basic accident compensation benefit for a single adult is about double the basic benefit for retired single people or the lone parent with one child, and just under three times the basic benefit payable to single unemployed people.

## CATEGORICAL ASSISTANCE

### Historical Resume

The first significant benefits in this category were introduced in 1912 for veterans of the Land Wars during the previous century. These benefits were expanded during and after the First World War to provide compensation for widows and rehabilitation for returning soldiers. In 1915 benefits were introduced for miners suffering from miner's phthisis, while the first benefits for the blind were introduced in 1924.

### *Unemployment Provision*

Benefit payment for the unemployed was first introduced by the 1938 Social Security Act. Throughout the economic depression of the late 1920s and early 1930s work camps were created for the unemployed. Participation in these camps and/or in some form of subsidized work was required to maintain eligibility for unemployment payment. "No pay without work" was the common slogan. Following the 1938 Social Security Act, the work requirement was dropped and all of the unemployed became eligible for payment. This remained the position until 1990 when the age of eligibility was increased to 18 years, with severely limited assistance for younger persons. The age of eligibility for full adult benefit for the unemployed was increased from 20 years to 25 years in 1991. In 1998, a work and organized activity test was introduced for the unemployed. Availability for work has always been required to maintain eligibility for unemployment benefit. The new criteria, from 1998, was a willingness to accept any referral to paid work or to training in some form, with the benefit being renamed as the "community wage," the term used to cover the previous categories of unemployment, sickness, widow's and invalid's benefit.

### *Lone-Parent Provision*

A discretionary benefit was introduced for lone parents in 1968. A statutory benefit—the Domestic Purposes Benefit—was introduced five years later following the findings of the Royal Commission on Social Security reported the previous year. Eligibility for this benefit was reduced in 1977 with limits being placed on eligibility immediately after separation and on eligibility for new lone

Table 7.2
Base Payment Rates for Each Form of Income Support

| Ingredient | Payment Rate | Special Notes |
|---|---|---|
| Categorical Benefits | NZ$147.89 for unemployed single person aged 25; NZ$154.04 (widow); NZ$211.82 lone parent, one child. | |
| Retirement Pensions | NZ$162.79 (married person, no other income); NZ$212.69 (single, no other income). | |
| Supplementary Payments | Maximum accommodation supplement varies between NZ$75 and NZ$150. NZ$32.75 maximum weekly for Child Disability Allowance, NZ$43.39 maximum for Disability Allowance. | Housing amount depends on income, locality and accommodation costs. Disability Allowance is income tested and is paid on basis of proven and approved costs. |
| Guaranteed Minimum Family Income/ Family Support/ Independent Family Tax Credit | IFTC is NZ$15 per week. Maximum FS NZ$60 for eldest child, NZ$40 for second and subsequent children over age 12, NZ$32 for second and subsequent child under age 13 (all figures are weekly). GMFI is currently NZ$286 per week. | Amount varies depending on income and work status. (IFTC is limited to persons in paid work.) |
| Safety Net Programs | SB calculated on standard living cost formula. Payment then linked to income. Maximum payment for SNG varies depending on purpose of grant. | |
| Accident Compensation | NZ$424.85. | Based on 80 percent of current average male taxable wage. |

*Note*: For the purposes of comparison, the benefits relate to those payable to an adult person; additional payments on behalf of dependent children or for other purposes such as housing costs are not included for the first two components.

*Sources*: Income Support data is taken from pamphlets supplied by Work and Income New Zealand. The ACC calculation is based on average wage statistics (New Zealand, Statistics New Zealand, 1998a).

mothers immediately after the birth of a child. This benefit was cut savagely in 1991, and a work and organized activity test was introduced in February 1999. Lone parents with a child under the age of seven are exempt from the requirements of this test. This test is also applied to widows who are in receipt of a separate widow's benefit, which was also reduced in 1991 but not as savagely as the DPB.

### Sickness Provision

A sickness benefit was first introduced by the 1938 Social Security Act, while the invalid's benefit appeared initially in the same legislation. These benefits were also reduced in the 1991 cuts. Eligibility is now subject to the satisfaction of the work-test requirements for a community wage, unless exempted on medical grounds. During the 1990s there has been a steady growth in surveillance and compliance demands placed on these beneficiaries, with requirements for medical testing by state-appointed medical practitioners in addition to the completion of medical certificates by the beneficiary's own doctor.

## As a Form of Political Marketization

The failure of markets to provide adequately levels of social well-being represented an important reason for the initial introduction of social assistance, culminating in the 1938 Social Security Act. Indeed, the full title to this Act hints at this:

An Act to provide for the payment of Superannuation Benefits and of other Benefits designed to safeguard the People of New Zealand from Disabilities arising from Age, Sickness, Widowhood, Orphanhood, Unemployment, or other Exceptional Conditions.

The electoral success of a Labour government in 1935 resulted in the election to Parliament of a large number of members with first hand experience of the deprivations arising from failures of the market during the late 1920s and early 1930s depression, which was most strongly evidenced in the experiences of the unemployed during this period. This electoral success, combined with the international acceptance of Keynesian economic prescriptions as the route out of economic depression, meant an active state role in attempting to reduce the levels of misery many had experienced (for an interesting and informative discussion of the experiences of these years, see Simpson, 1990). Moreover, the state took an active role in promoting full male employment as a fundamental feature of social security (Castles, 1985; Easton, 1980; Sutch, 1966).

However, it cannot be argued that failures of the market were directly instrumental in the introduction of the DPB in 1973, for its introduction followed the report of the Royal Commission on Social Security in the previous year. Many health, women's and social service groups had argued to the Royal Commission for a statutory form of benefit because of the impoverished experiences of lone mothers. The outgoing conservative National government was reluctant to act on the Commission's recommendation for the introduction of such a benefit (O'Brien, 1991). The introduction of the benefit followed after the election of a Labour government in 1972.

Politics and ideology were, however, much more explicitly drawn on for the 1991 benefit cuts. The Ministers of Finance and Social Welfare emphasized economic considerations, arguing that the growing cost of social assistance had to be reduced. The strength of political and ideological factors is clear from the budget documents of that year:

The state will continue to provide a safety net—a modest standard below which people will not be allowed to fall—provided they demonstrate they are prepared to help themselves. . . . These are the measures that protect all those who can demonstrate that matters beyond their control threaten to force them into poverty. The Government reaffirms its commitment to protect those who are unable to protect themselves. (Shipley, 1991:13)

Ruth Richardson (1995: 209), the Finance Minister responsible for the 1991 budget, elaborates:

Like many social policies, the introduction of the DPB affected social behavior in a way that was to have deep and undesirable consequences. It substantially altered the incentives and moral sanctions surrounding human relationships and child-rearing. For men, the DPB made it easier to be more casual about family ties. Suddenly, abandoning one's family became a less costly exercise. The DPB reduced the expected financial cost; just as important it reduced the cost of social disapproval. For women, the DPB also meant they had less at stake when investing in a relationship. For both men and women who were casual about relationships and careless about the consequences in the form of any child that might follow, personal irresponsibility was officially sanctioned.

The phrase "Welfare that Works," used both as an integral part of the title of the reforms and in subsequent public discussions by the then Minister of Social Welfare, Jenny Shipley, carries two quite distinct meanings, both through skillful use of the word "works" (referring, of course, to paid work). In the first instance, "works" is used to refer to an organizational system that is effective and efficient and produces the welfare results desired by government. Second, and more significantly, the linkage between "welfare" and "works" provides a basis for linkage between the words so that "welfare" and "work" become associated together in public and political discourse. Rather than "welfare" being provided for those unable to engage in paid "work," access to "welfare" now becomes contingent on acceptance of the primacy and superiority of "work." The multiple meanings of "works" in the 1991 budget title is reflected in the development of social assistance during the intervening years. "Work," in the narrow sense of paid work, quickly becomes the critical determinant in social assistance provision in two very concrete ways.

First, the "less eligibility" principle is regularly invoked as the basis for setting rates of assistance. This principle was presented as one of the reasons for the cuts of 1991: "They (benefits) are not intended to provide a standard of living better than is enjoyed by New Zealanders who work in paid employment to support themselves and their families" (Shipley, 1991: 23). "Through these moves (cutting benefit entitlement and eligibility) we will increase the rewards for moving from welfare to work by creating a greater margin between benefit rates and workforce earnings" (Bolger et al., 1990). These sentiments have continued to be used to justify impoverished benefit levels.

Second, the introduction of workfare represents a clear expression of the emphasis on paid labor. Benefit payments carry with them a continual reciprocal obligation incumbent on recipients to prepare themselves for work. Government information on social assistance payments emphasizes work responsibilities, as does the legislation on which it is based. For example, the latter defines the purpose of the work test as "To reinforce the reciprocal obligations of work-tested beneficiaries to seek work or take steps to improve their employment prospects as a condition of receiving the benefit" (New Zealand, Social Security Work Test Amendment Act, section 101). Perhaps the most poignant expression of this emphasis was given by the then responsible Minister, who said that the legislation created "a consistent set of sanctions designed to reinforce the message that "if you don't work, you don't get paid" (New Zealand, Social Security Work Test Amendment Bill 1998: ii).

The work and organized activity test that is fundamental to workfare is based around two fundamental assumptions about paid work. The first assumption is that work is available if beneficiaries obtained the necessary skills and qualifications and/or if they make an effort to obtain it. Making that effort includes being more energetic in the search for work, improving personal appearance by, for example, losing weight, and/or improving the quality of written job applications. The second assumption is that work remuneration will be adequate to meet individual and family needs. It should be noted, however, that the Chief Executive of the Department of Social Welfare commented in a radio program in 1997 that she was not worried about wage rates as long as people moved from benefit to paid work.

The market, through paid work, is presumed to be the most desirable source of primary income, against which all else is measured. This is the same position as prevailed prior to the 1938 Social Security Act. The reassertion of market primacy as the source of income—a reassertion that is implicit and explicit in the reshaping of social assistance—stems from the active pursuit of an agenda in which dependence on the state has been actively maligned. One of the key points in the attack on state dependence was a conference sponsored and carefully stage managed by the Department of Social Welfare in 1997 under the title "Beyond Dependency." Keynote speakers at that conference included Jean Rogers (1997) (from Wisconsin, the American home of workfare), Lawrence Mead (1997) and Frank Field, the then United Kingdom Minister for Welfare Reform. There were a small number of contributors presenting alternative views on dependency (Baker, 1997) and an alternative conference was organized preceding the departmental gathering (O'Brien and Briar, 1997). The theme of dependency has also been emphasized continuously in such key places as Departmental Briefing Papers to the Minister of Social Welfare (New Zealand, Department of Social Welfare, 1996) and has been a topic of frequent public debate by the Minister himself. These arguments and emphases from central political figures have been augmented by and simultaneously reinforced significant public hostility toward most groups of social assistance recipients. As recently as March 1999, the right wing political party, the Association of Consumers and Taxpayers (ACT), was calling for abolition of the DPB on ideological grounds. Its polling had indicated that this was one of the three issues likely to produce the most significant gain in its level of political support, then standing at 6 percent in the polls. Although this figure is low, the argument is significant because ACT is the major coalition partner of the governing National Party.

While securing accurate data on public opinion on welfare is difficult (Taylor-Gooby, 1985), the available sources do suggest that the level of support for the unemployed and lone parents as beneficiary groups is significantly lower than support for the elderly (New Zealand, Royal Commission on Social Policy, 1988). The success of the "political market" of social assistance has not been paralleled in the "failed market" of retirement pensions.

**Performance and Outcomes**

The evolution of a comparatively comprehensive system of social assistance since the beginning of the twentieth century meant that by the mid-1970s there was some form of protection and support in the event of any social security contingencies faced by individuals and families. Although there were clear inadequacies, particularly in the tardy introduction of support for lone parents, and although the benefit rates were never particularly high, a basic form of income protection, based on the principles of citizenship rights, was clearly in place.

That range of measures was significantly linked to the continued high rate of employment and was placed under some pressure—fiscal, ideological and political—by the growth of unemployment from the mid-1970s. This pressure was augmented by the changes in family structure, changes which were critical in this context because of the growing numbers of lone-parent households, most of which are headed by women. Currently, approximately 9 percent of recipients of the DPB are male; this percentage is the highest at any time since the benefit was introduced (New Zealand, Department of Social Welfare, 1999). (For a more comprehensive discussion of the ways in which changes in economic and social structures have impacted on social security, see Baldwin and Falkingham, 1994.)

Although these economic and structural changes do not in themselves serve as an explanation of the development of marketization of social assistance, they form an important backdrop. Their importance lies in that they were indicative of social and economic change in New Zealand that both generated and reinforced demands for new policy responses. These policy responses reached their zenith with the introduction of work testing, the seeds for which were laid many years earlier as the state moved initially to place more responsibility on individuals and families to meet income-support needs.

The major desired policy outcomes sought from the placing of increased responsibility on families and individuals and from the strengthening of the requirement to seek and prepare for paid work are achievable only if the labor market can generate adequate income and work opportunities for all New Zealanders. The forecasts of sustained high levels of unemployment (*The Jobs Letter*, January 25, 1999) suggest that the desirable outcomes sought are highly unlikely to be achieved. For many of those in rural communities with unemployment rates in excess of 9 percent, the income adequacy and work opportunity outcome is even less likely. Indeed, the most likely outcome is increased demands on families, which will produce greater relative poverty. In turn, this increasing acceptance of the legitimacy of the expectations of greater individual and family responsibility is likely to lead to continued pressure for a further lowering of the real levels of income-support assistance and for more rigid policing of those receiving social assistance. Furthermore, as increasing numbers of social assistance recipients are pushed into paid work and/or become available to organizations and firms under workfare, there will be increasing pressure to lower the wages of those in paid work. In turn, this will result in sustained increases in the incidence of those in paid work falling below the poverty line. In short, the likely outcome of marketization of categorical assistance—political marketization—is greater poverty for those receiving social assistance, and for those in insecure, low-paid work—the marginalized and insecure, to use Hutton's (1996) words—greater surveillance and policing of those receiving social assistance.

## RETIREMENT PENSIONS

### Historical Resume

The first old-age pension program was introduced in 1898. The pensions provided were both income and behaviorally tested and coverage was limited significantly on racial ground: "Asiatics" were explicitly excluded while most Maori were disqualified because of collective land ownership or because of the difficulty they had proving their age (McClure, 1998; O'Brien and Wilkes, 1993). The 1938 Social Security Act created two different payments for older people, a means-tested age benefit payable at age 60 and a universal payment payable to all over the age of 65. This remained the basic structure of superannuation until 1974 when the Labour government introduced a compulsory social insurance program with government supplementation as required. The change of government the following year resulted in this strategy being abandoned and replaced in 1977 with a universal, flat-rate payment to all people over the age of 60. The income-replacement rate was set at 40 percent for a married person and at 48 percent for a single adult. This program has remained in place since then, although some important modifications have been made. The basis of calculating the relationship to wages has altered, resulting in a lowering of the relative value of benefits in relation to wage rates. The minimum benefit level has been lowered to 60 percent of average wage for a couple. The age of eligibility has increased, and a surtax on other earned income for recipients of retirement pensions was introduced in 1985, increased in 1992 and abandoned in 1998 (for a fuller discussion of these and other changes, see St. John, 1999b).

Recent years have seen a range of political, policy and administrative efforts to move from this tax-funded, universal provision to some form of private insurance-based provision. A referendum in 1997 to consider a further proposal for a form of private insurance-based provision to replace the current national universal provisions was rejected by over 93 percent of the electorate (Else and St. John, 1998; St. John, 1999b). As part of this program, various measures were to be included to compensate for women's lower earnings including state top-up payments for those whose lifetime earnings did not reach a given minimum level. There was little support for the strategy from political and business leaders.

### As a Form of Failed Marketization

As with social assistance, the failure of markets was an important ingredient in the development of social security for elderly people. One of the important factors leading to the 1898 legislation was the increasing number of older people who were inadequately provided for because their earnings from paid work were insufficient to support themselves and their wives in their retirement (Hanson, 1980; McClure, 1998; Sutch, 1969). The extension of the retirement pension provisions in the 1938 Social Security Act reflected a slightly different argument. There were a large number of people who had contributed significantly to the development of the country during their working life, for whom the state had a duty to ensure adequate income support in their old age. The state, it was argued, had a responsibility to ensure that there was financial provision for older people. Hence, the introduction of the universal retirement pension, which was intended eventually to become the only form of retirement benefit, for the provision of means-tested benefit was to be only a temporary arrangement until the universal pensions caught up in value with the means-tested benefits (Hanson, 1980; McClure, 1998).

Subsequent developments have seen a significant struggle between, on the one hand, efforts to introduce greater reliance on market-based provision through some form of insurance scheme, and, on the other hand, the introduction and preservation of a universal provision. For example, the 1974 social insurance program lasted only until the general election the following year. In that election, the universal superannuation scheme was widely considered to be an important factor in the success of the conservative National government at the polls (Booth, 1977).

Retirement benefit provision provides a good illustration of failed marketization, failed in the sense that the efforts have been unsuccessful in moving from a state-provided, tax-funded universal program to an insurance-based strategy that connected retirement pensions to lifetime earnings. There have at various times been such powerful employer advocacy that the former strategy is unsustainable, for both fiscal and demographic reasons (see discussion in Else and St. John, 1998), and that the private insurance–based strategy proposed in the 1997 referendum was unsatisfactory. Nevertheless, these voices have been unsuccessful in shifting the ideological parameters of the debate; there is much stronger public support for tax-financed, universal retirement pensions than there is for the social assistance provisions. For example, the 1988 Royal Commission on Social Policy found that there was significantly stronger support for government use of taxation for income support for the elderly than for any of the other social assistance groups, with the exception of the sick (New Zealand, Royal Commission on Social Policy, 1988, vol. 1). The historical framework of provision through the state remains the dominant expectation. It seems that ideology has not influenced policy change.

Indeed, policy changes have been in the direction of protecting market-derived retirement income, a protection that gives the greatest advantage to those with private sources of retirement income. In 1998, the post-retirement, private income surtax that was first introduced in 1984, which was extended in 1992, was finally abandoned. Approximately 34 percent of older people paid the surcharge and hence the primary advantage from removing the surtax went to the most affluent older people. It is historical and political forces, particularly the power of the vote of older people, their increasing organizational strength and the historical framework of state provision which have served as the major factors shaping the failed marketization of public retirement income support.

**Performance and Outcomes**

The failure to marketize retirement pensions has resulted in a continued state provision of financial support for older people, which is certain to continue for the foreseeable future. The massive failure of the 1997 referendum suggests that the introduction of a compulsory private insurance-based retirement provision is extremely unlikely. That failure, however, does not make the financial position of older people secure, as is evidenced by the reduction in the floor level for national superannuation pensions. While the political strength of older people will provide some protection of their retirement income levels, it is noticeable that this political strength has provided the greatest gains for the most affluent older people (as can be seen from the recent abolition of the post-retirement, private income surtax). There has been much less attention to the adequacy of the level of national retirement provision for those older people who have little or no additional income.

The outcome of failed marketization thus far has been that those with limited additional income (and those still in the paid workforce in a comparable financial position) have been protected. The strength of that protection remains untested. In the short term it is likely that the position of the most financially impoverished older people would be enhanced by a change of government, but longer term security is much less certain. The emphasis on personal provision and on the superiority of the market over the state as a form of social organization is likely to place the poorest elderly under some financial pressure as increasing proportions of the most powerful and affluent make their own voluntary provisions for superannuation.

## HOUSING ASSISTANCE AND WAGE SUPPORT

### Historical Resume

#### Housing Assistance

Historically, there has been a range of state efforts to support home ownership (Mahar, 1984), but the major provider of housing has been the market, either through owner occupation or private renting. The most dramatic direct interventions occurred following the election of the Labour government in 1938 when the state embarked on major housing initiatives creating a pool of what came to be known as "state houses." The newly elected government of that time used state housing for both economic and social reasons. State housing provision served as a fiscal mechanism to overcome unemployment, as an integral part of a Keynesian economic management strategy that was also a response to the problem of squalid housing conditions in the major cities. The state was to work with a major private developer, Fletcher Construction, in the development of the program. (Fletcher Construction, now one of New Zealand's foremost companies, has been critical of many aspects of New Zealand's program of economic liberalization.)

In addition to its economic role, the state program was designed to provide cheap accessible housing. It was administered through a government organization and was the major form of housing assistance for low-income earners, both in paid work and in receipt of social security payments. Rental was fixed at 25 percent of income. Furthermore, the state also operated a system of subsidized housing mortgages, providing loans at below market interest rates to promote home ownership. This loan facility allowed significant numbers of families to secure their own home. In addition, an accommodation benefit was available to beneficiaries renting in the private sector (but not to low-income earners in paid work) and to low-income private mortgage holders. In addition to the state rentals, there was also a significant private rental market. Moreover, alongside the state involvement, the private market also operated as a lender for private ownership. Historically, New Zealand has had one of the highest rates of home ownership in OECD countries with 75 percent of New Zealanders living in their own home, either freehold or as a mortgagee (New Zealand, Statistics New Zealand, 1998b).

During the welfare state changes of the early 1990s, housing assistance changed to provision through the Accommodation Supplement (AS) paid directly to those who were eligible. The specific sum paid is calculated through a formula that incorporates income levels and rental costs with a maximum level of assistance. This maximum has some regional variations for more expensive housing markets, such as those in Auckland. Assistance is available to all who qualify, irrespective of whether they own or rent. Rental for state houses is set on the basis of a calculation of the market rental for that property, rather than being fixed at 25 percent of income. Management of the state's housing was handed over to Housing New Zealand in 1992, a government-owned enterprise with profit expectations. Properties that were unable to be rented were sold. In addition, the state gradually removed itself from the provision of finance to assist ownership, eventually selling off its mortgages.

## *Wage Subsidies*

In 1926, the first benefit for children was introduced. This was income tested, paid to the father, and limited to the third and subsequent children. A universal benefit for all children was introduced by the 1938 Social Security Act but was not fully implemented until 1945 when it was extended to all children without income testing. Maori had become eligible for payment, at the same rate as *pakeha*, from 1939, but a range of discriminatory discretionary actions by officials resulted in lower payments for a number of years (McClure, 1998). The universal family benefit was abolished in 1991 amid extensive benefit reforms that included benefit cuts for most beneficiary groups.

Until 1984, there was no direct state support for wage and salary earners or for the self-employed. The limited assistance that was available came from tax rebates and tax exemptions, coupled with a universal family benefit paid to the carer of all children under the age of 16 (other than those in state care). This had been the pattern since 1946 when the family benefit became universal (Easton, 1981). Prior to that (from 1924) there was income-tested assistance to families with three or more children. Social security had limited interaction with the market (other than for beneficiaries who were working part-time) until 1984. That is, until 1984 there was no direct payment through the income-support structures to low-income earners in paid work.

The period since 1984, however, has been characterized by an increasing use of various forms of wage subsidy, initially with close connection between wages and benefit through such programs as Guaranteed Minimum Family Income and Family Support, which is also paid to recipients of categorical benefits and eligible retirement pensioners. Over recent years, however, this relationship has become more distant. This is reflected in the latest wage subsidy program—the

Independent Family Tax Credit. This benefit is available only to those in full-time paid work (defined as in excess of 30 hours), the rationale being that this supports the "less eligibility" principle referred to above and acts as an incentive for beneficiaries to secure paid work (Birch, 1996).

## As a Form of Subsidized Marketization

Housing assistance and wage supplementation are linked together here because they share an important characteristic, namely that the market constitutes the major, almost exclusive, form of provision, with only limited state assistance to accommodate market failure. Hence their characterization as a subsidized market. The housing policy changes reviewed here have been shaped almost entirely by ideological considerations that emphasize both minimal direct state assistance and maximum freedom of choice. As with the accident compensation changes, there was some pressure from private interests, namely landlords, for changes to state housing, but this pressure was not as extensive as the private interest pressures that occurred with respect to accident compensation coverage.

Part of the initial thrust of wage subsidy in the 1980s came from research and technical work carried out within the bureaucracy that identified child poverty for those in work as a significant issue (Easton, 1981). More recent emphasis has been shaped by ideological considerations similar to those that shaped the social assistance policy discourse, namely the emphasis on the superior nature of paid work, in contrast to state-provided income (McClure, 1998). The development of the wage subsidy programs and of the social assistance benefit cuts have had inequitable outcomes: "Real assistance for low-income families has fallen since 1986; when coupled with core benefit reductions, this decline in assistance has resulted in a rapid rise in the number of those in need. Major problems arise from the imbalance between targeted and universal provision, and from the inappropriateness of Family Support as a major means of redistribution to families" (Shirley et al., 1997: 268). Childcare costs have been restricted to partial subsidization of the costs arising from participation in paid work or in training that is intended to lead into paid work. Eligibility is determined by income testing. Access has been narrowed to work and training participation from the wider social and educational goals that previously also provided grounds for access and financial support.

## Performance and Outcomes

The impact of these policies has been ambivalent. In the first instance, the subsidized housing market, through the development of the Accommodation Supplement, has produced results that are totally contradictory to those that the state explicitly sought. Most particularly, the cost to the state has increased dramatically and continues to do so beyond initial estimates (Murphy, 1999).

The most recent data demonstrate that the number of Accommodation Supplement recipients almost doubled between 1993 and 1998 (New Zealand, Work and Income New Zealand, 1999). Furthermore, the outcome has been negative for those directly affected by the switch to the market from income-related rentals. The results of these changes on the lives of those living in state housing are well demonstrated in a range of studies (Gunby, 1996; New Zealand Council of Christian Social Services and the Salvation Army, 1994). These studies clearly indicate that the move to market rentals and the accompanying introduction of the Accommodation Supplement have dramatically increased housing costs for low-income recipients. In a similar vein, Waldegrave et al. (1996) have estimated that housing costs make up 63 percent of the poverty gap.

The introduction of wage subsidization has failed to meet one of the critical expected outcomes, namely the reduction of levels of poverty among families, including families in paid work (Easton, 1995; Easton, 1997). Indeed, the subsidization programs have been extended in recent years with the introduction of Independent Family Tax Credit (IFTC) in 1998. The process of subsidized markets is replete with contradictions, inconsistencies and complexities, with take up rates for some programs being as low as 60 percent in the case of the accommodation supplement and 75 to 80 percent in the case of participants for Family Support (Boston and St. John, 1999).

## ACCIDENT COMPENSATION

### Historical Resume

A form of accident compensation for workers was first introduced under the 1900 Workers Compensation Act. Until 1972, compensation for loss of income as a result of an accident came either through this legislation or from pursuing legal action for damages against an employer or the driver of another motor vehicle. For those who did not qualify under either ground, sickness or invalidity benefits became their only source of income. In 1972, this process was changed totally, following the Report of the 1967 Royal Commission of Inquiry into Workers Compensation. The 1972 Accident Compensation Act ushered in a no-fault process, eliminating legal action completely. The accident victims had to give up their right to litigate to gain compensation set at 80 percent of income at the time of the accident, subject to a generous earnings ceiling (for a discussion of the political processes surrounding this transition, see O'Brien, 1983; Palmer, 1979).

The most significant changes took place in 1992, with the creation of the Accident Compensation and Rehabilitation Insurance Corporation (ACRIC) to replace the former Accident Compensation Corporation. In brief, lump-sum entitlements have been abolished, the employer contributions now only cover work accidents, employee contribution has been introduced for non-work accidents, the Appeal Authority has been abolished (appeals were to be heard in the Courts) and work-capacity assessment has been introduced.

While the no-fault principle remains formally in place, the courts' increasing use of punitive fines payable to industrial accident victims and the imposition of employer contributions suggests that in practice at least there have been substantial inroads into this principle. There have also been significant increases in the motor vehicle levy over time. And employers only cover work-related accidents. The organizational structure has also undergone significant changes. Initially, accident compensation operated as a de facto government department, but the administrative structure was corporatized in the public sector changes of the late 1980s and early 1990s. (For an overview and chronology of many of the key changes, see St. John, 1999a). As with sickness and invalid's benefit, recent years have seen significant development of work assessment tests for those receiving accident compensation, tests that have served to reduce eligibility. However, the most dramatic change is still to come with accident compensation coverage being opened up to competition in July 1999.

### As a Form of Renewed Marketization

The changes in provision for compensation as a result of an accident, particularly a work-related accident might be best described as a renewed market. The early forms of workers compensation were provided primarily through insurance companies and tort claims, a system that remained in place until the 1972 Accident Compensation Act. That legislation shifted the coverage to the state entirely with employer and employee contributions being paid to a state entity. Although the specific form of organization has changed over the intervening years, as has the specific benefit coverage and the basis of contributions, coverage has been a state responsibility since 1972. However, following the July 1999 changes, employers will have a choice of providers: insurance firms, or some other comparable organization, or the newly created state-owned enterprises. Insurance companies are currently actively promoting themselves as potential providers of competitively priced accident insurance coverage.

This process is characterized as a "renewed market" because the framework has changed from private market provision initially, to exclusive state provision, and to joint (competitive) public-private provision, with income loss caused by motor vehicle accidents remaining with the former state agency, ACRIC. The self-employed are also able to obtain accident compensation coverage through this agency. Unlike the two areas discussed previously, the change here has been driven almost entirely by ideological considerations combined with powerful economic interests. Ideology is reflected in the slogan "Free to Choose," used on the cover of the brochure sent to employers describing the changes. The choice, of course, belongs with the employer, not with employees. Business interests have, of course, increasingly identified potential financial advantages in being able to provide such mandatory accident insurance coverage.

## Performance and Outcomes

For some workers and their employers, the cost of accident compensation after the introduction of public-private (competitive) provision in 1999 may fall as a result of the re-establishment of the market. These reductions are likely to arise from such factors as lower insurance premiums as private carriers seek a competitive advantage in the re-created market by differentiating between high- and low-risk occupations. Similarly, while there is in the establishment legislation a requirement that coverage must be the same as that provided under the state program, it seems likely over time that there will be increased pressures for changes in this provision. Cost considerations and competitive advantage are likely to be major considerations in generating and shaping such pressures. The powerful political forces that pressed for and secured the creation of this renewed market will quickly move toward contesting the extent of compulsory cover.

Should this reduced coverage requirement materialize, then those who rely on some form of accident compensation to provide them with income support will also find themselves receiving both less income and insurance protection over a narrower range of accident risks. In this context, pressure for a return to tort rights (currently regularly pressed for by unions because of the deterioration in accident compensation resulting from changes since 1991) is also highly likely.

There is no evidence that the renewed market will generate a cheaper accident compensation system overall. Indeed the evidence is that administration costs as a percentage of total expenditure are lower in the public sector than in a private sector (St. John, 1999a). There are some significant indicators suggesting that this renewed market will result in uneven coverage, reduced entitlements and privatization of what has over the last 27 years been an integral part of the social rights of citizenship in New Zealand.

## CONCLUDING REFLECTIONS

This review of the development of marketization of social security in New Zealand highlights three significant dimensions that warrant more explicit attention. These are

- the multi-faceted nature of marketization,
- the ideological dimensions of the changing relationships between the market and the state, and
- the relationship between marketization and poverty.

It is common in both daily discourse and in academic treatises to treat "the market" as an undifferentiated entity with universalized properties and characteristics. This chapter has highlighted both the falsity of such an argument and the need for careful attention to the subtle shades and nuances contained within the concept of "marketization," particularly when applied to social security. The advantages of attending to these shades and nuances are that a more differentiated understanding, a more comprehensive analysis and better focused interventions become possible than can occur if a blunt universalist definition and description is used. "Political," "failed," "renewed" and "subsidized" marketization demonstrates the multiple hues when we examine the concept of the marketization. Certainly, marketization has a common central feature, namely the use of the marketplace as a delivery mechanism. However, if attention is confined to that central feature, many key elements will be missed.

Second, throughout any exploration of social security marketization run some very important ideological threads that vary through the different forms of marketization. The variations involve ideological contestations around the state, private provision, family responsibility and the role of private charity. Reflection on the New Zealand experience illustrates that this ideological contestation cannot be regarded as settled at any particular historical conjuncture. Rather, the contestation persists, and the outcome at any point will reflect the balance of forces at that time, a balance that will be different for different components of social security. Witness, for example, the contrast set out here between the retirement pensions and accident compensation. Having noted the different forms of contestation, it is pertinent to make one obvious point, namely that the more active the role of the state, the greater the protection of the most vulnerable.

Nowhere is the significance of the role of the state in that ideological contestation more critically illustrated than when assessing the implications of forms of marketization for poverty. This is most clearly illustrated in the development of the political market in social assistance. For example, the 1938 Social Security Act explicitly established a social minimum below which no one should fall. Reflecting this, the 1972 Royal Commission on Social Security argued that provision should reinforce social cohesion and reflect community living standards. The form of political market pursued over the last decade clearly resulted in substantial increases in poverty, both in numbers and in depth. There is more poverty, and those in poverty are further below the poverty line (Easton, 1995; Krishnan, 1995; Waldegrave et al., 1996). It is no accident that the political market over the last decade has been accompanied by significant increase in the use of such benefits as Special Benefits and the Special Needs Grants. Steps have been taken to restrict eligibility for both these benefits, including tightening eligibility criteria and the introduction of customized individual services, that enable beneficiaries to be counseled on money management and that permit closer monitoring of eligibility to take place minimizing fraud (New Zealand, Income Support Service, 1998).

Again, if we look at the failed market in retirement pensions, the more affluent elderly have been the most vociferous in protecting their financial position while the position of the poorest elderly has deteriorated with the very real possibility of intensified poverty, particularly among those with significant housing costs. Clearly this retrenchment of state provision means greater poverty. As with social assistance, development of state provision was significant in reducing levels of poverty among the elderly, both in the 1930s and in the 1970s. The failed market of the last decade has provided some continued protection. Sustaining that protection is, however, less certain, although the political power of the elderly will be a significant consideration in future marketization forms.

One critical thread weaves through this review, namely the ways in which politics and ideology find particular confluences in shaping the form of marketization. We have seen the significance of this in the renewed market in accident compensation, to a lesser extent in the subsidized market in housing, in the failed market in superannuation and in the political market in social assistance. This suggests that, although appearing rather bleak in the immediate future, the precise future forms of marketization of social security will also be the product of political and ideological contests. The critical question, as always in social security, is the extent to which those forms will meet the needs and aspirations of the poor.

## REFERENCES

Alcock, P. 1997. *Understanding Poverty*. Basingstoke: Macmillan.

Baker, M. 1997. Restructuring Welfare States: Ideology and Policies for Low-Income Mothers. *Social Policy Journal of New Zealand* 8: 37–48.

Baldwin, S. and Falkingham, J. (eds.). 1994. *Social Security and Social Change*. Hemel Hempstead: Harvester Wheatsheaf.

Birch, W. 1996. *Tax Reduction and Social Policy Programme. Details*. Wellington: GP Print.

Bolger, J., Richardson, R. and Birch, W. 1990. *Economic and Social Initiative—December 1990. Statements to the House of Representatives*.

Booth, C. 1977. The National Party's 1975 Superannuation Policy. In Palmer, G. (ed.), *The Welfare State Today*. Wellington: Fourth Estate Books.

Boston, J. and St. John, S. 1999. Targeting versus Universality: Social Assistance for All or Just for the Poor? In Boston, J., Dalziel, P. and St. John, S. (eds.), *Redesigning the Welfare State in New Zealand*. Auckland: Oxford University Press.

Castles, F. 1985. *The Working Class and Welfare: Reflections on the Political Development of the Welfare State in Australia and New Zealand*. Sydney: Allen and Unwin/Port Nicholson Press.

Cheyne, C., O'Brien, M. and Belgrave, M. 1997. *Social Policy in Aotearoa New Zealand: A Critical Introduction*. Auckland: Oxford University Press.

Easton, B. 1980. *Social Policy and the Welfare State in New Zealand*. Sydney: George Allen and Unwin.

Easton, B. 1981. *Pragmatism and Progress. Social Security in the Seventies*. Christchurch: University of Canterbury.

Easton, B. 1995. Poverty in New Zealand: 1981–1993. *New Zealand Sociology* 10 (2): 181–213.

Easton, B. 1997. *The Commercialisation of New Zealand.* Auckland: Auckland University Press.
Else, A. and St. John, S. 1998. *A Super Future?* Auckland: Tandem Press.
Gunby, J. 1996. *Housing the Hungry: The Third Report.* Wellington: New Zealand Council of Christian Social Services and the Salvation Army.
Handler, J. and Hasenfeld, Y. 1991. *The Moral Construction of Poverty: Welfare Reform in America.* Thousand Oaks, CA: Sage.
Hanson, E. 1980. *The Politics of Social Security: The 1938 Act and Some Later Developments.* Auckland: Auckland University Press, Oxford University Press.
Hutton, W. 1996. *The State We're In.* London: Vintage.
Krishnan, V. 1995. Modest but Adequate: An Appraisal of Changing Household Income Circumstances in New Zealand. *Social Policy Journal of New Zealand* 4: 76–97.
Mahar, C. 1984. Government Housing Policy: The Impact on Consumers. In Wilkes, C. and Shirley, I. (eds.), *In The Public Interest.* Auckland: Benton Ross.
McClure, M. 1998. *A Civilised Community.* Auckland: Auckland University Press.
Mead, L. M. 1997. Raising Work Levels among the Poor. *Social Policy Journal of New Zealand* 8: 1–28.
Murphy, L. 1999. Housing Policy. In Boston, J., Dalziel, P. and St. John, S. (eds.), *Redesigning the Welfare State in New Zealand.* Auckland: Oxford University Press.
New Zealand Council of Christian Social Services and the Salvation Army. 1994. *Housing the Hungry.* Wellington: New Zealand Council of Christian Social Services and the Salvation Army.
New Zealand, Department of Social Welfare. 1996. *Social Welfare in New Zealand. Strategic Directions.* Wellington: Department of Social Welfare.
New Zealand, Department of Social Welfare. 1999. *Statistics Report for the Year Ending 1998.* Wellington: Department of Social Welfare.
New Zealand, Income Support Service. 1998. *Quarterly Review of Benefit Trends, Period Ended 30 June 1998.* Wellington: Income Support Service.
New Zealand, Royal Commission on Social Policy. 1988. *The April Report. Report of the Royal Commission on Social Policy.* Wellington: Royal Commission on Social Policy.
New Zealand, Statistics New Zealand. 1998a. *Hot off the Press: Incomes of Persons.* Wellington: Statistics New Zealand.
New Zealand, Statistics New Zealand. 1998b. *New Zealand Now: Housing.* Wellington: Housing New Zealand.
New Zealand, Statistics New Zealand. 1999. *New Zealand Now: Incomes.* Wellington: Statistics New Zealand.
New Zealand, Work and Income New Zealand. 1999. *Quarterly Customer Profile, December 1998.* Wellington: Work and Income New Zealand.
O'Brien, M. 1983. Accident Compensation: Whose Interests? In Wilkes, C. (ed.), *Working Papers on the State, Volume 1.* Palmerston North: Massey University.
O'Brien, M. 1991. *The Problem of Poverty: Ideology, the State and the 1972 Royal Commission on Social Security.* Unpublished Ph.D. Thesis, Massey University, New Zealand.
O'Brien, M. and Briar, C. (eds.). 1997. *Beyond Poverty.* Auckland: Auckland Unemployed Workers Rights Centre.

O'Brien, M. and Wilkes, C. 1993. *The Tragedy of the Market*. Palmerston North: Dunmore Press.
Palmer, G. 1979. *Compensation for Incapacity: A Study of Law and Social Change in New Zealand and Australia*. Wellington: Oxford University Press.
Periodic Report Group. 1997. *Retirement Income Report: A Review of the Current Framework*. Wellington: GP Print.
Richardson, R. 1995. *Making a Difference*. Christchurch: Shoal Bay Press.
Rogers, J. 1997. Designing Work-Focused Welfare Replacement Programmes. *Social Policy Journal of New Zealand* 8: 67–77.
Shipley, J. 1991. *Social Assistance. Welfare That Works*. Wellington: GP Print.
Shirley, I., Koopman-Boyden, P., Pool, I. and St. John, S. 1997. Family Change and Family Policies: New Zealand. In Kammerman, S. and Kahn, A. (eds.), *Family Change and Family Policy in Great Britain: Canada, New Zealand and the United States*. Oxford: Clarendon Press.
Simpson, T. 1990. *The Sugarbag Years*. Auckland: Penguin.
St. John, S. 1999a. Accident Compensation in New Zealand: A Fairer Scheme? In Boston, J., Dalziel, P. and St. John, S. (eds.), *Redesigning the Welfare State in New Zealand: Problems, Policies, Prospects*. Auckland: Oxford University Press.
St. John, S. 1999b. Superannuation in the 1990s: Where Angels Fear to Tread? In Boston, J., Dalziel, P. and St. John, S. (eds.), *Redesigning the Welfare State in New Zealand: Problems, Policies, Prospects*. Auckland: Oxford University Press.
Sutch, W. 1966. *The Quest for Security in New Zealand: 1840 to 1966*. Wellington: Oxford University Press.
Sutch, W. 1969. *Poverty and Progress in New Zealand*. Wellington: A. H. & A. W. Reed.
Taylor-Gooby, P. 1985. *Public Opinion, Ideology and State Welfare*. London: Routledge and Kegan Paul.
Waldegrave, C., Stephens, R. and Frater, P. 1996. Most Recent Findings in the New Zealand Poverty Measurement Project. *Social Work Review* 8 (3): 22–24.

*Chapter 8*

# "Almost 12 People an Hour Leaving Welfare": The Marketization of Welfare in Ontario and the Decline of the Public Good

## Hugh Shewell

### INTRODUCTION

Since the mid-to-late 1970s, Canada, as elsewhere, has witnessed a steady decline in the idea of collective responsibility for welfare. The interventionist role of the state has been undermined by the pressures of global capitalism, buttressed by the attack of a variety of vested interests lobbies, such as the right-wing think tanks (notably, the Howe and Fraser Institutes, the Business Council on National Issues, the Canadian Manufacturers Association, and the Canadian Federation of Independent Business) and of the New Right, through its established parties and organizations (notably, the National Citizens Coalition and the Canadian Taxpayers Association). This weakening of collective state responsibility has been evidenced most notably by the incremental dismantling of Canada's, and hence of Ontario's, minimalist welfare state (Guest, 1997; Jeffrey, 1999; Pulkingham and Ternowetsky, 1999). What factors led to and continue to drive this relentless process? To answer this question, it is necessary first to understand Canadian social welfare in its more recent historical and ideological contexts.

### THE BREAKDOWN OF THE WELFARE STATE CONSENSUS

Although the international energy crisis and the subsequent economic and fiscal problems of the mid-1970s formed the basis for the end of the welfare state consensus in Canada, it was the 1980s that brought its final end. Several factors directly contributed to its demise in this period. As the Soviet Union struggled to survive, socialism lost credibility and, in this context, the fiscal crisis of the 1970s gave way to the "new reality" of the global economy and the rapid internationalization of capital (Leonard, 1997; Teeple, 1995). Computer technology hastened the ability of capital to move instantaneously throughout the world, and corporations sought greater freedom from national constraints, including the burdens they felt had been imposed by the welfare state (Leonard, 1997). Teeple describes the emerging global economy as being characterized by "such a high degree of productive capacity and interlocking trade and investment that it cannot be said to have a national home" (1995: 55). According to Teeple (1995: 55), capital, in this global environment, requires "freedom" from national controls or intervention and ultimately has no national allegiance. "The global economy," he writes, "produces its own demands that are distinct from those of the national economy."

The movement toward a global, capitalist economy has had, and continues to have, a profound effect on Canada and its welfare state apparatus. Keynesian economics, conceived primarily for the regulation of national economies and the protection of their capital and labor, were ill adapted for this rapid change and were discredited and largely abandoned after 1975 (Wolfe, 1989). Also, in 1982, two events fundamentally altered the future nature of Canadian society. The first was the strengthening of Canada's sense of independence by the Trudeau government's repatriation of the British North America Act (1867) from England and renaming it the Constitution Act (1982). Entrenched in the new constitution was a Charter of Rights and Freedoms. The charter essentially was intended to protect the individual civil and political rights of all Canadian citizens. While this was laudable in one respect, in retrospect it might be argued that the Charter has contributed to a greater emphasis on liberal individualism and individual rather than social justice in Canada (Joel, 1999).

These new forces hastened the move toward a free trade agreement with the United States, recommended by many "for the long-term good of the Canadian economy" (Guest, 1997: 219). The Royal Commission on the Economic Union and Development Prospects for Canada (RCEUDPC), which recommended in 1985 that Canada should seek a free trade agreement with the United States, was critical of the unemployment insurance system. The Commission alleged that it unduly interfered in the labor market and that eligibility requirements were too lenient and required "tightening." According to Guest (1997: 219), the RCEUDPC may also have wished to prepare Canadians for the low wages and underemployment to follow by suggesting "a form of minimal guaranteed income . . . financed by amalgamating a major portion of the social security network with certain personal tax exemptions and credits."

The timing of the Royal Commission's report in 1985 was auspicious: a new Conservative government under Prime Minister Brian Mulroney had been swept to power in 1984. While soft-pedalling on both the rhetoric of Thatcherism in Britain and Reaganomics in the United States, Mulroney pressed ahead with transforming the Canadian welfare state into what Chomsky (1996) refers to as the "nanny state." Although Mulroney had never campaigned on free trade, the report of the Commission played perfectly into his governing philosophy, which emphasized the application of market principles to government (Campbell and Christian, 1996). The new Conservative government had, according to Campbell and Christian (1996: 53), three broad goals:

First, it hoped to slim the state by reducing the budget deficit and minimizing the ways in which government intervened in the economy and in society. Second, it aimed to privatize much of the business activity of government by selling off state assets and contracting out services to private contractors. Third, it sought to restructure government along market lines.

Free trade with the United States offered the government the vehicle by which to achieve these objectives because it meant that Canada would have to negotiate a level playing field with its dominant neighbor, a nation intent on applying market principles and accustomed to market freedom. By 1988, Canada had entered into a free trade agreement with the United States, and protectionism, which, since confederation, had characterized Canadian economic policy and had played a major influence in promoting policy for the public good, was officially dead.

There was now a readiness for a coalescence of the demands of provincial business interests with the federal government's agenda to position Canada in the global economy. Mulroney's vision of Canada included the devolution of powers to the provinces so that they would feel less encumbered by central government interference and thus freer to pursue their economic interests. In 1987, the federal government and the ten provinces negotiated the Meech Lake Accord, which would have brought Québec into the constitutional fold (as it is not a signatory to the Constitution Act), and which accorded the provinces the right to withdraw from federally cost-shared social programs with full financial compensation. In effect this would have meant the elimination of national standards and the certain demise of the already shaky welfare state (Guest, 1997). The Accord was abandoned in 1990 when, after considerable public opposition, it failed to gain the approval of every provincial legislature.

What could not be accomplished by constitutional means could be achieved by administrative arrangements. Consequently, in 1990, the Conservative government began to place spending limits on the amounts it would cost-share with the richest provinces under Canada Assistance Plan 1966 (CAP) (Guest, 1997). In effect, this cap on CAP signaled an attack on Canada's poorest and most vulnerable populations and reduced the capacity and the will of the provinces to meet their needs. It is important to understand this action by the Mulroney government in the context of the Free Trade Agreement with the United States (FTA). The cap on CAP, together with other decisions taken by his government (namely not to implement the guaranteed income recommended by the 1985 Royal Commission, to restrict unemployment insurance and to terminate the provision of universal family allowances) was intended to eliminate the possibility that Canada's social programs might be viewed by the Americans as an unfair labor subsidy under the terms of the FTA.

Distrusted by the Canadian electorate, Mulroney's Conservatives were defeated in 1993 by the Liberals under Jean Chrétien. Although in opposition the Liberals had opposed free trade and the many anti-welfare measures taken by the Conservatives, once in office they revealed themselves as business liberals, determined to eliminate Canada's deficit quickly and dramatically and to strengthen Canada's position in the global marketplace. The Liberals were apologetic but firm in arguing that Canada had to be competitive in a world driven by market forces. The Radical Right, represented by the western province-based Reform Party, moved the Chrétien Liberals further to the right. The federal Liberals slashed government spending. They introduced extensive restrictions to unemployment insurance and, in a related move, reached agreement with the provinces further to devolve federal powers including employment and training programs. Of special importance, the Liberals rescinded the Canada Assistance Plan in 1995 and replaced it with the Canada Health and Social Transfer (CHST) (Campbell and Christian, 1996; Guest, 1997).

Under the CHST, the federal government now transfers funds in block to the provinces for health, post-secondary education, and welfare. National standards have been abandoned and the federal government has placed ceilings on the amounts to be transferred. An adverse effect of the CHST has been that, at the provincial level, it places social welfare in direct competition with health and education for scarce funds at a time when all three program areas have suffered prolonged budget cuts (Guest, 1997). Describing the CHST essentially as the final nail in the coffin of a national welfare state, Pulkingham and Ternowetsky (1999: 84) further argue that it "entrenches a decentralized welfare state and ushers in an era of declining and uneven citizenship rights, disintegrating safety-net provisions and increased insecurity for the most vulnerable groups, such as women, children, the poor and the unemployed." Just as important, the CHST opened the door for the provinces to institute "work-for-welfare."

The rise of neoliberalism, the return to a classical, decentralized model of the federal state, the implementation of free trade and the surrender to the "new reality" of the global economy have transformed the ideas of nation and community in Canada (Simeon, 1991). Indeed, the age of modernism, of universality and optimism, would appear to have collapsed (Leonard, 1997). Once most Canadians, while respecting regional differences, shared a sense of collective welfare and the national, public good. Now, increasingly, regionalism has become dominant, and Canadians have become consumed by the ethos of self-interest and the attitude exemplified by "I'm alright Jack." The poverty gap in Canada is widening, and there is an erosion of a distinct middle class (Shewell, 1998). Yalnizan (1998) revealed that, in 1973, for example, the richest families in Canada made, on average, 21 times more than the poorest but, by 1996, that disparity had increased fifteen-fold to 314 times that of the poorest. Similarly, during the same period, the proportion of the population who were very poor or very rich grew substantially (by about 6 and 8 percent respectively) while those clustered in the middle income ranges shrank by about 16 percent (Yalnizan, 1998). The effects of this, she argues, are calamitous. The less common our interests and experiences, the more likely it will be that one segment of society, the dominant class, will simply not understand, be interested in or have any sympathy for the needs of the other, more vulnerable classes, notably the working and non-working poor. It is precisely upon this indifference that the Conservative government of Ontario has crafted its transformation of social welfare policy.

## THE MARKETIZATION OF WELFARE IN ONTARIO

Within the context of these global, national and provincial forces, Ontario, Canada's largest and richest province, has sought to marketize its welfare or social assistance programs. Ontario has recently been transformed from a patriarchal, provincial state, one that is concerned with national unity and is strongly infused with Tory traditions of moral and social order, into a neoliberal society, determined, on the one hand, to minimize the state's presence in the marketplace but, on the other hand, to interfere in ways to promote the economy or to support market values. Although the forces for this transformation were already felt prior to 1995, it was directly precipitated by the election in that year of the Conservative Party which called for a "Commonsense Revolution," a plan to restore the province's fiscal stability and to restructure its public institutions, including health, education and welfare (Courchene and Telmer, 1998).

### Ontario: The Canadian Heartland

To understand the Commonsense Revolution (CSR) it is helpful to understand Ontario's historical dominance within Canadian confederation and the events leading up to the 1995 provincial election. With a population of 11 million—over one-third of Canada's entire population—the province geographically occupies the east–west core of the country. Courchene and Telmer (1998) describe Ontario as having been the heartland, the pre-eminent province of the nation for decades after the Second World War. So powerful was the province in this period that Canada's interests were Ontario's, and Ontario's Canada's, and everyone, including the federal government, understood this salient fact. By comparison with the other provinces, Ontario did not think of itself as a region of the country: it was the country (Courchene and Telmer, 1998: 3).

Ontario enjoyed this dominant position until the mid-1970s. The provincial economy flourished under Keynesianism and protective tariffs. Unemployment was as low as 2.3 percent, the labor force skilled, stable and prosperous. In terms of social assistance Ontario maintained a moralistic, intrusive approach, especially toward lone mothers and the employable unemployed. For the latter group it continually favored work-for-welfare but was dissuaded by senior Ottawa bureaucrats and the threat of a labor backlash (Struthers, 1994). Ontario deferred to Ottawa—though not always happily—on national welfare issues because national welfare measures were directed at the maintenance and reproduction of the labor force, and that directly benefited the province. In addition, Ontario took pride in its status as nation-builder and could afford to share its affluence with the other provinces (Courchene and Telmer, 1998).

## The Demise of the Heartland, 1973–1995

The 1970s and early 1980s were years of significant change for Ontario and the ruling Conservative Party. The erosion of the welfare state consensus was experienced most dramatically in Ontario. Importantly, the international energy crisis was instrumental in realigning the economic power base in Canada such that the energy-producing provinces asserted a much greater influence over national issues than in the past. While Ontario remained dominant, it was not as dominant. Critically, Ontario continued to rely on Ottawa to protect its interests and to secure cheap sources of energy for its enormous industrial base. This Ottawa-Ontario alignment pitted Ontario against the energy-producing provinces which, enjoying new leverage, lobbied for greater devolution of federal powers and for less federal intrusion into their affairs (Courchene and Telmer, 1998). This assertion of mainly western, provincial interests, combined with the rise of Québec separatism, undermined Ontario's economic dominance and role as nation-builder. Consequently, Ontario's economy faltered, the sustained success of post-war Keynesianism ended and Ottawa, in attempting simultaneously to accommodate the western provinces and to maintain its support of Ontario through the controversial National Energy Policy, effectively began to surrender its role as the senior government. Thus, the welfare state consensus began to disintegrate.

The 1980s and early 1990s proved central to what would unfold in Ontario by 1995. After 1982, while the rest of the country remained in recession, Ontario—and to some extent Québec—entered a period of economic growth (Courchene and Telmer, 1998). Importantly, for the first time since the Second World War, the rest of the country remained insulated from Ontario's prosperity. Nevertheless, while Ontario was economically strong, its political strength within the country declined. This was because significant political changes occurred at both the provincial and federal levels in Ontario and Ottawa.

The uninterrupted hegemony of the ruling Ontario Conservative Party gave way in 1985 to a form of coalition government by the Liberals and the New Democratic Party (NDP), a social democratic party. Nationally, in 1984, the Conservatives had been swept to power replacing the long reign of the Liberals. A sharp divide then emerged between Ottawa and Ontario regarding the economic and political directions of the country (Courchene and Telmer, 1998). The federal Conservatives, who had curried favor in Québec and the West in order to secure power, were not interested in maintaining the Ottawa-Ontario alliance and the continuation of a predominantly East–West economy. Instead, the Conservatives promoted regionalism and free trade with the United States. Their deep cuts to national social programs reflected this new, decentralized vision of Canada and the promotion of individual and corporate enterprise. In contrast, Ontario under Liberal minority (1985–1987) and majority governments (1987–1990) opposed free trade and pursued policies of welfare liberalism in defiance of Ottawa's new directions. Remarkably, Ontario enriched and expanded its social programs, especially social assistance (Moscovitch, 1997; Courchene and Telmer, 1998).

Social assistance benefits had not increased substantially in Ontario since the introduction in 1966 of the Canada Assistance Plan, which contributed to a significant rise in the province's overall welfare spending (Struthers, 1994). Nevertheless, Ontario, despite its enormous postwar affluence, remained very reluctant to engage in welfare reform and, relative to the rest of the population, recipients of social assistance remained not only well below the poverty line, but received allowances which were only 60 percent of basic adequacy (Struthers, 1994). When the Liberal/NDP coalition came to power, it was determined to address this long neglect of the poor—including the working poor—of Ontario. A Ministry of Community and Social Services (1998) report, *Transitions*, recommended substantial reforms to Ontario's antiquated and inadequate welfare system. Central to the report was the principle of restoring dignity and hope to Ontario's poorest citizens. This was to be accomplished by substantial increases in the assistance rates, comprehensive training and education programs, enriched and expanded child care, the extension of benefits to the working poor and streamlining the administration, which was divided between the provincial and municipal levels. As a result, Ontario raised social assistance rates on an annual basis, extended eligibility to the working poor and introduced the Steps Toward Employment Program (STEP) (Moscovitch, 1997). Courchene and Telmer (1998) assert that these reforms resulted in an increase in spending of at least C$420 million.

The Ontario reforms ran against the federal government's agenda and its stated determination to eliminate the country's debt and deficit. Courchene and Telmer (1998) argue that, in 1990, as a result of Liberal Ontario's "recklessness," Ottawa decided to place a ceiling on shareable costs under the CAP. Canada's richest provinces were held to annual increases of 5 percent over their actual 1989 welfare expenditures, effectively ending the 50/50 cost-sharing formula. The timing of the cap on CAP could not have been worse. By 1990, the effects of the FTA were being felt in Ontario's manufacturing sector. Companies—including American branch plants—shut down, relocated to, or consolidated their operations in the United States where labor and distribution costs were cheaper. Those that remained in Ontario restructured their operations. By 1994, over 660,000 jobs had been lost in Canada, most of them in Ontario (Barlow and Campbell, 1995). The onset of a recession in Ontario, mushrooming job loss and the impact of a more restrictive unemployment insurance program had one significant outcome: higher numbers in need of social assistance (Moscovitch, 1997).

In the provincial election of 1990, the New Democratic Party unexpectedly took power. The NDP government continued to oppose free trade and resisted Ottawa's attempts to decentralize powers, believing instead in a strong federal role in health and welfare and an economy based on a strong East–West union. Not surprisingly, the NDP continued both to reform social assistance and to increase monthly benefits (Moscovitch, 1997). By the end of 1990 and through to 1995, Ontario's social assistance benefits were the highest in the country at a time when its economy was spiraling downward (Courchene and Telmer, 1998). However, even with these continuous increases, the social assistance rates remained below the Canadian poverty line (National Council of Welfare, 1995). Although Courchene and Telmer (1998) ignore the social calamity that befell Ontario as unemployment soared to 13.1 percent, they are correct in stating that, at the time, the problem with its increased social spending and continued focus on protected East–West relations was that the federal government was withdrawing from its role in social programs and was fostering economic continentalism. The succession of the federal Liberal Party to power in 1992 merely accelerated this market agenda. The federal government, together with the United States, extended the Free Trade Agreement to Mexico under the North American Free Trade Agreement (NAFTA). In doing so, it slashed public spending and rescinded CAP, replacing it with the CHST.

The Ontario NDP government held on and succeeded in 1992 in introducing a moderate charter of social rights as part of a national referendum on constitutional reform. This was defeated and with it the political will of the country to maintain the semblance of a welfare state. Ontario's isolation from the social and economic directions of the country continued to grow even though geographically and economically it was ideally situated to become a strong, self-sufficient region. Nevertheless, there was something noble, if somewhat naïve, in the insistence of both the Ontario Liberal and NDP governments to restore to Canada a purposeful sense of national unity and economic independence.

### The Commonsense Revolution: Ontario Works and Work for Welfare

In its final days, the NDP was beleaguered by criticism from both the left and right. Ridiculed by the New Right, including its powerful media allies, for trying to tax and spend its way out of the recession, the NDP responded in 1993 with a plan to maintain public services while at the same time endeavoring to reduce costs by C$2 billion. Known as the Social Contract, all public service employees and their unions were obliged to renegotiate their contracts or face imposed salary cuts (Courchene and Telmer, 1998). For this they suffered a bitter labor backlash and a right-wing media which reveled in mocking the NDP for having betrayed its traditional ally. In the end, the NDP lost credibility with the public who came to see the government as fiscally incompetent and unable to manage the affairs of state.

In June 1995, a substantial portion of the electorate, believing Ontario to be near fiscal collapse, elected the Conservative Party led by Mike Harris and his "Commonsense Revolution." The "revolution," as described by both Courchene and Telmer (1998) and Clarke (1997), consisted of four broad objectives:

- the termination of the social agenda, which Harris believed had pre-occupied and imperiled Ontario;
- the restoration of fiscal responsibility, defined in business management terms and consisting of deep cuts to the provincial budget and a phased-in 30 percent reduction in provincial income tax;
- an economic agenda to make Ontario competitive in both the global economy and in north-south commerce, and realized by privatization, smaller, less intrusive government and the creation of 750,000 jobs; and
- the restructuring of Ontario's institutions, by reduction of public services, reduction of the power of public and private sector unions, promotion of individualism and the market and re-formulation and re-organization of the internal financing and delivery of public services such as health, education, welfare and municipal services.

It is in the context of these objectives that Ontario embarked on its restructuring of welfare institutions including the introduction of work-for-welfare—workfare—the first step in the marketization of social assistance in the province.

In 1995, Ontario had a welfare dependency rate of about 12 percent, representing 678,400 cases or 1.34 million recipients (including children) (Lightman, 1997; National Council of Welfare, 1998). No government, including the NDP, believed this to be an acceptable statistic. The question, however, was in how and where the problem was defined and located. Whereas both the previous Liberal and NDP governments had defined the problem mainly in structural, educational and labor market access terms, the Conservatives alleged that the social security system promoted indolence and complacence, that benefits were too high in relation to wages, that the system was rife with cheats and that the poor were largely responsible for their own misfortune (Lightman, 1997; Struthers, 1996). In the election campaign, the Conservatives promised to clean up the system and, offering "a hand up, not a hand-out," their platform stated "[w]e should prepare welfare recipients to return to the workforce by requiring all able-bodied recipients . . . either to work, or to be retrained in return for their benefits" (Progressive Conservative Party of Ontario, 1995). This was the call to workfare and the classic equation of welfare with the rules of exchange in the marketplace. In accordance with their promises, within four months of the election, the Harris government announced a 21.6 percent cut to social assistance rates—resulting in rates even further below the poverty line—and severely restricted eligibility for all categories of social assistance (Moscovitch, 1997). In addition, the government introduced a toll-free telephone "snitch" line, inviting citizens of Ontario to report suspected welfare fraud or, in effect, to turn in their relatives, friends and neighbors (Moscovitch, 1997). Finally, in June 1996, the government announced the introduction of work-for-welfare.

In order for workfare to be implemented efficiently the government was faced with restructuring the administration of the entire social security system. Until 1995, Ontario had a two-tier system of social assistance. Municipalities were delegated to administer short-term benefits under the General Welfare Assistance Act (1958) (GWA) to the employable: single adults, couples and two-parent families. The province, under the Family Benefits Act (1967) (FBA), administered all long-term benefits to the unemployable: disabled persons, the elderly and lone parents, mainly women. Compulsory work-for-welfare was first introduced in 1996 through Regulation 537, an amendment to the GWA regulations (Vosko, 1998). At first, only GWA recipients—those traditionally classified as employable—were required to participate. By 1998, however, GWA and FBA had been consolidated under the Ontario Works Act 1997, and work-for-welfare was fully incorporated in the new statute. Under the act the requirement to participate was extended to include all adult persons under the age of 65 years excepting disabled persons and lone parents with children under the age of 6 years—although these parents will likely be phased in at a later date. The extension of the work requirement to lone parents represented a continuing trend in Canada and the United Sates of reclassifying this group, for a long time regarded as unemployable, to employable (Clark, 1998) and has been interpreted as a direct attack on the rights of women.

Finally, in 1997, as part of the welfare re-structuring and in keeping with the objective of institutional reform, the government moved to consolidate and delegate the administration of all social assistance, save that of disabled persons, to the municipalities (Moscovitch, 1997). To do this, it retained the international firm, Andersen Consulting. Under the Common Purpose Procurement (CPP) program, Andersen Consulting was contracted to reconfigure the technology of the social security system and to find ways of reducing the numbers of persons on assistance for which they received a percentage of the savings so realized (Canada, Ontario, 1998a; Ontario Social Safety Network, 1998).

**The Workfare Principles**

The guiding principle of workfare in Ontario is the reduction of social assistance dependency and expenditure through "the shortest route to paid employment" (Gorlick and Brethour, 1998). Thus, the government believes that it has no real moral or legal obligations to support those in need and that recipients must accept any job, regardless of its personal suitability or wage level, if it renders them independent of state support. Having first established eligibility for social assistance, recipients who fall under the work-for-welfare requirement are assessed and referred to one of three program components: employment support, employment placement, or community participation. The workers and the recipients sign contracts of "agreement" on work-for-welfare plans that, according to Vosko (1998), signify that recipients had really agreed that they had no effective choice in the matter. Recipients are often required to participate in more than one component until employment is secured. For example, participants completing the community participation component may be referred to employment placement if they are then considered job ready.

The coercive nature of the program rests on failure to comply. Under the Ontario Works Act there are four types of non-compliance. They are the refusal to accept employment, referral to a placement or an offer of a placement, and the failure to make reasonable efforts to meet the requirements of the program. A finding of non-compliance will result in the termination or reduction of benefits or, in the case of a family with children, the termination of the adult's portion of the monthly benefit. A re-application for benefits will not be considered for three months following the first determination of non-compliance and for six months for each recurrence (Canada, Ontario, 1996).

**Evaluation: Facts or Fiction?**

The Ontario government has no evaluation mechanism for the work-for-welfare program and apparently has no plans to introduce one (Canada, Ontario, 1998a; Gorlick and Brethour, 1998). Consequently, the program's efficiency and effectiveness are rife with claims and counter-claims by both its proponents and opponents, rendering it an ideological battleground. The Provincial Auditor noted in its 1998 Annual Report to the Ontario legislature (Canada, Ontario, 1998a: 65) that "the Ministry [of Community and Social Services] did not have the necessary management information to assess the effectiveness of the Ontario Works Program. Instead, the information collected . . . measured program activity levels only, such as the number of registrants with completed participation agreements and the number of participants in Employment Support, Community Participation and Employment Placement activities."

A ploy of the Conservative government has been to announce "dramatic" statistics, such as the rate per hour at which people are leaving welfare, as though they are products on an assembly line, or the number of cases and/or beneficiaries by which the welfare rolls have decreased over one-month periods. For example, in March 1999, the Minister responsible for welfare claimed that almost 12 people an hour had been leaving welfare since 1995 (Canada, Ontario, 1999). As well, in October 1998, the same minister asserted that nearly 20,000 persons had left welfare the previous month and that since May 1998, the caseloads had declined by 8 percent and the number of beneficiaries by 7 percent (Canada, Ontario, 1998b). These numbers were all attributed to the success of workfare. Despite these claims there is no convincing evidence directly linking the decline in rolls to the program's effectiveness (Ontario Social Safety Network, 1998). To be sure, work-for-welfare has had an impact, but not likely the one the government so blatantly proclaims. The government has not accounted for those persons who found work on their own before their four month phase-in to Ontario Works occurred, nor has it attempted to factor in the usual, shorter length on assistance for various employable groups. In other words, employable persons who are on assistance for job-related reasons such as re-structuring, normally find employment quickly as the labor market improves. Thus, their time on assistance is usually relatively short (National Council of Welfare, 1998). This is the case in Ontario where, since 1995, and before the election of the Conservatives, the province had already begun to emerge from the recession.

Another problem with the government's claim to the success of work-for-welfare—but thought to be a part of its strategy—is that the rules of eligibility and the administrative surveillance while on assistance have either eliminated many recipients from the rolls or frightened and deterred many from applying. One consequence of the rates reduction in 1995 and the tightened rules of eligibility is an unprecedented rise in homelessness especially in Toronto (Canada, Toronto, 1999) and Ottawa. Thus, while welfare caseloads may be down, absolute destitution is rising.

Despite glossy government brochures filled with personal testimonies to the miracle of workfare, the results of preliminary, external evaluations by social planning councils in Ottawa and Toronto are more tempered. The Monitoring Ontario Works project of the Social Planning Council of Ottawa-Carleton conducted a limited, two-phase study of 75 participants in Ontario Works between May and November 1998. The study followed their experiences only in the community placement and employment support components since employment placement was not fully operational in Ottawa at the time. Although many felt that the experience had been positive, several reported "that they had not gained anything useful or relevant from their . . . placement" and, since it had not led to employment, most felt more discouraged than before they began (Monitoring Ontario Works, 1999: 25). Participants in the employment-support component recorded similar responses.

Of most interest in the Ottawa study was the nature of the labor market itself. Four of the study's 40 follow-up participants had, within the six-month time frame, been employed temporarily and then were obliged to re-apply for assistance. The study concluded "this may reflect the fact that it is normal for a percentage of individuals on assistance to cycle on and off the system, depending upon the availability of work. . . . Furthermore, a number of individuals . . . earn income from employment but are not able to get ahead . . . as a percentage of their earnings is deducted from their welfare cheque" (Monitoring Ontario Works, 1999: 26). Five participants who were off assistance were earning only slightly more than what they had received while on assistance.

The findings of the Ottawa and Toronto studies, as preliminary and limited as they are, tend to support the evaluation of other workfare programs, especially in the United States. There, the successful programs occurred in areas where there was rapid economic growth and low unemployment (Lightman, 1997). While Ottawa and Ontario generally are expanding rapidly, the growth is occurring in high technology, areas which require high educational and skill levels. Ontario's workfare program, with its objective to provide the shortest, least expensive route to employment, is simply not intended to prepare people for this sector of the economy. Instead, as Vosko's (1998) research suggests, workfare is deliberately intended to service the under-educated underclass, preparing them for an endless cycle of temporary, low-wage employment, usually in the service sector, relieved only by miserable spells on assistance before being coerced and shunted off again by the system. Workfare is the new unemployment insurance for the underclass and the final answer to the call for discipline in a marginal but necessary labor force (Chomsky, 1995 and 1996). In conclusions very similar to Ottawa's, the Toronto study (Canada, Toronto, 1999: 11), stated:

Our participants' hope that Ontario Works would help them get decent jobs is a fair one. Ironically, the Ontario Works focus on rapid labor force entry and dismissal of longer term training and education work best for those who need it least—relatively well-educated or highly skilled workers. But most Ontario Works participants do not fit into this category. Employment opportunities are rising for the well-educated, stagnant at best for high school graduates and falling for people with less than high school education. For people with limited education and skills, Ontario Works is simply a recipe for continued low wages and poverty.

## Problems and Issues: The Future of Social Assistance in Ontario

What is the real agenda underlying these reactive social measures in Ontario? Courchene and Telmer (1998) argue that, in response to global economic forces and Ottawa's devolution of powers, Ontario under the current Conservative regime has completely repositioned itself within the confederation. No longer is it the benevolent, heartland province, the senior leader of national unity and the economic engine of the country. Now it is poised to become a North American region state, virtually autonomous, and an economic engine unto itself. Simeon (1991), while implicitly despairing of this scenario, agrees that this is the apparent future of Canada, a fractured union of provinces more interested in their own destinies than that of the nation as a whole. Although he believes that there is still a role for the nation-state, he is not clear what that is. In the meantime, Ontario is certainly clear: Ottawa is an incidental player to a future which lies with strong economic and political ties to the United States and to the largely privatized world of global capitalism (Clarke, 1997; Courchene and Telmer, 1998; Jeffrey, 1999).

In this world there is no room for community or the social contract: that was tried and it was too expensive. In fact, there is no community, there are only self-interested individuals in the Lockean and utilitarian sense. Social programs are an imposition on, and a contradiction to, the state's ultimate responsibility of ensuring the conditions necessary for the unfettered pursuit of capitalism and the unrestricted accumulation of private wealth. How far should this notion reach into the functions of the state? According to a report of the Fraser Institute by

Law et al. (1997), it should reach very deep indeed. The Fraser Institute, in extolling the virtues of privatization, concluded:

> Hence, there is reason to believe that many public services and industries now run by the public sector could be transferred over to private enterprise ... the presence of competition ensures that private suppliers will produce as efficiently as possible. A private garbage-collection service that does not produce efficiently can be replaced when its contract expires; public garbage-collection services cannot be so easily replaced. That this same logic can be applied to many other industries and services yields the following general policy conclusion: governments should privatize all businesses and services that can be more efficiently produced by the private sector. This will free scarce resources for more productive uses in other sectors. (1997: 5)

The Fraser Institute appraised the Ontario Conservative government's record on privatization by reviewing its record against its stated objective to reduce the size and scope of the public sector. Noting that it still had some way to go, the Institute recommended the privatization of nine prominent Crown corporations and added,

> this is only the tip of a very large iceberg. ... [T]here is a multitude of smaller ... public sector services which could be contracted out to private suppliers. For instance, the chartered banks could take over the responsibility for issuing welfare cheques. (1997: 5)

The privatization of social assistance is clearly part of the Conservative agenda in Ontario. In this respect, the roles of Andersen Consulting, of private employment agencies, of private employment training firms and of private profit and non-profit work placements are crucial. First, the Ontario Works program, under the less visible and transparent guidance of Andersen Consulting, has been so constructed that the role of public administration is becoming irrelevant. In fact, it is increasingly obvious that the role of the public welfare administrator is rapidly becoming only that of a broker, assessing and referring persons to the appropriate private agency providing the service required for the shortest route possible to employment. It is entirely conceivable that even this role could simply be privatized or incorporated into one of the three components of Ontario Works. Within the headquarters of Ontario Works in Toronto, persons with business education and training are now the employees and intern students of choice over social workers. Who, of course, knows better than a person with such training the best and most cost-efficient methods of ridding the province of welfare dependents? Apparently not social workers, who are too closely linked with the history of the social contract—the costly experiment that failed.

Equally troubling is the system of incentives used for incorporating private sector involvement in the re-design and implementation of social assistance in Ontario—Andersen Consulting—and in the use of private, for-profit agencies in the three components of Ontario Works. Andersen Consulting was retained despite a known history in Canada and the United States of missed deadlines and fees and costs charged far in excess of original projections (Canada, Ontario, 1998a; Ontario Social Safety Network, 1998). In Ontario, Andersen Consulting was retained for fees and incentives totaling at least C$180 million, at least three times in excess of their original estimates (Canada, Ontario, 1998a). Under terms of their agreement, the Ontario government passes on to Andersen Consulting the savings realized by the reduction or termination of benefits to recipients under the former Family Benefits Act. Yet, according to the Ontario auditor, the C$15.5 million savings realized by March 31, 1998, really could not be attributed to Andersen Consulting. None of this seems to have bothered the fiscally conscious Ontario Conservatives, who have extended the contract by at least a year.

The concerns with the private sector involvement in the administration of social assistance in Ontario are both ethical and practical. It is an ethical concern that, because of the use of financial incentives, the recipients of benefits have been reduced to targets for the measurement and achievement of efficiency and have been made visible prey to the profitable success of contracted service agencies. This is true both in the Andersen Consulting contract and in the incentives offered to employment placement agencies. The structural and underclass issues that are the actual cause of their poverty are ignored and denied: they, the recipients, are the problem. Moreover, the use of the private sector to administer the basic means of survival to victims of its own inability to create enduring jobs with acceptable wages, adroitly removes the issue from public consciousness and responsibility and relocates it to where it can be carefully contained and managed (Lightman, 1997; Torjman, 1996).

A practical yet ethical issue is the degree of accountability of the private sector for the expenditure of public funds. Private corporations are not spending their own money on public enterprise; they are spending or charging public funds to make a profit. Yet their accountability is to their shareholders, not to the general public. In commenting on Andersen's bill of millions of dollars in excess of estimates for welfare automation, the Nebraska state auditor stated, "It's like pouring money down a deep dark hole" (cited in Ontario Social Safety Network, 1998). The meaning is clear: public auditors may only audit government (public) accounts. The accounts of Andersen Consulting, or any other private contractor, are not open to public scrutiny. In the case of Ontario, for example, the auditor could only surmise, based on government records and on what would have been the government's costs had it performed the same tasks, that Andersen Consulting's claim to have directly saved the government millions of dollars was a gross exaggeration (Canada, Ontario, 1998a). The issue of private sector accountability for the expenditure of public funds is studiously ignored by proponents of privatization. For example, Law et al. (1997) of the Fraser Institute, dwell entirely on the economics of privatization but naïvely or purposely avoid the real discussion of public accountability and the ethics of spending public money for what is the private not public good. In noting that much of the debate surrounding privatization is "severely misinformed," Law et al. (1997: 11) so absolutely adhere to the ideology of the market that they seem unable to think through to the ultimate outcome of their position: the tyranny of the private sector (Chomsky, 1996).

Finally, there is the real concern that the implementation of work-for-welfare in Ontario is intended to create a cheap, ready supply of temporary and casual labor with the intent, deliberate or otherwise, of depressing wages and/or supplanting unionized labor in the service sector and of displacing public sector employees as government services are privatized or abandoned (Lightman, 1997; National Union Research, 1997; Monitoring Ontario Works, 1999; Torjman, 1996; Vosko, 1998; Workfare Watch, 1996 and 1999). Certainly, the introduction of workfare must be understood not only as an attack by conservative and neoliberal ideologues on the poor and their suspect morality and work ethic (Struthers, 1996; Lightman, 1997), but also in the broader context, an attack on labor, women and minorities, which, thus far, has included the repeal of employment and pay equity legislation, the freezing of the minimum wage and the enactment of new labor legislation restricting collective bargaining rights and making union certification more difficult and, conversely, decertification easier (Kitchen, 1997; Watson, 1997). These measures are deliberately designed to bring Ontario more in line with limited labor rights in the United States and Mexico.

## CONCLUSION: WHAT IS TO BE DONE?

"Government," said John Dewey, "is the shadow cast by big business" (cited by Chomsky, 1996). By this statement Dewey meant, in part, that in liberal democracies the influence of large and powerful companies—today's corporations—pervades the inner working of government, demanding that their interests receive unquestioned priority, threatening the very structure of the democracy and rendering the democratic process useless. At a deeper level he also implied that society was in danger of subjection to private tyranny through its control of cultural mechanisms by which people could be subdued and made to believe in very distorted ideas of freedom. Chomsky (1996) takes this idea one step further: so adept is the corporate world in manipulating public opinion that we blame government for the ills of society.

Ralph (1997:15) repeats this sentiment in its Canadian context: "[W]e are at war, a worldwide class war of capital versus everyone else, a war which the bubble of the Keynesian welfare state temporarily obscured." She continues:

capital has forged a unified coalition of business, politics, and fundamentalist religion. It owns most of the national and local media. Through massive campaign donations it has bought the loyalty of the Liberal, Reform, and Tory parties, and through threats to withhold credit, it has coerced the reluctant support of the NDP. By its control of over $1.2 trillion in assets, members of the Business Council on National Issues can grant or withhold credit and job-creating investment. And through speculative manipulations, they have the power to disrupt the entire Canadian economy. As a result they wield enormous influence over all levels of government and public opinion. (p. 15)

The fiscal burdens associated with eliminating government debts and deficits, with restructuring the economy and with persistently high levels of unemployment have been shifted to the poor, the working and middle classes. Struthers (1996) observes that historically in Canada the demand for the imposition of compulsory labor on the unemployed has nearly always followed the existence of such conditions, especially when prevailing economic theory fails to explain their occurrence. Moreover, he argues, "workfare ... represents an attempt to shift the causal location of ... high unemployment away from structural changes within the economy and towards the inner moral character or values of the victims of these changes" (1996: 7).

Workfare is merely the late twentieth century's re-invention of the parish workhouse and entails the secularization of a so-called moral issue by turning it into a profoundly ideological project: the marketization of government. Workfare is not simply a solution for welfare dependency, it is a transformation of the idea of public good and public responsibility. According to Lightman:

workfare is ... one part of a broader political strategy to dismantle government, resulting in the elimination of public responsibility for social services, relentless downward pressure on the wages and employment rights of those still working for wages, and victimization of those sectors of society unfortunate enough to depend on social assistance for economic survival.... [T]he public obligation to assist those dependent on welfare ... disappeared from the Conservative agenda. (1997: 107)

If this were not the case, then the Ontario government would not have terminated, as it did, the evaluation units of nine successful pilot projects for opportunity planning. Through the use of community economic development strategies (CEDS), social assistance recipients partnered with the administering public agency in developing action plans for employment, which included the identification and removal of barriers to employment and complete support, not coercion into meaningful jobs. Though not without problems, CEDS offers a far more enlightened, constructive and socially beneficial approach to welfare dependency (Lalonde, 1997; Torjman, 1996).

Solutions offered through CEDS, however, probably will not suffice. Chomsky (1996) argues that democracy flourishes only in countries where labor movements are strong. Thus, if the privatization agenda of the Ontario government is to be halted and reversed, then, arguably, the labor movement in Ontario must become stronger and, in turn, re-commit itself to social reform and social justice. To counteract the strength of the business lobby, labor could form coalitions with the academic left, public agencies, community-based planning and watchdog organizations, co-operatives, credit unions and the new social and environmental movements. Such coalitions might then form the basis for raising awareness among Ontario's citizens of how and why the government's objectives undermine the democratic process and for developing strategies of resistance to these objectives. Finally, the labor movement and its allies could also advocate the entrenchment of a charter of social rights in the Canadian constitution, assuring all Canadians a meaningful level of social security and social justice, including access to meaningful participation in society. Although the enactment of these measures would not in themselves solve the broader issues surrounding global capitalism, they would form an important bulwark against those who, by engaging in the marketization of welfare and the privatization of the society, oppress the poor and working people.

## REFERENCES

Barlow, M. and Campbell, B. 1995. *Straight through the Heart: How the Liberals Abandoned the Just Society.* Toronto: HarperCollins.

Campbell, C. and Christian, W. 1996. *Parties, Leaders, and Ideologies in Canada.* Toronto: McGraw-Hill Ryerson.

Canada, Ontario. 1996. *Program Guidelines for Early Implementation of Ontario Works.* Ministry of Community and Social Services. Toronto: Queen's Printer for Ontario.

Canada, Ontario. 1998a. *1998 Annual Report of the Provincial Auditor to the Legislative Assembly.* Toronto: Queen's Printer for Ontario.

Canada, Ontario. 1998b. Almost 20,000 People Leave Welfare in a Single Month. News Release, Communications and Marketing Branch, October 7. Toronto: Ministry of Community and Social Services.

Canada, Ontario. 1999. Almost 12 People an Hour Leaving Welfare since June 1995. News Release, Communications and Marketing Branch, March 5. Toronto: Ministry of Community and Social Services.

Canada, Toronto. 1999. *Taking Responsibility for Homelessness: An Action Plan for Toronto.* Report of the Mayor's Homelessness Action Task Force. Toronto: City of Toronto.

Chomsky, N. 1995. *Class War: The Attack on Working People.* San Francisco: AK Press Audio.

Chomsky, N. 1996. *Class Warfare: Interviews with David Barsamian.* Monroe, ME: Common Courage Press.

Clark, C. 1998. *Canada's Income Security Programs.* Ottawa: Canadian Council on Social Development.

Clarke, T. 1997. The Transnational Corporate Agenda behind the Harris Regime. In Ralph, D., Régimbald, A. and St-Amand, N. (eds.), *Open for Business/Closed to People.* Halifax: Fernwood Publishing.

Courchene, T. J. with Telmer, C. R. 1998. *From Heartland to North American Region State: The Social, Fiscal and Federal Evolution of Ontario.* Monograph Series on Public Policy. Centre for Public Management, Faculty of Management. Toronto: University of Toronto Press.

Gorlick, C. and Brethour, G. 1998. *Welfare-to-Work Programs: A National Inventory.* Ottawa: Canadian Council on Social Development.

Guest, D. 1997. *The Emergence of Social Security in Canada* (3rd ed.). Vancouver: UBC Press.
Jeffrey, B. 1999. *Hard Right Turn: The New Face of Neo-Conservatism in Canada.* Toronto: HarperCollins.
Joel, S. 1999. Personal communication. York University, Toronto, July 6.
Kitchen, B. 1997. Common Sense Assaults on Families. In Ralph, D., Régimbald, A. and St.-Amand, N. (eds.), *Open for Business/Closed to People.* Halifax: Fernwood Publishing.
Lalonde, L. 1997. Tory Welfare Policies: A View from the Inside. In Ralph, D., Régimbald, A. and St.-Amand, N. (eds.), *Open for Business/Closed to People.* Halifax: Fernwood Publishing.
Law, M. T., Markowitz, H. I. and Mihlar, F. 1997. The Harris Government: A Mid-term Review. In *Critical Issues Bulletin.* Vancouver: The Fraser Institute.
Leonard, P. 1997. *Postmodern Welfare: Reconstructing an Emancipatory Project.* Thousand Oaks, CA: Sage Publications.
Lightman, E. S. 1997. It's Not a Walk in the Park: Workfare in Ontario. In Shragge, E. (ed.), *Workfare: Ideology for a New Under-Class.* Toronto: Garamond Press.
Monitoring Ontario Works Project. 1999. *Plain Speaking: Hope and Reality, Participants' Experience of Ontario Works.* Ottawa: Ottawa-Carleton Social Planning Council.
Moscovitch, A. 1997. Social Assistance in the New Ontario. In Ralph, D., Régimbald, A. and St.-Amand, N. (eds.), *Open for Business/Closed to People.* Halifax: Fernwood Publishing.
National Council of Welfare. 1995. *Welfare Incomes 1994.* Ottawa: Supply and Services Canada.
National Council of Welfare. 1998. *Profiles of Welfare: Myths and Realities.* Ottawa: Minister of Public Works and Government Services Canada.
National Union Research. 1997. *There's Nothing Fair about Workfare.* Ottawa: National Union of Public and General Employees.
Ontario, Ministry of Community and Social Services. 1988. *Transitions.* Report of the Social Assistance Review Committee, George Thomson, Chairman. Toronto: Queen's Printer for Ontario.
Ontario Social Safety Network. 1998. *Andersen and the Auditor.* Toronto: Workfare Watch Project.
Progressive Conservative Party of Ontario. 1995. *The Common Sense Revolution.* Toronto.
Pulkingham, J. and Ternowetsky, G. 1999. Neo-liberalism and Retrenchment: Employment, Universality, Safety-net Provisions and a Collapsing Canadian Welfare State. In Broad, D. and Antony, W. (eds.), *Citizens or Consumers? Social Policy in a Market Society.* Halifax: Fernwood Publishing.
Ralph, D. 1997. Introduction. In Ralph, D., Régimbald, A. and St.-Amand, N. (eds.), *Open for Business/Closed to People.* Halifax: Fernwood Publishing.
Shewell, H. 1998. Canada. In Dixon, J. and Macarov, D. (eds.), *Poverty: A Persistent Global Reality.* London: Routledge.
Simeon, R. 1991. Globalization and the Canadian Nation-State. In Doern, G. B. and Purchase, B. B. (eds.), *Canada at Risk? Canadian Public Policy in the 1990s.* Toronto: C. D. Howe Institute.

Struthers, J. 1994. *The Limits of Affluence: Welfare in Ontario, 1920–1970*. Toronto: University of Toronto Press.

Struthers, J. 1996. *Can Workfare Work? Reflections from History*. Ottawa: Caledon Institute of Social Policy.

Teeple, G. 1995. *Globalization and the Decline of Social Reform*. Toronto: Garamond Press.

Torjman, S. 1996. *Workfare: A Poor Law*. Ottawa: Caledon Institute of Social Policy.

Vosko, L. 1998. Workfare Temporaries: Workfare and the Rise of the Temporary Employment Relationship in Ontario. *Canadian Review of Social Policy* 42: 55–79.

Watson, S. 1997. Ontario Workers Take on the Common Sense Revolution. In Ralph, D., Régimbald, A. and St.-Amand, N. (eds.), *Open for Business/Closed to People*. Halifax: Fernwood Publishing.

Wolfe, D. 1989. The Canadian State in Comparative Perspective. *Canadian Review of Sociology and Anthropology* 26 (1): 95–126.

Workfare Watch. 1996. *Workfare Watch Bulletin*. 1 (2). Toronto: Ontario Social Safety Network and the Social Planning Council of Metropolitan Toronto.

Workfare Watch. 1999. *Broken Promises: Welfare Reform in Ontario*. Toronto: Community Social Planning Council of Toronto.

Yalnizan, A. 1998. *The Growing Gap: A Report on Growing Inequality between the Rich and Poor in Canada*. Toronto: Centre for Social Justice.

*Chapter 9*

# Why Privatization Is Not on the United States' Social Security Policy Agenda

## Max J. Skidmore

**INTRODUCTION**

The United States' policy agenda for its long-term social security contingency programs—old age, survivors' and disability insurance (collectively, in popular usage, Social Security, or OASDI) and health benefits for the aged (Medicare)—does not include privatization, nor is it likely to do so. There is consistent and strong support for the employment-related, contributory, public provision approach. There is, however, a powerful and well-financed campaign to encourage privatization. A number of organizations seek to replace Social Security with mandatory, private, defined-contribution plans—individual accounts—sometimes supplemented with a minimal or residualist government program for the needy. Others advocate private plans that at first would supplement and then gradually replace social insurance. There is also a related movement to secure changes that in themselves would not make the system private but would so revise the nature of the system that privatization would be the likely ultimate result.

Journalists in both print and electronic media have treated press releases from the special interest groups behind the campaigns as though they were legitimate news items. One of the most evident examples of this (although far from the only one) is the unquestioning coverage afforded the Concord Coalition—a conservative organization with an explicitly anti–Social Security agenda—by the *Kansas City Star*, a powerful Midwestern newspaper with regional influence. *The Star* is unusual not only in the extent to which it has made the campaign of a special interest group its own but also in that its subservience toward that group has been thoroughly documented in a scholarly study (Ekerdt, 1998).

Such journalism has ensured considerable publicity for forces opposed to social insurance. As those forces intended, the publicity has generated an atmosphere of crisis. Consequently, an unwarranted belief that bankruptcy is imminent has lowered confidence in Social Security, and misinformation is widespread.

To be sure, considering the speed with which developments can occur in American politics, these factors could result in a shift of policy. Nevertheless, the counterforces that exist are strong. They and the enormous popularity that Social Security has sustained through its nearly three-quarters of a century's existence continue to suggest that privatization is unlikely.

## CHARACTERISTICS AND PRINCIPLES OF THE UNITED STATES' SOCIAL SECURITY SYSTEM

The Social Security Act of 1935 and its numerous amendments established and refined the United States' OASDI programs. Subsequently, a contributory program of hospital benefits for the elderly and the optional companion program of medical benefits were established. (Additional provisions of the Social Security Act provide benefits to the unemployed and some assistance to the indigent. There also are other laws that provide other in-kind benefits, such as food stamps to assist the poor in purchasing food. While all of these are part of the United States' social security system in its broadest sense, they will not form a part of this discussion because of their non-contributory nature.)

The Social Security program is compulsory for all covered workers and is funded by an income tax surcharge with matching employer contributions. As of 1999, a tax surcharge of 6.2 percent applies to the first U.S.$72,600 of wages. Although the amount of wages taxed rises with inflation, there currently is no increase scheduled in the tax rate. In view of the anti-tax climate that a generation of politicians has stimulated in the United States, there is virtually no likelihood of an increase in the near future. The revenue collected funds retirement, survivors' and disability benefits. An additional 1.45 percent tax for Medicare provision applies to the full income. The employer matches the employee's contribution bringing the total to 15.3 percent of the first U.S.$72,600 of wages, the same amount that the self-employed pay. A tax totaling 2.9 percent (1.45 percent each on the worker and on the employer) is added for any amount above the U.S.$72,600 limit. The tax applies only to wages, not to dividend, interest or other income.

Social Security covers virtually all employees. Only a few positions in state and local government remain outside the system. The system provides portability—workers retain coverage when they change jobs. Benefits are not means tested. They are an earned right for qualified beneficiaries, who do not need to prove poverty. They therefore are not required to humiliate themselves before a government official in order to qualify.

Workers may retire and receive benefits as early as age 62. The age for full retirement benefits, however, is currently 65. Early retirement brings a substantial reduction in benefits for every year the worker is below the age of 65, which is a permanent entitlement.

Because of increasing life expectancy and changing demographics, the retirement age for full retirement is being increased. For those born in 1938, the full retirement age is raised to 65 years and two months. The increase will continue depending upon the year of birth until the full retirement age becomes 67 for those born in or after 1960.

The minimum age for retirement benefits will remain at 62. For workers whose full retirement age is 67, however, such early retirement will bring an even greater reduction of benefits than it does currently. Retirement at 62 for these workers will bring their benefits down permanently to a mere two-thirds of the full benefit. For most workers the loss is even greater than the formula would indicate because an additional five years of earnings at the end of their careers would likely have increased their average lifetime earnings and therefore would have increased their benefits. Presumably, though, it evens out actuarially because retirement at 62 will bring benefits for five additional years.

Several features of Social Security reinforce the notion that benefits are an earned right. Individual workers and their employers support the program through their tax contributions. Benefits are related to wages and are calculated on the 35 years of highest earnings.

Although the tax is regressive, applying to the first dollar of earnings and exempting earnings above the U.S.$72,600 limit (except for Medicare), the benefit structure is not. It is redistributive. The formula provides comparatively greater benefits to lower-paid workers—in relation to their contributions—than to those with higher earnings. Moreover, workers with extremely low wages can receive an Earned Income Tax Credit that effectively offsets the Social Security tax burden.

In contrast to private pensions and income from investment annuities, Social Security benefits are protected against inflation. Cost of living adjustments (COLAs) increase payments annually in relation to the Consumer Price Index. Their value therefore does not erode as the cost of living increases.

Social Security also provides numerous other benefits. At retirement age, the spouse of a retired worker also receives a retirement benefit, generally 50 percent of the amount paid to the primary beneficiary. If the spouse also has a wage record, he or she may draw benefits either as a spouse or as a primary beneficiary, whichever would be more advantageous to the recipient.

If retired workers have dependent children, they also receive payments until they are 18 years of age. A divorced spouse of a retired worker can receive a parent's benefit based on the worker's record provided that the spouse cares for the worker's dependent children for as long as those children receive benefits. If the marriage lasted for at least 10 years and the divorced spouse currently is not married, then a spouse's benefit is payable to a former spouse of retirement age (benefits may even be payable to a former spouse who is married, if that marriage took place after the age of 60). Payment to a former spouse is excluded from calculation of the maximum benefits payable to a family and therefore does not affect the amount the worker's family can receive. There is yet an additional benefit: if a primary beneficiary has dependent parents, those parents also receive benefits.

Social Security also provides survivors' benefits. For retired workers, these include benefits to a surviving spouse whose payment is adjusted upward to the amount that had been paid to the primary beneficiary. They also include benefits to surviving minor children below the age of 18. If the children are below the age of 16, the surviving parent also receives a benefit.

The Social Security Administration has calculated the value of these survivors' benefits. To duplicate them privately would require, for the average worker, a $307,000 policy. The total amount of life insurance that the Social Security system provides far exceeds the total value of all the private life insurance in effect in the United States (Ball and Bethell, 1997: 277).

Social Security also provides disability benefits. The average value of these benefits, if duplicated on the private market, would require a policy of approximately $207,000. Thus, Social Security in the United States is vastly more than a retirement system. The protection that it provides, even disregarding its pension features, is substantial.

## CONCERNS FOR THE SOCIAL SECURITY SYSTEM'S STABILITY

The 1983 amendments to the Social Security Act sought to deal with a cash-flow problem that was developing. Major revisions included progressively raising the age for full retirement from 65 to 67 and adopting a schedule of increasing taxation. The current rate of 7.65 percent on both employee and employer (including Medicare) is the culmination of that schedule.

Actuarial calculations at that time projected that the trust funds would maintain a small surplus indefinitely. For some years the annual reports released by the Board of Trustees continued to project the surplus. In the 1990s, however, the "intermediate projections" of the annual reports began to reflect a deficit. It is these later projections that fuel concern for the system's stability.

Through 1997, the reports of the Trustees predicted that increasing costs would come to exceed income and that in 2029 the trust funds would be exhausted. Note that the projections were remaining virtually constant despite the huge expansion of the economy that was taking place at that time. The 1998 projections finally took note of the country's unprecedented economic strength and re-calculated the year of exhaustion as 2032. In one year's time, that is, the "crisis" date jumped three years into the future. The 1999 report extended the date another two years to 2034.

The projected dangers to the system received enormous publicity, publicity generated by carefully designed and lavishly funded advertising campaigns. Few analysts—and almost no journalists—even asked why the projections suddenly had become pessimistic when for years they had anticipated a surplus. Even when the system's supporters tried to defend it, they played into the hands of its opponents. They argued that all would be well until 2029, or 2032, and that after that even if there were no reforms, three-quarters of current benefit levels could still be paid from the system's income. Thus, friend and foe alike assumed that "reform" would be essential, and almost no one was left to ask whether that assumption was really valid.

One approach could have been to analyze the trust funds to see whether their performance had fallen short of that projected in 1983. In fact, the performance of the trust funds had been considerably better than anticipated, as had the performance of the economy itself. In fact, there was no economic or demographic reason why the projected surplus turned into a projected deficit.

According to the Trustees themselves, there was only one reason why the projections changed from surplus to deficit: the actuaries had adopted different and considerably more stringent methods of calculation (Board of Trustees, 1991: 3). The new and exceedingly cautious calculations assumed among other things a growth rate far below that of actual experience and a life expectancy that would increase annually, and forever.

The reports of the Trustees are cautious in another way that journalists have not been. The Trustees warn that their projections "are not intended to be exact predictions of the future status of the OASDI program" (Board of Trustees, 1991: 38). They point out that all long-range projections as complex as theirs are uncertain. "In general, a greater degree of confidence can be placed in the assumptions and estimates for the earlier years than for the later years," they say, but "even for the earlier years, the estimates are only an indication" of what might occur (Board of Trustees, 1998: 11).

Nonetheless, rarely have even the most sober sources treated the intermediate projections with any skepticism. Equally rarely have they recognized that the Trustees reports also include more favorable, "low-cost" projections, which anticipate no difficulty with the trust funds—ever. For example, the American Association of Retired Persons (AARP), although purporting to be a strong supporter, builds all of its discussions around the notion of trust-fund exhaustion requiring "reform" (Dentzer, 1999).

The congressional research service, which is both non-partisan and scholarly in orientation, similarly persists in making such statements as

While no plan envisions making Social Security voluntary, the program's foundation is about to be scrutinized more closely than at any time since it began in 1935. The conventional wisdom that Social Security is too popular to be overhauled seems to be weakening. At the core of this shift in attitudes lies the inescapable fact that without major changes, Social Security will not be able to keep up with the retirement of the Baby Boomers. Best-guess estimates are that the system will be unable to provide full benefits to retirees by 2029. (CQ, 1997: 71)

Even the Social Security Administration sounds the same theme. An official statement on April 24, 1997, about the release of the Trustees' 1997 report, for example, was headed "Social Security's long-range financing outlook unchanged; trust funds solvent until 2029."

These and other pressures have brought about official government consideration of reforms, culminating in President Clinton's proposals in his 1999 State of the Union address. As will be apparent these official proposals are hardly likely to lead to privatization. Some from the Advisory Council would have incorporated partial privatization, but the Clinton proposals seem to have preempted them. Opponents of Social Security, of course, would tend to welcome even the most modest amount of privatization as "a foot in the door."

## OFFICIAL PROPOSALS TO REFORM SOCIAL SECURITY

On January 6, 1997, the Advisory Council on Social Security issued its report. After more than two years of work, the 13-member panel had been unable to agree on a proposal. All members of the highly divided group did, however, agree that some action was necessary; they all accepted the intermediate projections by the Board of Trustees that anticipated exhaustion of the Social Security Trust Funds in the year 2029 unless there were corrective measures.

The inconclusive result reflected the enormous differences in the backgrounds, presuppositions and approaches of the group's members. The Secretary of Health and Human Services, Donna Shalala, no doubt had sought diversity when she appointed the Council. She clearly achieved that goal, if none other.

Six of the members supported an option to maintain the program's current structure, with some revisions. Under this plan some 40 percent of the trust funds would have been invested in private sources, and it called for an increase of the Social Security tax in 2045 by an additional 1.6 percent. Two members supported a plan for individual accounts which would have added a 1.6 percent tax to finance a program of government-managed mandatory accounts for each worker, leaving the existing system to pay whatever benefits the current structure would support. This plan also called for increasing the age for full retirement as life expectancy increases. Five members called for "personal security accounts." This plan would make a small identical payment to beneficiaries each month and in addition would require each worker to invest about 40 percent of the current payroll tax into an individual retirement savings account. It, too, would increase the full retirement age (Advisory Council on Social Security, 1997).

The work of the Advisory Council appeared to satisfy no one, including some of its members. At best, a product consisting of varied minority reports hardly carried with it an aura of authority, and in any event a rising budget surplus—unanticipated earlier—added a new dimension to the debate. President Clinton's proposals in his 1999 State of the Union address appear to have superseded the Council's efforts entirely.

Clinton's plan carefully avoided privatization, but skillfully incorporated some elements calculated to undermine the privatizers' arguments. It sought reform by diverting some 62 percent of the budget surplus into the Social Security trust funds. Clinton proposed devoting an additional percentage into the Medicare fund. Some of the trust funds could be invested into the market to achieve a higher rate of return than paid by the government bonds that are currently Social Security's sole investment. On top of the current system would be private accounts, "Universal Savings" or "USA Accounts." These would be personal accounts funded and managed by the government for each worker. Thus, he proposed an add-on benefit that would not interfere with the existing system.

Although President Clinton's proposals have received a varied response, the idea of earmarking much of the surplus to the trust funds had been popular across much of the political spectrum. The "USA Accounts" would accomplish what some of the privatizers have advocated but in addition to the current system rather than as a replacement for it. Investment of some of the trust funds into the stock market had been strongly supported by many of the system's critics, but when the president proposed it as a real possibility, many figures from Right to Left advanced numerous objections.

These official proposals have reflected some of the pressures for privatization. At the same time the more influential proposals, especially those of President Clinton, have been tailored to resist those pressures. Those pressures have taken varied form and have resulted from a wide range of sources.

## ARGUMENTS (AND THEIR SOURCES) ADVANCED IN FAVOR OF PRIVATIZING AMERICAN SOCIAL SECURITY

The arguments advanced in support of privatization typically assert that Social Security is unsustainable in principle, or at least that it faces serious and irreparable financial difficulties. They virtually all allege as their primary rationale that participants would receive a greater return on investment in private pension funds than they do from what they put in to the current public system. They use a variety of calculations to compare Social Security rates of return unfavorably with returns earned on the stock market. Among the many different proposals, none exceed those from the Cato Institute in calling for radical change. This is to be expected. The Institute is a libertarian group with an anti-government orientation so strong that it is quasi-anarchistic.

The Cato Institute has employed a former labor minister of Chile, José Piñera, as a spokesman. He speaks around the country praising the Chilean system and condemning that of the United States. His theme is that if the United States follows Chile's example, its workers all can become capitalists. His efforts—which the Cato Institute presents as objective analyses despite his status as a paid publicist—are part of a much broader "Cato Project on Social Security Privatization."

Piñera is co-chairman of the project along with William Shipman, Principal of State Street Global Advisers (affiliated with Boston's State Street Bank, which has financed extensive advertising favoring privatization). State Street Global Advisers is an enormous pension fund management company, one of the largest in the world. The project's advisory committee consists largely of investment fund executives and doctrinaire economists. It also includes former Reagan political appointee Paul Craig Roberts and Dorcas Hardy who was Reagan's Commissioner of Social Security (Tanner, 1996). It might be noted that Reagan himself campaigned with bitter intensity against Social Security before becoming president (Dugger, 1983; Ritter, 1968; Skidmore, 1970, 1989 and 1999).

Michael Tanner, Director of Health and Welfare Studies at the Cato Institute, also directs its Project on Social Security privatization. He speaks and writes prolifically. His efforts have received coverage—on the whole, admiring coverage—from major American news magazines. (When I debated him at a forum in late 1997, he responded to my allegation that Cato was spending U.S.$2 million to undermine public confidence in Social Security by saying that I was incorrect. The figure was $3 million! In all likelihood it has escalated far beyond that since then.)

The Cato Institute's criticism of Social Security alleges that it has been unsound from the very first. "It is a program that was flawed from its initial design, an unsustainable pyramid scheme" (Ferrara and Tanner, 1998: 1). The theme that Social Security "resembles the type of pyramid or 'Ponzi' schemes that are illegal in all 50 states" (Ferrara and Tanner, 1998: 37–38) recurs throughout Cato literature and in fact through much of the argument for privatization.

Milton Friedman has echoed the "pyramid" charge. Friedman, a committed advocate of an unfettered free market, strongly supports complete privatization. In an op-ed piece titled "Social Security Chimeras" in the *New York Times* for January 11, 1998, he said of Social Security that what supporters call a compact between generations, "opponents call a Ponzi scheme." Note that Friedman carefully avoided applying the label himself—he is, after all, the holder of a Nobel Prize in economics and thus surely knows what a Ponzi scheme is (and is not)—but he was quite willing to refer to the charge without dispelling it.

Another core argument from the Cato Institute is that Social Security represents a poor rate of return on investment. It maintains that individual private investments inevitably would produce higher returns. Despite the progressive nature of the system's benefit structure, the Cato Institute argues that it is unfair to those of low income and that, in Tanner's words, privatizing Social Security would be "A Big Boost for the Poor" (Tanner, 1996), the argument for which runs as follows: "By providing a much higher rate of return, privatization would raise the incomes of those who are most in need." Private investment of the amount paid in Social Security taxes would have enabled a low-income worker to receive an income about 41 percent higher if invested in bonds or almost 350 percent higher if invested in stocks than Social Security would bring. Privatization would "give the poor ownership in America," and it "would bail out a system hurtling rapidly toward insolvency." It would benefit the poor directly "by providing them with higher benefits and removing the link between benefits and longevity." Because in general the poor have shorter life spans, the Cato Institute argues, the return that they receive on their investment is lower than the return to other classes, despite the progressive benefit formula. Privatization would permit them to retire on the interest from their accumulated "nest eggs" and then leave their heirs with an inheritance (Tanner, 1996).

The Concord Coalition is less overtly hostile to Social Security compared with the Cato Institute and purports to be interested in saving the existing public system. Implicitly, however, it is equally hostile. Concord's influence, because of its wide acceptance by the news media and by policy makers, no doubt is considerably greater than the Cato Institute's. That acceptance owes much to skillful public relations. In portraying the organization as "bi-partisan," Concord's leaders have induced some widely respected figures to lend their names to its efforts.

The Concord Coalition is ostensibly the creation of two former United States Senators, Democrat Paul Tsongas and Republican Warren Rudman. From the beginning, however, much of its energy has come from Peter Peterson, an investment banker and former Secretary of Commerce. Peterson's opposition to Social Security is so zealous that it has led him to charge even that it was "a direct cause" of the federal government's budget deficit (Peterson and Howe, 1988: 43).

Indirectly, the roots of the Concord Coalition date back to 1984 when a Republican Senator, David Durenberger, founded "Americans for Generational Equity (AGE)." AGE's purpose was to oppose the national government's old-age insurance benefit programs, and it popularized the notion of "generational inequity." Whatever the justification of the idea, it will henceforth be necessary—as Jill Quadagno (1998) has pointed out—to take it into account in making policy choices.

Despite AGE's public relations successes, it disbanded after a few years when Durenberger's financial irregularities brought him into disrepute. Peterson stepped into the resulting vacuum and in 1992 helped to found the Concord Coalition. Despite its many conscientious members, it has served as a powerful tool for Peterson in his efforts to undermine Social Security.

Some of the most thoughtful social policy analysts in the United States have remarked that the Concord Coalition, although "nominally dedicated to the purpose of educating Americans about the hard financial choices the nation will be confronting," in fact "reiterates the conservative position that government spending favors older, more affluent Americans at the expense of a younger generation that is already under financial distress." They have proceeded to say that "in addition to encouraging younger Americans to see themselves as needy and to see the elderly as an affluent group not deserving of public support," the coalition is not above "the use of scare tactics. It has warned, for example, that the failure to transform Social Security may bring on a generational war. And given their own residualist political agenda, Peterson and other coalition members have been ready to lead it" (Marmor et al., 1997: 204).

The Concord Coalition has generated vast numbers of pamphlets, brochures and bulletins calling for Social Security to be put on a "fiscally sustainable and generationally equitable basis" (Concord Coalition, 1998). Currently, they say, the system is unsustainable because of unfavorable demographics. Concord Coalition's solution involves introducing defined-contribution rather than defined-benefit programs and reducing public pension benefits by raising the retirement age and imposing means tests. Peterson has called for a mandatory scheme of pensions based upon private investment, a scheme that he sees as increasingly substituting for Social Security (Peterson, 1996: 80–82).

Echoing the charge that Social Security is based on a pyramid scheme, Concord Coalition publications refer to the system as a "chain letter." They assert the remedial measures that are needed to address what they believe to be the public pension system's deficiencies will require sacrifices from everyone. Concord Coalition's position is that there must be reforms, and that they must include private ownership—individual retirement savings accounts—and a fair return on investment "to every cohort and income group" (Howe, 1996).

There are many other groups seeking ultimately to eliminate Social Security. Among them are Citizens for a Sound Economy, the National Center for Policy Analysis, Economic Security 2000, and Third Millennium. Sam Beard of Economic Security 2000 argues that "with a private, invested system, the middle class would retire as millionaires" (Ferrara and Tanner, 1998: 3). He has even written—apparently seriously—that it would enable a very low-paid worker, one who earned U.S.$8,000 per year, to retire with savings of nearly U.S.$500,000 (Lieberman 1997).

Third Millennium inundates the media with press releases and op-ed pieces and purports to speak for youth. This is the group that was responsible for the famous finding that young people believe that they are more likely to encounter a UFO than ever to receive Social Security. That finding produced dramatic headlines but was spurious. Third Millennium's survey had one item on UFOs as question number five and another on Social Security as question number fourteen. It did not ask for a comparison. A survey that did ask for a direct comparison brought an entirely different response:

A 1997 survey by the Employee Benefit Research Institute (EBRI) offered respondents the direct choice that Third Millennium falsely claimed to have posed. EBRI asked, "Which do you have greater confidence in: receiving Social Security benefits after retirement or alien life exists in outer space?" EBRI found that Americans overwhelmingly sided with Social Security over UFOs by a whopping margin of 71 percent to 26 percent. (Even among Generation X, respondents aged 33 or younger, the margin remained a stunning 63 percent to 33 percent.) (Jacobs and Shapiro, 1998: 364)

One of the best arguments for privatization comes from Harvard economics professor Martin Feldstein, who does not rely on charges that Social Security is a Ponzi scheme and who recognizes that, with regard to Social Security,

> the notion of bankruptcy has no real substance. Social Security is said to be heading toward bankruptcy only because it uses earmarked taxes and has a trust fund. Other federal programs like education and defense have no earmarked taxes and no trust fund and would therefore never be perceived to be bankrupt. Social Security will only be bankrupt and unable to pay benefits if taxpayers grow unwilling to raise taxes to pay for those benefits. (Feldstein, 1997: 27)

He does, however, argue that such a prospect is increasingly likely, and he points out that Congress already has cut Social Security substantially by making benefits taxable and raising the age for full retirement. Moreover, he accepts questionable demographic figures that suggest that health and Social Security benefits could come to more than 35 percent of GDP (Feldstein, 1997). However shocking these unlikely figures are, they lose some of their shock value if contrasted with the magnitude of military expenditures during the Cold War.

## FLAWS IN ARGUMENTS FOR PRIVATIZATION

As Richard C. Leone has pointed out—and the Social Security Trustees have warned—just as politics is not an exact science,

> neither is predicting economic, demographic, and social trends. Fertility experts, for example, foresaw neither the beginning nor the end of the American baby boom. And 2030—the year of peak U.S. boomer retirement—is as far away from us now as 1964. How many, 30 years ago, could have predicted stagnation of wages, the decline in birthrates, the rise of computers, the fall of the U.S.S.R.? (Leone, 1997: 39)

Although nothing can be assured, the performance to date of the Social Security system has been exemplary and gives no indication of impending trouble.

The allegation that the program is actuarially unsustainable is based on the false and deliberately misleading assumption that it is a Ponzi, or pyramid, scheme, which are, indeed, unsustainable. They are unsustainable because they depend upon geometric progression. Social Security, by contrast, simply involves one generation taking care of another and thus incorporates no trace of geometric progression. Hence, it incorporates no trace of a Ponzi or pyramid scheme, a fact that should be clear to anyone who examines the system.

It is only fair to concede that some of those who allege that Social Security represents an unsustainable pyramid arrangement may misunderstand either the nature of the system or of a pyramid scheme. It is doubtful though that writers from the Cato Institute are so ignorant or that such figures as Nobel Prize winning economist Milton Friedman could be unaware of the nature of Ponzi schemes. It is difficult to escape the conclusion that they mislead deliberately in an effort to strengthen their argument.

Whether partially funded or fully pay-as-you-go, Social Security involves one generation taking care of another. Not only is this completely sustainable but also, in one form or another, every generation in human history has done this. Those of one generation who produce have always taken care of those who, because they are too old or too young to do so, cannot.

Social Security is designed to provide greater benefits in relation to contributions for those at the lower end of the wage scale than for those who are more affluent. Disregarding the element of risk, a privatized defined-contribution system provides return based on contributions. This, by definition, would benefit those of higher earnings by eliminating the redistributive element; eliminating that redistributive element would, also by definition, penalize those whose earnings are lower. Writing in *The Christian Century*, Donn Mitchell notes that such a privatized system "would be transformed from 'social security' to mandatory individual risk-taking. This change would create new categories of winners and losers and would offer a bonanza to the brokerage industry, which would collect fees on the trading of upwards of 100 million new portfolios" (Mitchell, 1998: 861). If it were not already obvious, this explains why the financing of the privatization campaign is so massive.

Although the literature on Social Security privatization glows with the assurance of greater returns on investment, any such greater return is associated with greater investment risk. Greater risk also implies a disparity of return. Under such a privatized system, the winners clearly would come disproportionately from the ranks of those with more income while the losers would be those who already have lost out in the economic race. The social benefits of shared risk would be eliminated.

Rarely if ever do privatizers concede the administrative efficiency of the Social Security system. It operates at an administrative cost of less than 1 percent of income. No private program can compare. Individual retirement savings accounts would be whittled away quickly by investment fees and other administrative costs. Privatizers forget that the United States and all countries once had completely privatized systems of income support. Those systems failed so utterly that entire populations were at risk, and social insurance systems came to be recognized as essential—even in a country so ideologically committed to free market capitalism as the United States.

As for demographics, it is a matter of fact that the total dependency rates in the United States "in 2030 will not be much different from 1960 levels." Actually, it may well be more favorable. "Today, 46 percent of Americans are in the labor force; when the boomers are all retired in about 2030, that number will decline slightly to 44 percent. In 1964, when the baby boomer population peaked, however, only 37 percent of Americans were in the labor force—a ratio considerably 'worse' than can be expected in the 21st century" (Leone, 1997:

41). How can a population age without its labor force shrinking? A major part of the answer is the huge influx of women into employment since the 1960s.

The boomer generation itself was not as much of an aberration as Social Security's opponents have portrayed it. A report from the National Academy on an Aging Society makes this clear. "Many commentators talk about the 76 million baby-boomers as if no children would have been born in the absence of the baby boomers," it said. "If fertility rates had remained at pre–World War Two rates, there would still have been 64 million children born from 1946 to 1964. The real 'baby boomers' are the 12.3 million additional children born in those years." Moreover, "all this attention to the growth of the elderly population overlooks the fact that there will be growth in the non-elderly population as well. Baby boomers had fewer children than their parents, but there are more parents now than ever." In fact, the number of babies born during the time identified as the "baby boom" is not greatly different from the number being born today. The 72 million births in the past 18 years are almost as many as the 76 million born "during the 18 years of the baby-boom" (Friedland and Summer, 1999: 9).

The projections that portend trouble for Social Security assume an annual growth rate in the economy of about 1.4 percent over the next 75 years, far below the rate actually experienced for the last 75 years. Those arguing for privatization point out that the stock market historically has yielded between 7 percent and 9 percent, and they assume that it will continue to yield at that rate. For it to do so, the economy will have to continue to expand at somewhere near its historic rate.

If the economy does continue to grow at its historic levels, the Social Security system clearly will remain in balance. If, however, the economy does actually grow at only 1.4 percent, the capital market could not yield anywhere near the rate that the privatizers assume, and it would be impossible for the stock market to continue to deliver a yield five to six times the economic growth rate. They argue both ways. On the one hand, they say that the economy will perform poorly, and that will doom Social Security, which must be privatized. On the other hand, they say that a privatized system will thrive because the economy over the long term always performs well.

Privatizers distort their figures in another way. They assume that a worker would be able to invest the full Social Security tax, including the employer's share because "that is part of his wages." Unless the government forced employers to add that amount to a worker's salary, it is naive to assume that it would occur when many employers already are utilizing as many part-time workers as possible to avoid paying fringe benefits, and others are moving their operations to Third World countries to take advantage of cheap labor. They also ignore the portion of the Social Security tax that pays not for retirement benefits but for disability and survivors' protections.

The privatizers' comparisons typically ignore the inflation protection built into Social Security benefits and compare real and nominal returns as though there were no distinction. They also ignore benefits for a spouse who has low or no earnings and for dependents. It is not necessary to turn to the more hysterical rantings of the extremists, such as Peter Peterson, to find such distortions. Even the more careful arguments, such as those of Martin Feldstein, are typically based inappropriately on "return on investment," and consider only retirement benefits while ignoring coverage for survivors, dependents, disability, or health care (Feldstein, 1997).

As the financial writer Jane Bryant Quinn has pointed out, those who argue that Social Security provides a puny return on investment compared to market returns "are making false comparisons." Social Security's actuaries have compared the return from Social Security with that from individual retirement savings accounts, including the costs of continuing to support current beneficiaries, and "the returns from privatized systems are in the same ball park as Social Security's returns. In many cases, you might even get less from the privatized plans than straight Social Security might pay," she remarked, "because in privatization plans, Social Security benefits go down. The payroll tax money diverted into your private account is supposed to make up for the benefits you lost. But," she said, "according to the actuaries' report, it often doesn't work that way" (Quinn, 1999). "From both a moral and a social standpoint, there is nothing wrong with current wage earners financing the retirement of their parents' generation. The arrangement is problematic only if one believes that people should never get anything they did not personally earn—as if we all showed up ready for work at birth and paid our own way throughout life" (Mitchell, 1998: 860).

Investing a portion of the trust funds in the market, including that part of President Clinton's proposal, is undesirable for a number of reasons. For one thing, a huge influx of government funds could overheat the market, which could also be flooded when it became necessary to sell large blocks of stock to pay benefits, making it impossible to obtain the return required. Ultimately such government dependence upon the market, in competition with private investors, could lead to economic catastrophe such as has devastated Japan.

Moreover, there is the likelihood that such public investment in the capital market—with the best of intentions—might reflect political rather than economic considerations. Also, investment of the trust funds in the market would "force workers to invest in business corporations while denying them the rights of ownership enjoyed by all other shareholders—rights such as proposing or voting on shareholder resolutions, electing boards of directors and approving mergers" (Mitchell, 1998: 861). Finally, because of the nature of the global economy, government investment in the capital market would result in a constantly increasing foreign ownership of America's public debt.

## CONCLUSION

The case for privatizing Social Security is seriously flawed. Privatizers have misrepresented the nature of the existing public system and have exaggerated any troubles that it faces. Moreover, they have exaggerated the potential benefits of privatization while minimizing its risks. Many of those considering privatization do so because they have been convinced that the projections forecasting shortfalls in the Social Security trust funds are accurate, reasonable and in fact are prophecies rather than the guesswork that they inevitably are. The impetus, however, comes from anti-governmental ideologues with access to huge amounts of funding from interests that would benefit enormously if only a small portion of the system were to be privatized.

Much of the media have been closed to argument questioning the assertion that radical reform is required, and thus debate has been stifled. The question has been not "whether" Social Security is in trouble—which it is not—but rather "how" can it be "saved" or "reformed." The answer often has been that it will be necessary to take steps that would replace it.

Despite the subservience of the media to Social Security's opponents, however, the case for Social Security now is being made. At least two major books are analyzing the realities of the situation (Baker and Weisbrot, 1999; Skidmore, 1999), and several organizations are launching campaigns to counter the anti–Social Security propaganda. Skidmore (1999) exposes the long history of opposition to Social Security that was underground until the Reagan presidency made it politically possible for it to emerge and be conducted in the open.

The American people have strongly supported Social Security since its beginning in the 1930s. Arguably, the United States has never had a more popular public program. This popularity will stand it in good stead as Americans are called upon to consider the nature of the existing system and to evaluate the objections to it. The likely result will be that the people, and policy makers, will conclude that there is no need any longer to consider privatization of the American Social Security system. It is performing well as it is, and relatively minor adjustments from time to time are likely to be adequate to keep the program in balance without strain. It would be foolish to radically restructure a functioning program, when the only argument for doing so is based upon vague projections extending 30 years into the future—projections that come with the clear warning that they are not prophecies.

## REFERENCES

Advisory Council on Social Security. 1997. *Report of the 1994–1996 Advisory Council on Social Security*. Washington, DC: U.S. Government Printing Office.

Baker, D. and Weisbrot, M. 1999. *Social Security: The Phony Crisis*. Chicago: University of Chicago Press.

Ball, R. M. with Bethell, T. 1997. Bridging the Centuries: The Case for Traditional Social Security. In Kingson, E. R. and Schulz, J. H. (eds.), *Social Security in the 21st Century*. New York: Oxford University Press.

Board of Trustees. 1991. *1991 Annual Report of the Board of Trustees of the Federal Old-Age and Survivors Insurance and Disability Insurance Trust Funds*. Washington, DC: Social Security Administration.

Board of Trustees. 1997. *1997 Annual Report of the Board of Trustees of the Federal Old-Age and Survivors Insurance and Disability Insurance Trust Funds*. Washington, DC: Social Security Administration.

Board of Trustees. 1998. *1998 Annual Report of the Board of Trustees of the Federal Old-Age and Survivors Insurance and Disability Insurance Trust Funds*. Washington, DC: Social Security Administration.

Concord Coalition. 1998. *Saving Social Security: A Framework for Reform*. Washington, DC: Concord Coalition.

Congressional Quarterly (CQ). 1997. Debate Looms as Congress Turns to Social Security Rescue. *CQ Weekly Report*, January 11: 71–76.

Dentzer, S. 1999. Raising the Stakes: How Will You Fare When Congress Makes Its Move? *Modern Maturity* 42 (1): 42–50, 56–57.

Dugger, R. 1983. *On Reagan: The Man and His Presidency*. New York: McGraw-Hill.

Ekerdt, J. 1998. Entitlements, Generational Equity, and Public–Opinion Manipulation in Kansas City. *The Gerontologist* 38 (5): 525–36.

Feldstein, M. 1997. The Case for Privatization. *Foreign Affairs* 76 (4): 24–38.

Ferrara, P. J. and Tanner, M. 1998. *A New Deal for Social Security*. Washington, DC: Cato Institute.

Friedland, R. B. and Summer, L. 1999. *Demography Is Not Destiny*. New York: National Academy on an Aging Society.

Howe, N. 1996. The New Debate over Social Security Reform: Parts I, II, and III. In *Facing Facts, Fax Alert from the Concord Coalition*, April 15, July 8, and July 23.

Jacobs, L. R., and Shapiro, R. Y. 1998. Myth and Misunderstandings about Public Opinion and Social Security. In Arnold, R. D., Graetz, M. G. and Munnell, A. (eds.), *Framing the Social Security Debate*. Washington, DC: National Academy of Social Insurance.

Leone, R. C. 1997. Stick with Public Pensions. *Foreign Affairs* 76 (4): 39–53.

Lieberman, T. 1997. Social Insecurity: The Campaign to Take the System Private. *The Nation* 264: 11–18.

Marmor, T. R., Cook, F. L. and Scher, S. 1997. Social Security Politics and the Conflict between Generations: Are We Asking the Right Questions? In Kingson, E. R. and Schulz, J. H. (eds.), *Social Security in the 21st Century*. New York: Oxford University Press.

Mitchell, 1998. Against Privatization: The Genius of Social Security. *The Christian Century*, September 23–30: 860–62.

Peterson, P. 1996. Will America Grow Up Before It Grows Old? *The Atlantic Monthly* 277 (5): 55–86.

Peterson, P. and Howe, N. 1988. *On Borrowed Time: How the Growth of Entitlements Threatens America's Future*. San Francisco: Institute for Contemporary Studies.

Quadagno, J. 1998. Generational Equity and the Politics of the Welfare State. *Politics and Society* 17 (3): 353–76.

Quinn, J. B. 1999. Social Security Returns Aren't as Bad as Suggested. *Kansas City Star*, February 7: G6.

Ritter, K. 1968. Ronald Reagan and "The Speech": The Rhetoric of Public Relations Politics. *Western Speech* 32 (1).

Skidmore, M. J. 1970. *Medicare and the American Rhetoric of Reconciliation*. Tuscaloosa: University of Alabama Press.

Skidmore, M. J. 1989. Ronald Reagan and "Operation Coffeecup": A Hidden Episode in American Political History. *Journal of American Culture* 12 (3): 89–96.

Skidmore, M. J. 1999. *Social Security and Its Enemies: The Case for America's Most Efficient Insurance Program.* Boulder, CO: Westview Press.

Tanner, M. 1996. Privatizing Social Security: A Big Boost for the Poor. In *The Cato Project on Social Security Privatization* SSP No. 4 (July 26).

*Chapter 10*

# An Assessment of the Marketization of Social Security in Zimbabwe

## Edwin Kaseke

**INTRODUCTION**

This chapter makes an assessment of the market-driven approach to the provision of social security in Zimbabwe. The discussion begins by providing a socio-economic and political profile of Zimbabwe before examining the forces that have molded the market-driven approach to social security. The chapter then describes and assesses the market-driven approach, and finally it identifies some lessons to be drawn from Zimbabwe's experience.

**SOCIO-ECONOMIC AND POLITICAL BACKGROUND**

Zimbabwe is located in Southern Africa and shares borders with South Africa in the south, Mozambique in the east and Zambia in the north. The country gained its independence in April 1980 after sixteen years of armed struggle waged by the indigenous population against British minority rule. In the census of 1992, Zimbabwe's population was put at 10.4 million although it is anticipated that the population has since increased to between 11 million and 12 million. The indigenous African population constitutes about 98.8 percent of the population with persons of European and Asian origin constituting only 1.2 percent. About 69 percent of the population lives in the rural areas where they are largely dependent on agriculture for their sustenance. The majority of rural people engage in subsistence agriculture although a sizeable proportion now grows cash crops.

The population growth rate of 3.1 percent is high when compared to the economic growth rate that has averaged 1.4 percent in the last five years. According to the United Nations Development Program (UNDP), Poverty

Reduction Forum and Institute of Development Studies (1998), "fertility rates are higher in rural areas (4.85 in 1994) than urban areas (3.09) and also inversely related to educational standards." The same authors also observe that life expectancy for males is 48.1 and females 50.1, and it is argued that life expectancy is declining as a result of the AIDS pandemic.

Zimbabwe has a modestly diversified economy with agriculture constituting the backbone of economic activity. Agriculture's share of Gross Domestic Product (GDP) is about 14 percent, and it is the biggest employer. Mining and manufacturing are also strong pillars of the economy. In the mid-1980s the economy of Zimbabwe began to experience a downturn resulting in a growing debt burden. This forced the government to embark on an economic structural adjustment program in 1990. This program sought, among other things, to reduce the budget deficit, inflation, and the civil service; to increase investment and savings; and to attain sustainable levels of growth in GDP. It was assumed that these measures would put Zimbabwe's economy on the road to recovery and would ultimately improve the standards of living for the majority of the people. Unfortunately, these expectations have not been realized.

The economic structural adjustment program has impacted negatively on poor and vulnerable groups, mainly because of the introduction of cost-recovery measures and the removal of subsidies that have seen the cost of basic commodities escalating. Not only has the economic structural adjustment program impacted negatively on poor and vulnerable groups but also the country's economic performance has actually worsened. As the UNDP, Poverty Reduction Forum and the Institute of Development Studies (1998) observe, "Zimbabwe's economic performance has deteriorated since 1990, falling behind that of the sub-Saharan region as a whole."

Politically, Zimbabwe has been governed by one dominant party since independence—the Zimbabwe African National Union–Patriotic Front (ZANU PF). In the present parliament only three members out of a total of 150 members do not belong to the ruling party. During the first decade of independence, the country was a de facto one party state, but in the early 1990s, the country embraced multiparty democracy. At independence, the ruling party adopted scientific socialism as its ideology. This ideology was based on three central values, namely equality, freedom and fellowship.

According to this ideology, it was considered necessary for government to interfere with market forces in order to protect the poor and create an environment that allows all citizens to realize their potential. The pursuit of egalitarian ideals was therefore seen as a cornerstone of this ideology. This ideology influenced the government to introduce free health services for persons earning not more than Z$150 per month and free primary education. The fact that the country had a highly regulated economy during the first decade of independence can be attributed to the government's ideological orientation. The adoption of the economic structural adjustment program with its emphasis on free market and deregulation saw the government abandoning its scientific socialism, albeit reluctantly.

It should be pointed out that when Zimbabwe embarked on the economic structural adjustment program, it did not have a mandatory public social insurance system (Hampson and Kaseke, 1987; Kaseke, 1998). Although a minority of the population had occupational and private pensions as forms of social protection, the majority relied (and still do) on informal social security systems usually based on kinship ties. These informal social security systems operate on the basis of the principles of solidarity and reciprocity. Although economic hardships and westernization are undermining the viability of the extended family system, it still remains an important source of social protection for the majority of the population, particularly in the absence of a comprehensive public social security system.

## FORCES THAT HAVE MOLDED THE MARKET-DRIVEN APPROACH TO SOCIAL SECURITY

The forces that have molded the market-driven approach to social security in Zimbabwe are historical and can be traced back to the country's colonial past. Public provision of mandatory social security benefits is a recent development. Prior to this, it had not been seen as a critical area of concern for the government. Consequently, colonial governments adopted a laissez-faire attitude toward extending social protection to the majority of the population.

First, colonial governments assumed that the indigenous people did not need formal social security systems as they were perceived to have simple needs that could easily be met within the extended family system. Even those employed in the urban areas were considered temporary urban residents who were expected to retire to their rural homes under the cushion of the extended family system and the peasant economy. The extended family system and the peasant economy were considered appropriate channels through which post-retirement needs for Africans would be met (Kaseke, 1993).

Second, the white colonial administrators for a long time maintained their links with Britain and were assured of social protection in the event of their deciding to go back to their country of origin. As a result, colonial governments did not see any justification for introducing a mandatory public social insurance system apart from the pension scheme for civil servants which was introduced largely for the benefit of the white settler community.

It is noted that colonial governments also embraced the liberal values of individualism and freedom that emphasized non-interference by the state in the affairs of its people. This was also interpreted to mean that the state had a limited role to play in the provision of social welfare services. Consequently, it saw its role as that of providing an enabling environment. Individuals were therefore expected to use the market as the source of their social protection. This philosophy was also embraced by the majority government during the formative years after independence, resulting in unprecedented growth in the private insurance industry. This is clearly in line with the residual model of social welfare that perceives the family and the market as the preferred channels for the fulfillment of human needs (Titmuss, 1990).

This model of social welfare is influenced by the liberal ideology that views inequality in society as both necessary and inevitable. The ideology also views the market as the most efficient means of allocating resources and assumes that jobs are available to those who need them. Consequently, institutional provision of social welfare is considered wasteful and only serves to encourage people to be lazy and unproductive. Thus, the involvement of state in the provision of social welfare is kept to the minimum, and only the most needy are considered deserving of state assistance (Titmuss, 1990).

Residualism also holds that where individuals are unable to make use of the family or market economy, the state should come in but only in a temporary capacity. The assumption is that individuals can pull themselves up and be able to utilize their preferred channels of support. It is for this reason that successive governments have adopted non-contributory forms of social security that are wholly funded by the state. For example, the colonial government introduced the Old Age Pension Act of 1936 that provided means-tested old age pensions to all non-Africans over the age of 60 years. At independence, the majority government enacted the Social Welfare Assistance Act in 1988 to streamline the provision of social assistance to needy members of society. These non-contributory schemes are intended for the benefit of those who, due largely to circumstances beyond their control, are unable to insure their social security risks on the market and are therefore left without any source of support.

Third, because those in formal employment constituted a small percentage of the population (less than 20 percent), coverage of any public social insurance would have been low. Furthermore, wages for the African population were low, a situation which would have resulted in any form of mandatory social insurance becoming unduly burdensome to most wage earners.

It was therefore not until October 1994 that the government introduced a mandatory public social insurance system. This was preceded by the enactment of the National Social Security Authority Act in 1989, which among other things, provided for "the compulsory payment of contributions by employers and employees, the rates of such contributions and the deduction of contributions payable by employees from any salary, wages or other moneys payable to them" (Zimbabwe, 1989).

The Pensions and Other Benefits program is contributory with both employee and employers each contributing 3 percent of the employee's insurable earnings which provides protection against the contingencies of old age, invalidity and death. This program, still in its first phase, currently excludes public servants and the military. These groups are supposed to be covered in phase two. Indications are that it will take some time to extend coverage to these groups because the government does not have the resources to finance its contributions as an employer. There is a fear that bringing in public employees would only worsen the government's budget deficit at a time when the government is under scrutiny from the International Monetary Fund and the World Bank.

## VOLUNTARY SUPPLEMENTATION OF MANDATORY PUBLIC PROVISION BY PRIVATE PROVISION

The voluntary supplementation of mandatory public provision by voluntary private provision is carried out in accordance with the principle of co-existence between private and public provision. This voluntary private supplementation is made possible through the Pension and Provident Funds Act of 1987 and the Insurance Act of 1987. There are a number of registered private insurance companies in Zimbabwe providing different forms of social protection but mainly pension plans and life insurance policies. There are two types of pension plans, namely occupational defined-benefit plans and personal defined-contribution (retirement annuity) plans.

The occupational pension plans are provided through employers and underwritten by private insurance companies. Contributions usually come from both the employer and employee, with the employer typically matching the contributions of the employee, and are usually within the range of 3 and 7.5 percent of pensionable earnings. The benefits provided are usually linked to the final salary and the contributory period.

Contributions to retirement annuity and life insurance plans come from employees only and the level of contributions, or premium, is determined by the level of benefits required. Persons taking out membership in pension plans and life insurance policies are required to undergo medical examination. Furthermore, persons taking out life insurance policies with a value above Z$100,000 are required to undergo an HIV test, and those who test positive are denied membership. This requirement came as a result of a sharp increase in the number of claims being paid out by companies, a factor which has been attributed to the AIDS pandemic. This was therefore perceived to threaten the viability of the pension and insurance schemes, hence the requirement for an HIV test.

Contributions to the different voluntary retirement annuity plans are tax deductible. The tax adjustments are made when individuals complete their annual tax returns. Making them tax deductible serves as an incentive for individuals to take out private insurance as a way of enhancing their own retirement insurance. However, life insurance policy contributions are no longer tax deductible. If members are unable to continue contributing to a pension plan due to circumstances beyond their control such as unemployment or retrenchment, they can either withdraw their contributions together with accrued interest or have the contributions plus accrued interest invested in a voluntary preservation pension fund that can only be accessed upon death or upon reaching retirement age.

As there is no mandatory health insurance scheme in Zimbabwe, people seeking health insurance have to rely exclusively on voluntary private plans. These plans cover the cost of medical treatment including surgery and the purchase of drugs. The plans vary depending on the level of protection required including ability to contribute, and they therefore range from basic to executive plans. The more basic the plan is, the higher the shortfalls to be incurred by the members. Shortfalls occur, particularly when members receive specialist treatment or purchase expensive drugs. These shortfalls have to be settled by members although the shortfalls are also tax deductible. Contributions to health insurance plans, popularly known as medical aid societies, normally come from both employers and employees, and employers are free to determine their share of the contributions. However, it is common practice for employers to contribute 50 percent of the premiums. A few employers provide non-contributory medical aid plans.

## PERFORMANCE OF THE MARKET-DRIVEN APPROACH TO SOCIAL SECURITY PROVISION

The performance of the market-driven approach to social security in Zimbabwe has been undermined by the AIDS pandemic that is claiming about 240 lives a day. It is also projected that Zimbabwe will have 600,000 AIDS orphans by the year 2000 (O'Donogue, 1995). Consequently, insurance companies are facing financial losses as there is a growing mismatch between the inflow and outflow of funds. Insurance companies are therefore being forced by circumstances to insist on an HIV test in order to safeguard their viability.

Many potential beneficiaries are reluctant to undergo an HIV test because they may fail. Instead, they prefer to take out insurance coverage that is below Z$100,000. This does not of course provide sufficient protection, particularly given Zimbabwe's current inflation rate of about 50 percent.

The other problem that has undermined the effectiveness of occupational pension plans in Zimbabwe over the years has been the absence of the principle of portability (Mbanje, 1986). This means that employees resigning from their jobs cannot transfer their pension entitlements to the next employer. Employees receive a refund of their contributions plus accrued interest. The refund can be payable directly to the member or, as pointed out earlier on, it can be invested in a voluntary preservation pension fund. The benefits are, however, much lower than those that would accrue in a situation where all contributions are transferred to another occupational plan.

The principle of co-existence between the mandatory public social insurance provision and voluntary pension plans and life insurance policies has not worked and has only served to undermine private schemes. Employers resisted the introduction of mandatory public social insurance because this would have increased payroll taxes. Private insurance companies also resisted the introduction of mandatory public social insurance as they felt that this would undermine the viability of their own pension plans and life insurance policies. It is true that the introduction of mandatory public social insurance has impacted negatively on occupational and private pension plans. For instance, before the introduction of mandatory social insurance, most occupational pension plans required workers to contribute about 7.5 percent of their pensionable earnings, but the percentage has since gone down to 4 percent or 5 percent for pension plans. Employers allege that they cannot afford to maintain their contributions at the original rate in view of the additional scheme and the harsh economic climate. As employers cannot opt out of the mandatory social insurance system, they can only do so with voluntary pension plans.

Employees also find the mandatory public social insurance burdensome as contributions to both this and voluntary pension plans only serve to reduce their disposable income. It is common for members to fall behind in the payment of their pension plan contributions and life insurance premiums with the result that the policies lapse. The level of protection provided by voluntary pension schemes has therefore shrunk, much to the detriment of the members, particularly those in the low-income groups.

Given the problem of co-existence between mandatory public provision and voluntary private provision and the AIDS pandemic, private pension plans and life insurance policies are not in strong demand thereby making it difficult for them to achieve economies of scale. This will also eventually increase the administrative costs incurred and thus undermine the benefits that accrue to members. This will further reduce the size of the population covered by voluntary private provision.

Lastly, a major weakness of private provision is that the benefits that accrue to members depend on the yields of the investments made by the insurance companies. Under such circumstances there is no sharing of risks, a situation that undermines the social protection of the members, particularly in the event of death. Some plans, however, are based on risk sharing and pooling of resources, as there are guaranteed insurance benefits payable to members.

The absence of risk sharing is even more glaring in defined-contribution (money purchase) plans, which by their nature do not have any insurance elements. Consequently, individuals carry their own investment risk, which undermines the social protection provided. Furthermore, these benefits are not indexed against inflation and are inadequate to meet the basic needs of members. Perhaps their greatest weakness, however, lies in the use of lump sum payments instead of periodic payments. Lump sum payments do not provide income-maintenance but rather a one-off payment that the members can exhaust within a few months. The problems caused by inadequate benefits would be minimal if there was a comprehensive social insurance system providing good first tier protection.

## LESSONS FROM ZIMBABWE'S EXPERIENCE WITH THE MARKET-DRIVEN APPROACH TO SOCIAL SECURITY

It is clear from Zimbabwe's experience with the market-driven approach to social security that it is suitable only in circumstances where there is a comprehensive first tier mandatory public social insurance system to provide basic social protection which is an integral component of the Reluctant Collectivist approach to social security. In its absence voluntary private provision only offers social protection to a small percentage of the population, given that 69 percent of the population are not in wage employment. This means that the overwhelming majority of the population are not covered by private provision. This is also not helped by a mandatory social insurance system that is not inclusive and discriminates against the rural population.

Although the rural people expected to be covered in phase three of the implementation of the Pensions and Other Benefits Scheme, indications are that this will not be done soon. The groups that are currently excluded by the mandatory public social insurance system are also the same groups that are largely excluded by voluntary private provision. Similarly, those who are covered by the mandatory public social insurance system are overrepresented in voluntary private provision. This exacerbates existing inequalities in society. There is, therefore, a need to ensure that there is a minimum floor of social protection for the majority of the population. The challenge for Zimbabwe is to extend mandatory public social insurance to groups that are currently not covered, namely the informal sector workers and the peasants. While most of the groups do not have the capacity to contribute to mandatory public social insurance on a monthly basis, they can, however, pay annual premiums which can be subsidized by the rest of the membership or by government, in line with social justice and egalitarian ideals.

It is also clear from Zimbabwe's experience that low-income earners do not join voluntary private pension plans or purchase life insurance policies because they find this unduly financially burdensome. The wages are too low. It, therefore, does not make sense to expect people who are failing to meet their immediate consumption needs to make voluntary private provision against a future social security contingency. There is thus a need to pay wages that are adequate to support a reasonable standard of living to enable employees to protect themselves against future contingencies. Currently, most wages for unskilled and semi-skilled workers fall below the poverty line (Kaseke, 1998). Thus paying adequate wages will increase the predisposition of low-income earners to contribute to voluntary private provision.

Another important lesson that can be drawn from the experience of Zimbabwe is that there can never be meaningful co-existence between mandatory public and voluntary private provision in a harsh economic environment unless private provision is also made mandatory. There is no real competition between mandatory and voluntary provision, a situation that forces the mandatory provision to undermine voluntary provision, not necessarily because members do not want to supplement mandatory public provision but because this overstresses their resources. Of particular importance, however, is the need to make occupational pensions not only mandatory but also portable.

Governance is another problematic issue. Although the Pension and Provident

Funds Act stipulates that "a registered fund shall, within six months after the end of its financial year, submit to the Registrar audited accounts and such other statements and reports as may be prescribed." But many funds have problems in meeting this requirement, which underscores the difficulties experienced by the government in regulating the operation of private pension plans. As the reports are often delayed, it is therefore difficult to detect problems earlier, which may disadvantage fund members.

## CONCLUSION

The discussion has shown that voluntary private provision does not provide the answer to the problem of social protection for the majority of the people in Zimbabwe. In a developing economy where the overwhelming majority of the population is dependent on subsistence agriculture and where unemployment levels are high and wages low, the take up rate for voluntary provision is low. Consequently, coverage is low and voluntary provision becomes elitist, much to the detriment of the poor. What the poor need is a mandatory public insurance system based on risk sharing and pooling of resources in order to guarantee acceptable minimum benefits to members. There is also need for a non-contributory public social assistance program to operate alongside a contributory public social insurance system in order to capture those that may miss the contributory safety net. In view of this, it would appear that Zimbabwe's circumstances are not conducive for a market-driven approach to social security provision, a prerequisite for which is enhancing the productive capacity of the majority of the people, particularly the rural population and the urban poor. The creation of income earning opportunities will enhance the participation of the poor in the market and ultimately enhance their capacity to participate in market-driven social security provision.

## REFERENCES

Hampson, J. and Kaseke, E. 1987. Zimbabwe. In Dixon, J. (ed.), *Social Welfare in Africa*. London: Croom Helm.
Kaseke, E. 1993. *Rural Social Security Needs: The Case of Zimbabwe*. Harare: School of Social Work.
Kaseke, E. 1998. Zimbabwe. In Dixon, J. and Macarov, D. (eds.), *Poverty: A Persistent Global Reality*. London: Routledge.
Mbanje, R. 1986. *Social Security for the Elderly in Zimbabwe*. Harare: School of Social Work.
O'Donogue, J. 1995. *Zimbabwe's AIDS Action Programme for Schools*. Harare: UNICEF.
Titmuss, R. M. 1990. *Social Policy: An Introduction*. London: Unwin Hyman.
United Nations Development Program (UNDP)/Poverty Reduction Forum/Institute of Development Studies. 1998. *Human Development Report*. Harare: UNDP.

# Index

Accountability of private social security institutions, public, 181
Administration of private social security institutions, quality of, 106
Administrative contracting-out. *See* Contracting-out, administrative services
Afghanistan, 28
Aging population, 76, 128, 198–99
AIDS. *See* HIV
Andersen Consulting, 176, 180–81
Anti-statism, 30, 193
Arenas de Mesa, A. Z., 54
Argentina, 28, 35, 58
Asian (Confucian) values, 12
Australia, 28

Banks, social security role of: the Netherlands, 99–100; the United States, 194
Belgium, 91
Benefit dependency. *See* Welfare dependency
Benthamite tradition, 31
Beveridge, W., 13
Beveridge legacy: the Netherlands, 87; the United Kingdom, 124–27
Bismarck legacy in the Netherlands, 87
Bolivia, 28
Brazil, 58; current system, 66–74; 1998 reforms, 80–84; proposed reforms, 77–80; social security system history, 65–66
Britain. *See* United Kingdom, the

Capital market and social security: Chile, 49, 54, 56–57; the United States, 198
Cerney, P., 31, 32
Chile, 28, 35, 78, 84, 85, 193; mandatory individual capitalization system since 1980, 50–52; neoliberal transformation (1973–1980), 46–47; reform impact, 53–60; social security system (1924–1973), 43–46
Chomsky, N., 168, 183
Citizenship: obligations, 11, 12, 17, 33; rights, 7, 8, 10, 12, 33, 153, 170
Collective responsibility for social security, 1, 3, 167
Collectivism, Reluctant. *See* Reluctant Collectivism
Colombia, 28, 35
Commissions charged by private social security institutions, 35–36, 49, 55–56, 198
Communist Collectivism, 3, 4, 6, 17, 21
Communitarianism, 33

Community (social) solidarity, 30, 47, 48, 59, 88, 207
Complementary benefit provision, private provision: Brazil, 66–67, 71–74, 81, 83–84, 85; the Netherlands, 102; privatized provision, 20, 27–28, 65. *See also* Joint public–private provision
Confidence of public in private social security institutions, lack of, 86
Confidentiality of personal data held by private social security institutions, 106
Contracting-out, 4, 14, 20
Contracting-out of administrative services: Canada, 180–82; the Netherlands, 96, 99, 101, 103–8, 113–15, 116–17; the United Kingdom, 133–36
Contracting-out of coverage, 28; the Netherlands, 96, 100, 102–4, 110; New Zealand, 161–62; the United Kingdom, 128–29. *See also* Joint public–private provision
Cóstabal, M., 49
Côte d'Ivoire, 28
Courchene, T. J., 173, 179
Coverage marketization, 21, 29. *See also* Contracting-out of coverage
Coverage privatization, Chile, 48, 49–50, 50–51, 53–54

Dahl, R., 33
De-commodification, 3, 16–17, 21
Defined-benefit plans, 20, 28, 36, 71, 72, 83, 196, 209
Defined-contribution plans, 20, 28, 29, 35, 71, 72, 85, 196, 198, 209, 211
Democracy, 15, 33, 60, 61
Deng Xiaoping, 9
Denmark, 91
Dependency. *See* Welfare dependency

Economic efficiency principle, 15; Canada, 181; the Netherlands, 88; Zimbabwe, 208
El Salvador, 28
Employer responsibility for social security: the Netherlands, 96, 98–99, 100, 101, 102, 113; the United Kingdom, 132, 134. *See also* Occupational plans

Equality of opportunity, 29
Equality principle, 7; the Netherlands, 88; Zimbabwe, 206
Esping-Andersen, G., 3, 16, 21
Ethnic minorities, 148, 154
Etzioni, A., 11
European Union, the, 89, 93, 130

Feldstein, M., 197, 200
Fellowship 7, 8, 206. *See also* Social cohesion
Field, F., 21, 152
Fiji, 28
Financial disclosures by private social security institutions, 106
Finland, 28
France, 28, 76
Fraudulent behavior by private social security institutions, 85, 86
Freedom, 7, 14, 206; negative liberty, 14–15; positive liberty, 7
Freud, S., 7
Friedman, M., 16, 194, 197

Galbraith, J. K., 12–13
Gender inequalities and social security privatization, 54–55
Germany, 76, 91
Giddens, A., 10–11
Governance: and public interest, 27, 32–33, 34, 35, 37; socio-political, 34. *See also* Regulation of private social security institutions, public
Government subsidies to private social security institutions, 33, 35–36, 47, 50, 58–59
Greece, 28
Guatemala, 29
Guest, D., 168

Harris, R., 31
Health benefit plans, 28, 47, 209–10
HIV, 209, 210, 211
Hong Kong, 28
Hungary, 28

Incentive-driven social security, 4, 6, 11, 20

Income inequalities, 4, 13; Canada, 170–71; Chile, 45
India, 28
Individual accounts (plans) (individual capitalization), 28; Brazil, 83; Chile, 47–50; New Zealand, 155–56; the United Kingdom, 128, 129, 130, 131; the United States, 187, 192, 196; Zimbabwe, 207, 209, 210–11
Individual responsibility for social security, 1, 3, 10, 11, 12, 13, 14, 16, 29, 30, 32, 37, 47, 48, 59, 123, 127, 207
Individualism, Reluctant. *See* Reluctant Individualism
Insurance companies: Brazil, 83; the Netherlands, 99–100, 115; Zimbabwe, 208, 209, 210, 211
International financial institutions, 2–3, 209
Investment portfolio: proposal to privatize U.S. social security trust, 193; regulation of private social security institutions', 52, 85

Japan, 28, 76, 200
Joint public–private provision, 4, 11, 12, 17. *See also* Complimentary benefit provision; Contracting-out

Keynes, J. M., 12
Kingson, E. R., 32
Kooiman, J., 34
Kotlikoff, L., 2

Law, M. T., 180, 181–82
Lenin, V. I., 4
"Less eligibility," principle of, 16, 151–52, 159
Liberalism, 30, 173
Lightman, E. S., 183
Long-term care, proposal for the privatization of in the United Kingdom, 127, 133

Malaysia, 28
Market entry regulation of private social security institutions, 100, 102–3, 104, 105

Market failure, 3, 7, 12–13, 15, 16, 109–10
Market-oriented social security provision. *See* Complementary benefit provision, privatized provision; Contracting-out; Coverage marketization; Coverage privatization; Incentive-driven social security; Joint public–private provision; Private social security institutions; Tax-induced voluntary private social security provision
Markowitz, H. I., 180, 181–82
Martin, B., 2
Marx, K., 4
Maydell, B. von, 29
Mead, L., 10, 152
Mesa-Lago, C., 45, 56, 59
Mexico, 28, 174, 182
Mihlar, F., 180, 181–82
Mishra, R., 2
Montecinos, V., 54
Murray, C., 15

Neoliberalism, 15, 30–32, 46, 52, 57, 59, 60, 170, 171, 182
Netherlands, the: lessons, 115–18; proposed market-driven reforms, 95–97; public social security system, 87–92; reform context, 92–95; reform discourse, 102–8; reform evaluation, 108–15; social security reforms, 97–102
New Right, 3, 4, 6, 7, 11, 14–16, 21, 167, 174. *See also* Radical Right
New Zealand: marketization elements, 148–61; performance and outcomes, 163–64; social security system structure, 145–48
North American Free Trade Agreement, 169, 173

Occupational plans, 28; Zimbabwe, 207, 209, 210–11, 212
Organization for Economic Cooperation and Development (OECD), 158
Ownership concentration of private social security institutions, 51, 56, 99–100

Papua New Guinea, 28
Personal plans. *See* Individual accounts (plans)
Peru, 28
Piñera, J., 53
Poland, 28
Poverty, 13; Canada, 170, 173, 179; Chile, 45; New Zealand, 162; the United Kingdom, 124, 125, 131, 136–38
Prinz, C., 2
Private social security institutions. *See* Accountability of private social security institutions, public; Administration of private social security institutions, quality of; Commissions charged by private social security institutions; Confidence of public in private social security institutions, lack of; Confidentiality of personal data held by private social security institutions; Financial disclosures by private social security institutions; Fraudulent behavior by private social security institutions; Investment portfolio, regulation of private social security institutions'; Market entry regulation of private social security institutions; Ownership concentration of private social security institutions; Regulation of private social security institutions, public
Pulkingham, J., 170

Quadagno, J., 195

Radical Right, 170. *See also* New Right
Ralph, D., 182
Regulation of private social security institutions, public, 31, 32, 34–35, 49–50, 52, 57, 85, 101, 105, 106, 116, 213
Reluctant Collectivism, 3, 12–14, 21, 48, 212
Reluctant Individualism, 3, 9–12, 17, 21
Riker, W. H., 31
Rousseau, J., 33

Seldon, A., 31
Silburn, R., 29

Simeon, R., 179
Singapore, 28
Smith, A., 15
Social assistance: Brazil, 66, 81; Canada, 169, 170, 171, 173, 174, 175, 176, 177–78, 179–82; the Netherlands, 88, 94, 101–2, 112; New Zealand, 150, 151, 152, 153, 155; the United Kingdom, 124, 125, 126; the United States, 188; Zimbabwe, 208, 213
Social cohesion, 7, 8, 10, 29, 37. *See also* Fellowship
Social contract, 179
Social exclusion, 13
Social insurance, 4, 44, 69–71, 83, 87, 100, 101, 102, 107, 108, 116, 118, 124, 155–56, 188–90, 207, 208, 210, 211, 212, 213
Social justice, 29, 37, 168, 184, 212
Social Reformism, 3, 4, 6–9, 11, 12, 21, 48
Social security administration, public, contracting out: Canada, 180–82; the Netherlands, 96, 99, 101, 103–8, 113–15, 116–17; the United Kingdom, 133–36
Social security administration, public, corporatization: New Zealand, 161; the United Kingdom, 134–35
Social security expenditure, public: crisis, 30, 45, 73–74, 188, 190–92, 193, 194–95, 196; escalating cost burden, 1, 30, 44; retrenchment, 88, 91, 108, 123, 175
Solomon Islands, 28
Soviet Union, 167
Sri Lanka, 28
Stalin, J., 6
State failure, 3, 9, 10, 11–12, 30, 31, 109
Structural adjustment, 206–7
Struthers, J., 183
Sweden, 91
Switzerland, 28
Sztompka, P., 10

Tax-induced voluntary private social security provision, 4, 13, 20, 123–24, 128, 129–30, 209, 210

Teeple, G., 168
Telmer, C. R., 173, 179
Ternowtsky, G., 170

Underclass, the, 15, 16, 29, 179, 181
Unemployment, 1, 12, 15; Brazil, 75, 77; Canada, 171, 173, 174, 183; Chile, 47, 48, 57–58; the Netherlands, 93; New Zealand, 152, 153, 157; the United Kingdom, 125; Zimbabwe, 213
United Kingdom, the, 28, 91, 205; administrative privatization, 134–36; Beveridge legacy, 124–27; familialization, 138–39; privatization of poverty, 136–38; privatizing social security, 123–24; social security and the private sector, 127–33
United States, the, 76, 85, 110, 168, 169, 173, 174, 176, 179, 182; flaws in the privatization argument, 197–200; official reform proposals, 192–197; social security system characteristics and principles, 188–92
Universalism, 8, 17, 102, 154, 155, 158, 170
Uruguay, 28

Vanuatu, 28
Venezuela, 28
Voluntary private social security provision, 16, 17, 20; Brazil, 67, 69, 71–73, 79; the Netherlands, 99–100, 101; the United Kingdom, 123–24, 125, 130–31; Zimbabwe, 209, 210, 211, 212, 213. *See also* Tax-induced voluntary private social security provision
Vosko, L., 179

Wage subsidies, 97, 112, 144, 158–60, 169
Walker, A., 123
Welfare dependency, 125, 152, 153, 175, 183
Welfare frauds, 175
Welfare state, 7, 16, 32, 36, 87, 167–68, 169, 172
Williamson, J., 32
WOOPIES (well-off older people), 126
Work ethic, 15
Workfare (welfare-to-work), 6, 7, 10, 11, 13–14, 89, 91; Brazil, 84–86; Canada, 170, 171, 175, 176–79, 180, 182, 183; New Zealand, 151, 152; the United Kingdom, 125
Wright, V., 36

Yalnizan, A., 170

Zambia, 28
Zimbabwe: marketization context, 205–7; marketization forces, 207–9; marketization lessons, 211–12; performance of private provision, 210–11; voluntary complimentary private provision, 209–10

# About the Contributors

SYLVIA BORZUTZKY is a Professor in the Department of Social and Decision Sciences at Carnegie-Mellon University, Pittsburgh, Pennsylvania, United States.

HENK-JAN DIRVEN is a Statistical Researcher in the Department of Socio-Economic Statistics of Statistics Netherlands, Amsterdam, the Netherlands.

JOHN DIXON is Professor of International Social Policy in the Department of Social Policy and Social Work at the University of Plymouth, Plymouth, United Kingdom.

SÔNIA MIRIAM DRAIBE is an Associate Professor in the Institute of Economics at the State University of Campinas, Campinas, Brazil.

MARK HYDE is a Senior Lecturer in Social Policy in the Department of Social Policy and Social Work at the University of Plymouth, Plymouth, United Kingdom.

EDWIN KASEKE is the Principal of the School of Social Work, Harare, Zimbabwe.

ALEXANDER KOUZMIN is Professor of Organizational Behaviour in the Cranfield Business School at Cranfield University, Cranfield, United Kingdom.

MILKO MATIJASCIC is a Researcher in the Center for Public Policy Studies in the Institute of Economics at the State University of Campinas, Campinas, Brazil.

RUUD MUFFELS is in the Research Unit on Work and Social Security in the Work and Organization Research Centre at Tilburg University, Le Tilburg, the Netherlands.

MICHAEL O'BRIEN is a Senior Lecturer and Head of the School of Social Policy and Social Work at Massey University, North Shore, New Zealand.

HUGH SHEWELL is an Assistant Professor in the Department of Social Work at York University, Toronto, Canada.

MAX J. SKIDMORE is Curator Professor of Political Science in the Department of Political Science at the University of Missouri–Kansas City, Kansas City, United States.

CAROL WALKER is Professor of Social Policy in the Department of Policy Studies, University of Lincolnshire and Humberside, Nottingham, United Kingdom.